GROWTH MINDSET
FOR TEACHERS

EDITED BY
SHERRIA HOSKINS

GROWTH
MINDSET
FOR TEACHERS

CORWIN

CORWIN
A SAGE Publishing Company

A SAGE company
2455 Teller Road
Thousand Oaks, California 91320
(0800)233-9936
www.corwin.com

SAGE Publications Ltd
1 Oliver's Yard
55 City Road
London EC1Y 1SP

SAGE Publications India Pvt Ltd
B 1/I 1 Mohan Cooperative Industrial Area
Mathura Road
New Delhi 110 044

SAGE Publications Asia-Pacific Pte Ltd
3 Church Street
#10-04 Samsung Hub
Singapore 049483

Editor: Amy Thornton
Senior project editor: Chris Marke
Marketing manager: Dilhara Attygalle
Cover design: Wendy Scott
Typeset by: C&M Digitals (P) Ltd, Chennai, India
Printed in the UK

Library of Congress Control Number: 2019939055

British Library Cataloguing in Publication data

A catalogue record for this book is available from the British Library

ISBN 978-1-5264-6023-3
ISBN 978-1-5264-6024-0 (pbk)

At SAGE we take sustainability seriously. Most of our products are printed in the UK using responsibly sourced papers and boards. When we print overseas we ensure sustainable papers are used as measured by the PREPS grading system. We undertake an annual audit to monitor our sustainability.

CONTENTS

ABOUT THE GROWING LEARNERS TEAM

"I DON'T DIVIDE THE WORLD INTO THE WEAK AND THE STRONG, OR THE SUCCESSES AND THE FAILURES ... I DIVIDE THE WORLD INTO THE LEARNERS AND NON LEARNERS."

(BENJAMIN R. BARBER)

Who are we?

We are a group of education research psychologists who are passionate about supporting schools and parents to improve their children's expectations and attainment using evidence-based practice to support them to become resilient, confident and effective learners. Everything that we offer is underpinned by psychology and education theory, and applied research showing what works.

Professor Sherria Hoskins leads Growing Learners – a group of education research psychologists who work directly with schools to improve their pupils' aspirations, expectations and attainment, using evidence-based practice. Sherria is Professor and Dean of Science at the University of Portsmouth.

Dr Victoria Devonshire is Senior Lecturer in the Department of Psychology at the University of Portsmouth. Before studying psychology, Victoria was a primary school teacher for eight years. Her research interests are around children's learning of reading and spelling.

Dr Frances Warren is a Lecturer in the Department of Psychology at the University of Portsmouth. Frances is also Honorary Assistant Psychologist at the University of Reading on a Randomised Clinical Trial aimed at investigating the effectiveness of childhood anxiety treatments.

Dr Emily Mason-Apps is a Research Fellow in the Department of Psychology at the University of Portsmouth. Emily is currently working as a research fellow on the Learning Gains Project, funded by the Higher Education Funding Council for England (HEFCE).

Dr Joanna Nye is a Lecturer in the Department of Psychology at the University of Portsmouth. Joanna's research interests relate to child development and issues relating to educational psychology.

Dr Liam Satchell is a lecturer in psychology at the University of Winchester. He studies theoretical and applied psychology, particularly focusing on personality psychology (normative aggression and psychopathy), ecological psychology and research design.

Ms Mathilde Chanvin is a Research Assistant in the Department of Psychology at the University of Portsmouth. Mathilde's current research focuses on the efficacy of a conservation education programme to influence children, parents and school teachers' knowledge, habits and attitudes towards their local environment.

INTRODUCTION

SHERRIA HOSKINS

Why did we write this book?

It would be rare to speak to a policy maker, educationalist or teacher in the US or the UK who hasn't heard the term 'growth mindset'. Indeed, one might describe it as an educational zeitgeist. It seems that as many people who have heard of mindsets have an opinion on it, exercised in the staff rooms of educational institutions, newspapers and Twitter, to name a few. The perspectives on mindsets, at least within the UK, are polarised, ranging from evangelical support to disdain (what we call the fad or fix-all debate), and arguments on both sides are commonly littered with misunderstandings and misrepresentations.

We certainly don't claim to be 'the' authority on mindsets, but we have worked with mindsets both as researchers and practitioners, and would like to share our dual perspectives with you. While this book does contain some practical tips for teachers, it certainly doesn't advocate mindsets as the best or only way to support learning, neither does it deal with this psychological theory within a learner deficit framework – e.g. teach that child to cope with life. Rather, we take a reflective and open-minded look at mindsets, based on the research available and our own systematic trials in the classroom. This book will explore some of the research evidence, the debates and myths surrounding mindset, and what we have found has worked, what has not worked and perhaps, most importantly, what we still don't understand about mindsets.

> **"THIS BOOK WILL EXPLORE SOME OF THE RESEARCH EVIDENCE, THE DEBATES AND MYTHS SURROUNDING MINDSET, AND WHAT WE HAVE FOUND HAS WORKED, WHAT HAS NOT WORKED AND PERHAPS, MOST IMPORTANTLY, WHAT WE STILL DON'T UNDERSTAND ABOUT MINDSETS."**

Where did our mindset journey begin?

I began as a lone educational researcher within a psychology department in 1999, eventually moving to the dizzy heights of employing one research assistant paid for by small externally funded research projects. One such project was brought to us in 2011 by our local council. The problem that they wanted us to explore were the Key Stage 2 Standard Attainment Tests (SATs) results in the city. These had been lower than the national average year on year since 2006. We were given unprecedented access to their historical pupil data (carefully managed to adhere to the then Data Protection Act and their Data Sharing Policy and notices).

Our City Council colleagues had a theory about what was causing the low attainment – a poverty of aspiration in the city. Their theory is understandable. Certainly, pupil aspiration nationally has been a huge focal point. One of the main priorities of the UK Government is to increase the aspirations of young people so that they aim higher. There appears to be a Government belief that young people who live in certain types of a neighbourhood are less likely to have high aspirations and these are associated with high levels of deprivation (Sinclair et al., 2010). The Government worked with the idea that low aspirations lead to low achievement. Their underlying assumption was that some people from certain areas have a lack of high aspiration that affects the way they live their lives. It is believed that raising these aspirations will help to break this cycle (Turok et al., 2009).

Specifically, we did two things to unravel whether this was the case for the pupils in the city in question:

- explore all the evidence (research literature on pupil attainment and over 100 Government reports);
- explore their data set of over 1,500 pupils over a five-year period.

We identified what might, according to theory and research, impact attainment, and then scrutinised the data for clues why this was or wasn't happening for pupils in the city.

So what of the poverty of aspiration theory?

First, we needed to unravel what is meant by 'aspirations' and its difference to other key concepts – specifically, expectation.

Educational *expectations* refers to the education that the individual *expects* to achieve; *aspirations* refers to what individuals *hope* to achieve. We could not explicitly explore this, as neither expectation nor aspiration were part of the city data sets shared – in fact, this data is not measured. We were able to report the following from our examination of the literature.

- It is said that expectations are better predictors of attainment than educational aspirations, as hopes are not likely to incorporate any self-assessment of ability, whereas expectations might (Goyette, 2008).
- Research demonstrates that young children generally have more positive expectations: 'As we grow up, and in the process experience disappointment, we develop negative expectations, mostly as a way to protect ourselves' (Brandt, 1984, p. 206).
- When teachers expect students to do well and show intellectual growth, they do; when teachers do not have such expectations, performance and growth are not so encouraged and may, in fact, be discouraged in a variety of ways (Rhem, 1999; Rosenthal and Jacobson, 1992).
- Aspirations and expectations from parents and children were high, even for pupils from the poorest backgrounds (Goodman and Gregg, 2010).

Certainly, our data analysis showed that demographic factors did not significantly predict attainment; low and high attainment was found across all groups based on, for example, ethnicity, gender and socioeconomic status. Further, we found what appeared to be a negative attainment spiral. Some pupils were just slightly below national attainment expectations at Key Stage 1. It was largely the same pupils who were lower at Key Stage 2 (by this time on average 5% lower) and the same pupils who were lower by their GCSE examinations (but this time, on average 10% lower).

In particular, the only consistently strong predictor of achievement of those analysed in the project was the Fisher Family Trust's model 'Estimate based on Prior Attainment'. The principal component of this model is prior attainment at KS1 (for KS2 score) and KS2 results (for GCSE). From these analyses, it seems likely that KS1 is an important area to focus on improving, as small differences in underachievement begin here and develop into a downward spiral of underachievement from KS1 to KS2 to GCSE.

In essence, considering the pupil data and the extant evidence when pupils faced early challenge or failure (in lower than expected attainment), this led to a downward spiral of lower and lower attainment, likely due to the lowering of expectation (teacher and pupil) and a subsequent self-fulfilling prophecy. Based on this, we made three key recommendations to the city policy makers.

- Utilise early challenge and failure indicators as flags for early intervention.
- Focus that intervention not just on cognitive skills (study skills and knowledge development), but also on non-cognitive elements of pupils and teachers (specifically expectations) in order that we avoid self-fulfilling prophecies resulting in downward spirals in academic attainment.
- Theory and research in implicit theories of intelligence (aka mindsets) could be a useful framework for the development of non-cognitive interventions.

I was extremely curious to test this theory in practice. Could it work? I was awarded a series of significant grants to support this work and the 'I' became 'we'. Specifically, we are a core team of eight applied researchers from disciplinary backgrounds in psychology, education and sociology. Our research over the last seven years into the question 'Could mindsets work?' is explored in this book.

> "OUR GOAL IN WRITING THIS BOOK IS TO ENCOURAGE EDUCATIONAL PRACTITIONERS TO TAKE THE SAME ANALYTICAL APPROACH TO MINDSETS, TO SUPPORT THEM IN MAKING A CONSIDERED DECISION ABOUT WHETHER AND HOW TO USE MINDSETS IN THEIR CLASSROOMS, AND HOW TO CRITICALLY EXPLORE ITS IMPACT IN PRACTICE."

Our goal in writing this book is to encourage educational practitioners to take the same analytical approach to mindsets, to support them in making a considered decision about whether and how to use mindsets in their classrooms, and how to critically explore its impact in practice. Ultimately, then, the debates may become better evidenced and less polarised, and the mindsets practice more effective.

PART
ONE

ALL ABOUT MINDSETS

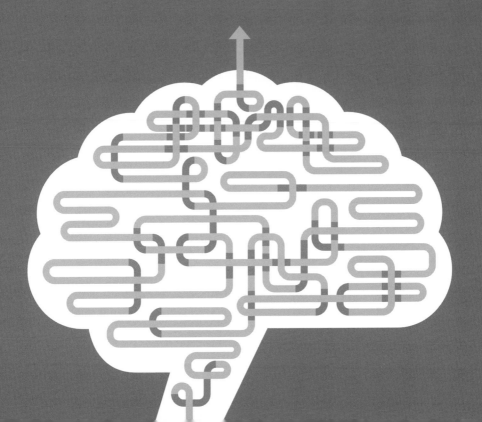

CHAPTER 1

WHY DID WE DESIGN THE GROWING LEARNERS MINDSET INTERVENTION?

SHERRIA HOSKINS

Establishing the need for intervention

As a teacher, you will know better than any research psychologist/sociologist the challenges that are faced every day in schools. I barely need to cite the figures that you will already be aware of, but to provide a national perspective I will summarise a few around pupil attainment and behaviour.

> "THERE IS GROWING CONCERN IN BOTH PRIMARY AND SECONDARY SCHOOLS THAT THE DISRUPTIVE BEHAVIOUR OF PUPILS IS LEADING TO POOR ATTAINMENT LEVELS AND IN WORST CASES EXCLUSION."

There is growing concern in both primary and secondary schools that the disruptive behaviour of pupils is leading to poor attainment levels and in worst cases exclusion (House of Commons Education Committee, 2010–11). It is generally acknowledged that male and female behaviour in the classroom is different. Boys' behaviour tends to be more disruptive and inattentive, and this in turn influences the level of academic achievement; the deficits are small but consistent. It has been claimed that if boys and girls exhibited the same behaviour in the classroom, there would be no evidence of any consistent gender-related differences in school achievement (Fergusson and Horwood, 1997).

Ministers expect the majority of pupils to achieve at least *at expected standard* in English and in Mathematics by the end of Key Stage 2 (typically age 11). Whether this is achievable with the current funding and resource constraints is a debate we will leave for another day. Taking this expectation as our benchmark, the National Pupil Database indicates that in 2012, 79% of pupils achieved this. The attainment gap is evident in clear differences across girls (82%) and boys (77%). For those receiving free school meals, the proportion was 66% compared to all others at 83%. Unfortunately, it is not possible to make easy comparisons between 2012 attainment data and earlier years due to a change in the way that English was measured from 2012, although the attainment gap can be compared. For free school meal pupils, the gap has decreased from a 20% difference in 2011 to a 17% difference in 2012.

GCSE attainment has been improving. In 2009, 50% of pupils achieved five good GCSEs, 54% in 2010, 60% in 2011, with the figure remaining stable into 2012. Research consistently shows that there is a small gender divide in pupil achievement.

"RESEARCH CONSISTENTLY SHOWS THAT THERE IS A SMALL GENDER DIVIDE IN PUPIL ACHIEVEMENT."

Girls achieve better results than boys educationally at the age of 16 years, and a higher proportion of girls than boys continue into education to degree level (Ofsted, 2011). In 2012, 38% of disadvantaged pupils achieved five good GCSEs, including English and maths, or equivalent qualifications, versus 65% of other pupils (Laws, 2013).

Clearly, there is still much to do in terms of supporting schools to improve the educational attainment of pupils (with schools being one route to supporting attainment, and parents and communities being another). The Growing Learners team have had the pleasure to work on two initiatives that aim to bring teachers and teaching leaders together with a researcher academic (in our case, a psychologist) in order that schools are supported with evidence-based interventions. The first for us was the Education Endowment Foundation project in which we worked with 36 schools across

Hampshire; the second is this, the National College for Teaching and Leadership, Closing the Gap project. These are fantastic initiatives because rarely do we, as academic researchers, effectively disseminate what we learn to practitioners. You will, I am sure, come across many educational consultants, and many do great work in schools, but many do not and cannot provide an evidence base for their work. They simply don't know if it works or not – it just sounds feasible.

> "YOU WILL HAVE, I AM SURE, COME ACROSS MANY EDUCATIONAL CONSULTANTS, AND MANY DO GREAT WORK IN SCHOOLS, BUT MANY DO NOT AND CANNOT PROVIDE AN EVIDENCE BASE FOR THEIR WORK, THEY SIMPLY DON'T KNOW IF IT WORKS OR NOT, IT JUST SOUNDS FEASIBLE."

As a psychologist, my goal is not to advise you on how to teach your pupils – you will have a wealth of experience on this. What I can do is tell you about what the theory and the robust and credible research suggest will work to inform your practice and provide potentially useful additions to your toolkit. It is psychology theory and robust applied research that we have based the Growing Learners intervention on.

Focusing on motivation: helping pupils to become Growing Learners

While many educational interventions will work for pupils, we are focusing here on what we call non-cognitive skills – those that impact motivation to learn rather than techniques for learning. However, there is evidence that some non-cognitive skills can have an impact on classroom behaviour and attainment.

> "THERE IS EVIDENCE THAT SOME NON-COGNITIVE SKILLS CAN HAVE AN IMPACT ON CLASSROOM BEHAVIOUR AND ATTAINMENT."

Some have been more powerful than direct behavioural or educational interventions. This is because sometimes you can provide inspiring teaching, encourage effective learning techniques and good classroom behaviour, but a child simply does not have the motivation to use these strategies or attend to the teaching. In addition, supporting the development of some non-cognitive skills will often create a Growing Learner for life, not just for a specific learning task or situation.

"SUPPORTING THE DEVELOPMENT OF SOME NON-COGNITIVE SKILLS WILL OFTEN CREATE A GROWING LEARNER FOR LIFE, NOT JUST FOR A SPECIFIC LEARNING TASK OR SITUATION."

Our main goal in this intervention is to help schools and teachers to support pupils to become a Growing Learner – that is, pupils who are engaged (both in terms of school attendance and persistence in learning) in positive classroom behaviour that works towards closing the attainment gap.

Here, I introduce the theory and research that underpins the Growing Learners intervention. We explore a range of non-cognitive elements that relate to learning behaviour and attainment.

Laddishness

There is currently research to suggest that 'laddishness' attitudes affect the motivation and commitment of children and young adolescents in education. Laddishness is described as an anti-learning attitude, manifesting directly as disruptive behaviour in the classroom, or indirectly through withdrawal of effort and avoiding the appearance of working (Jackson, 2006) – more specifically: procrastination, intentional withdrawal of effort, avoidance of the appearance of working and disruptive behaviour. Jackson describes it as a strategy aimed at self-protection. For example, if a pupil has a spelling test but they don't practise for that test, and if they don't perform well as a result, they can tell themselves that they didn't practise rather than evaluate their ability in relation to the outcome in a way that would damage their self-esteem.

It is suggested that these anti-learning attitudes are also admired by peers, which leads to an exacerbation of disruptive and non-conformist behaviours (Warrington et al., 2003). Laddishness behaviours are considered as a result of a need for acceptance within a dominant social hierarchy, meaning that laddishness-type behaviours can affect a whole year group. This exerts strong negative influences on engagement and leads to severe costs concerning children's attainment levels (Skelton, 2001).

However, laddishness is not limited to male learners. Recently, the problem has also been reported to affect the female population, although this was identified in a relatively small-scale study assessing only eight schools. Females reported in interviews that they engaged in similar types of disruptive behaviour such as being abusive to teachers and fighting with peers (Jackson, 2006). It has been suggested that this is due to a change of attitudes to femininity, with women becoming more confident and assertive (Harris, 2004). This has resulted in women becoming more loud and boisterous in the classroom, and therefore having negative effects on the classroom environment and disrupting other students' learning. 'Laddette' behaviours outside school also have negative outcome for learning as research suggests that there is an increasing problem of binge drinking, unsafe sex and risk-taking behaviours that can impede future success (Harris, 2004). Therefore, disruptive behaviour is problematic across genders. It is important not to perceive laddishness as a male-only issue.

Nevertheless, existing research into disruptive behaviour in schools focuses mostly on a male population due to a decline in male achievement (Francis, 2000).

"EXISTING RESEARCH INTO DISRUPTIVE BEHAVIOUR IN SCHOOLS FOCUSES MOSTLY ON A MALE POPULATION DUE TO A DECLINE IN MALE ACHIEVEMENT."

This has led to government research and interventions that aimed to improve attainment levels and male engagement to learning (Department for Education and Employment, 1998). An example of an intervention is the 'Raising Achievement in Boys' project which was intended to assess the differential achievement gap between boys and girls. The research was completed over a four-year period, covering 50 primary schools, although it only assessed achievement levels in pupils in Key Stages 2 and 4. The findings showed that the main issue relating to male under-achievement is their struggle to maintain a masculine status and protect their self-worth. Therefore social-cultural strategies have been put in place in order to try to combat the problem such as leadership schemes and citizenship initiatives. However, previous attempts to implement social-cultural strategies have failed as a result of the complexity of the issue and time-restraints of the project, meaning that staff found it difficult to fully commit to the project (Younger et al., 2005). These barriers made it difficult to address laddishness behaviours in schools. This is rather a negative point on which to end our exploration of laddishness, but I will pick this up again later with a possible solution.

Aspiration

One of the main priorities of the UK Government is to increase the aspirations of young people so that they aim higher. There is a Government belief that young people who live in certain types of neighbourhood are less likely to have high aspirations and these are associated with high levels of deprivation (Sinclair et al., 2010). The Government works with the idea that low aspirations tend to lead to low achievement. It is believed that raising these aspirations will help to break this cycle (Kintrea, 2009).

Aspirations have a significant social basis (Genicot and Ray, 2010). They begin to develop long before children start their educational experience. Through family interaction at home and involvement in the community, children learn of expectations at an early age.

"THROUGH FAMILY INTERACTION AT HOME AND INVOLVEMENT IN THE COMMUNITY, CHILDREN LEARN OF EXPECTATIONS AT AN EARLY AGE."

Aspirations of close relatives, parents, teachers and peers all have differential effects on students' educational expectations (Cheng and Starks, 2002). Interpersonal relationships have been found to affect individual educational aspirations. Significant others seem to mediate the effects of socioeconomic class and occupational attainment. Parents and peers emerge as the strongest shapers of students' aspirations, but teachers are also important. The type of school the student attends can also affect their student aspirations; the closer the school is to the parents' education, the greater the influence of peers and parents; the less close the school is to the parents' education, the less influence the parents and peers have (Buchmann and Dalton, 2002).

Ethnicity seems to play a role in students' aspirational goals, although other factors such as the home educational aspirations are also important. Students who had career aspirations were more likely to have family members as role models.

"STUDENTS WHO HAD CAREER ASPIRATIONS WERE MORE LIKELY TO HAVE FAMILY MEMBERS AS ROLE MODELS."

Parents of black students seem to encourage their sons to do better, whereas parents of white students did not want their children to suffer disappointment or angry feelings. Similar patterns in ethnic groups have been found in other research.

Ashmore (2009) claims that current UK Government policies are based on a 'Poverty of Aspiration' thesis, which asserts that lower class families and neighbourhoods have low aspirations. This leads in turn to under-achievement, which then leads to low participation in post-compulsory education, which can lead to low social mobility, thereby reinforcing a cycle of disadvantage. However, Ashmore challenges this 'Poverty of Aspiration' thesis as research from the Department for Children, Schools and Families (DCSF, 2009) has shown that students in Year 7, for example, have high aspirations regardless of socioeconomic background. In addition, those students in Year 7 were well aware of what job they wanted, for logical reasons, and had held these beliefs for many years. The DCSF (2009) research found no difference in aspirations based on socioeconomic status (SES) background, although some students had a poor knowledge of the educational choices available. Further evidence that expectations are more important predictors than aspiration comes from the results of a longitudinal exploration of schools in Glasgow, London and Nottingham (Turok et al., 2009). The study demonstrates that young people do think about their future and many aspire to be in professional jobs. Young people are realistic when thinking about the qualifications they need to get their ideal jobs. Parents are an important influence, but it was found that many parents in deprived areas had strong educational and vocational aspirations for their children. There was little evidence to show that living in a disadvantaged area affects young people's aspirations at the age of 13.

"THERE WAS LITTLE EVIDENCE TO SHOW THAT LIVING IN A DISADVANTAGED AREA AFFECTS YOUNG PEOPLE'S ASPIRATIONS AT THE AGE OF 13."

Further support for the conclusions of Turok et al. (2009) that SES does not affect aspirations comes from a study in a deprived area of Glasgow that found no evidence of secondary school children having low aspirations or a readiness to work (Sinclair et al., 2010).

To summarise the research, only some of which we have mentioned here, it can be said that the assumption that low SES is a cause of low aspiration is an oversimplification. In much of the research, this assumption is not evidenced. Although it is clear that aspirations are influenced by the adults in children's lives, it is not necessarily the case that regional poverty leads to low aspiration.

It should be made explicit here that aspirations are not the same as expectations. Expectations refer to the education and experience that the individual *expects* to achieve; aspirations refers to what individuals *hope* to achieve.

"EXPECTATIONS REFER TO THE EDUCATION AND EXPE-RIENCE THAT THE INDIVIDUAL *EXPECTS* TO ACHIEVE; ASPIRATIONS REFERS TO WHAT INDIVIDUALS *HOPE* TO ACHIEVE."

It is said that expectations are better predictors of attainment than educational aspirations, as hopes are not likely to incorporate any self-assessment of ability, whereas expectations might (Goyette, 2008). Thus, government policy may have misdirected its efforts.

Self-efficacy

Self-efficacy is one of the oldest non-cognitive phenomena researched in psychology that taps into pupil expectations (rather than aspiration). Bandura (1977, 1997) describes self-efficacy as a key motivating factor in goal achievement. Outcome expectations – i.e. the expectation that certain behaviour will lead to the goal (outcome) are a part of motivation. However, it is argued that outcome expectations alone are not sufficient to explain the behaviour of an individual. An individual may expect that certain behaviours will result in a desired outcome, but it does not necessarily follow that they will complete the necessary behaviour. Bandura (ibid.) argued that this could be understood in terms of efficacy expectations; an individual must be aware of the required behaviour *and* be confident that they have the ability to execute that behaviour. A person who has low efficacy regarding their ability to successfully complete a task and reach a goal will avoid the situation or expend little effort, whereas an individual with high efficacy will feel capable of tackling the situation and subsequently may use more effort.

"A PERSON WHO HAS LOW EFFICACY REGARDING THEIR ABILITY TO SUCCESSFULLY COMPLETE A TASK AND REACH A GOAL WILL AVOID THE SITUATION OR EXPEND LITTLE EFFORT, WHEREAS AN INDIVIDUAL WITH HIGH EFFICACY WILL FEEL CAPABLE OF TACKLING THE SITUA-TION AND SUBSEQUENTLY MAY USE MORE EFFORT."

Decisions regarding self-efficacy, according to Bandura, are learned from a person's own experience and vicarious experience (seeing others achieve and comparing self to others). The effect of failure is temporal in that it is dependent upon the timing of the failure within a success/failure sequence. For example, an early failure is liable to result in a larger decrease in self-efficacy than a failure that follows a string of successes (particularly if it is then followed by more success). In the absence of personal experience, efficacy expectations may be formed through vicarious experience – i.e. observing other individuals' experience of a similar task. The degree to which vicarious experience affects efficacy expectations is mediated by the characteristics of the other person involved. There is a larger increase in efficacy when 1) the other individual displays characteristics similar to those of oneself and 2) they have experienced difficulty with the task but persisted and succeeded. This effect is heightened when more than one other person has been successful in achieving the goal. Discussion and reflection may influence efficacy judgements since verbal persuasion is another reference point for such judgements (Bandura, op. cit.).

Bandura's 'self-efficacy' theory is an important approach to consider for non-cognitive interventions in schools because it involves behavioural change. It is students' *perceptions* regarding their ability (non-cognitive skill), rather than actual levels of ability (cognitive skill), that is important. Bandura suggested that low self-efficacy causes avoidance behaviour, whereas high self-efficacy is coupled with motivational behaviour and a driving force to succeed.

"LOW SELF-EFFICACY CAUSES AVOIDANCE BEHAVIOUR, WHEREAS HIGH SELF-EFFICACY IS COUPLED WITH MOTIVATIONAL BEHAVIOUR AND A DRIVING FORCE TO SUCCEED."

Here we return to laddishness, as it has been suggested to result from feelings of inadequacy and lack of self-worth, similar to low self-efficacy. Certainly, self-efficacy has been found to affect several aspects of educational development. For example, Salomon (1984) demonstrated that self-efficacy is positively related to achievement in a task involving learning from material perceived as difficult. Haycock et al. (2011) investigated participants' self-efficacy expectations in relation to their performance on an important project and found a significant correlation between a stronger self-efficacy expectation and less procrastination. Therefore, developing pupils' self-efficacy in learning may be a route to addressing laddishness. However, based on Bandura's (1997) self-efficacy theory, which implies that through repeated failure self-efficacy would be re-evaluated and lowered, lower achievement levels are reached. Research also found that low self-efficacy is coupled with a fear of failure, meaning that individuals are less likely to work towards goals and try to improve their performance (Malouff et al., 1990). Therefore, self-efficacy cannot explain how a learner becomes persistent in the face of challenge or failure, a situation that is likely during Standard Attainment Tests (SATs) periods or at key educational transitions.

Where does this leave us?

If laddishness interventions are hard to commit to, if aspiration doesn't impact behaviour and attainment as much as expectation, but the best current measure of expectation, self-efficacy, only predicts attainment until a pupil faces a challenge and failure – where do we go from here? I believe that self-theories of intelligence (commonly known as mindsets) are one way ahead. The focus on non-cognitive skills, relating to attainment and behaviours, could provide a protection against laddishness and positive mindsets can be developed in pupils fairly easily.

Self theories of intelligence (mindsets)

"IT IS NOT ABILITY (COGNITIVE SKILL) OR BELIEF IN THAT ABILITY (SELF-EFFICACY, A NON-COGNITIVE SKILL) THAT PREDICTS RESILIENCE AND PERSEVERANCE IN THE FACE OF CHALLENGE AND FAILURE; RATHER, IT IS AN INDIVIDUAL'S BELIEF ABOUT THE NATURE OF ABILITY."

Dweck (1999) asserts that it is not ability (cognitive skill) or belief in that ability (self-efficacy, a non-cognitive skill) that predicts resilience and perseverance in the face of challenge and failure; rather, it is an individual's belief about the nature of ability.

Nussbaum and Dweck (2008) suggested that implicit theories of intelligence affect how pupils cope in the face of failure.

Dweck's model of implicit theories of intelligence consists of two self theories: entity and incremental. Pupils who hold an entity theory of intelligence believe that intelligence is fixed and cannot be improved through effort; they therefore are believed to focus on performance goals – i.e.

their result in order to appear intelligent. On the other hand, people who hold an incremental theory of intelligence believe that intelligence is malleable and can be cultivated by applying effort; this is believed to lead them to focus on learning goals – i.e. seeking challenging tasks in order to develop their skills and knowledge, and reflecting on what they learned from that task, rather whether their score made them look clever (Dweck and Leggett, 1988).

These expected differences in learning orientation are reported to be due to the difference in children's meaning systems; failure has different meanings for those with a either a growth mindset or a fixed mindset. For those with a growth mindset, effort is seen as a necessity in order to achieve in life (Dweck, 1999). However, fixed theorists believe that high effort indicates low ability and are therefore fearful of being perceived in these terms, avoiding persistent effort, leading them to sabotage long-term goals (Dweck, 1999). For those with a fixed mindset, failure is attributed not to effort but to their own ability; thus, failure is damaging to self-esteem.

"FOR THOSE WITH A FIXED MINDSET, FAILURE IS ATTRIBUTED NOT TO EFFORT BUT TO THEIR OWN ABILITY; THUS, FAILURE IS DAMAGING TO SELF-ESTEEM."

This is a negative state that can be evaded by avoidance of the task or avoidance of effort in the task if forced to confront it. Thus, the individual protects themselves from future failures that can be attributed to their ability (by themselves or others).

Implicit theories of intelligence have been studied extensively. First, I want to explore the evidence that mindsets really do relate to or impact on the way in which students approach their learning – are those with a growth theory of intelligence more engaged, resilient and persistent?

First, reaction to failure and challenge. Nussbaum and Dweck (2008) demonstrated that the implicit theory of intelligence a person holds affects the remedial action they will take in the face of failure, with entity theorists more likely to defend their self-esteem even though this does not improve their ability, while incremental theorists are more likely to take remedial action in order to learn rather than protect their self-esteem. Zhao and Dweck (1994) cited by Dweck et al. (1995) explored how people with different mindsets deal with failure. They gave participants actual and hypothetical failures and asked them to rate their responses to these scenarios. Entity theorists gave more negative responses to failure, whereas growth theorists were more likely to directly confront the situation and seek to challenge themselves to avoid failure in the future. However, this study used hypothetical situations, meaning that participants may not have responded accurately. Licht and Dweck (1984) revealed that when students with a helpless orientation were confronted with a confusing passage of a task, only 35.6% of students mastered the task compared to 71.9% of mastery orientated children. Diener and Dweck (1978) explored the differences between helpless children and mastery orientated children in fifth and sixth grade (UK Years 5 and 6). This study was based on anagrams: the first eight anagrams were possible to solve, but the next four anagrams were far too difficult for children of their age. As expected, the helpless children attributed their failure to lack of ability and quickly doubted their intelligence when faced with failure. They lost their motivation to perform the task.

It is clear that having a helpless orientation to learning can hinder an individual's ability to work to their full potential. Students who adopt a mastery orientation tend to demonstrate more pride and satisfaction in their success and have less anxiety in the event of failure than students who adopt a performance goal orientation (Ames, 1992).

"STUDENTS WHO ADOPT A MASTERY ORIENTATION TEND TO DEMONSTRATE MORE PRIDE AND SATISFACTION IN THEIR SUCCESS AND HAVE LESS ANXIETY IN THE EVENT OF FAILURE THAN STUDENTS WHO ADOPT A PERFORMANCE GOAL ORIENTATION" (AMES, 1992).

A similar relationship is found for theory of intelligence, with individuals with a fixed theory of intelligence adopting a helpless reaction to failure. This leads to negative cognitions such as self-blame, resulting in a decline in academic achievement for many individuals (Dweck, 1996).

In terms of general learning orientations, correlational studies indicate that students who espouse a mastery goal orientation are more likely to monitor their understanding of what is being learned – e.g. Meece and Holt, 1993; Middleton and Midgley, 1997, employ organising strategies such as paraphrasing and summarising (Archer 1994), and make positive, adaptive attributions for occasional failures compared to students who adopt performance goals. Hong et al. (1999) demonstrated the substantial influence of implicit theories in their study. They carried out three studies exploring implicit theories and their effects on attributions and coping. Schunk (1996) manipulated the goal orientation of children aged 9 to 11 while doing maths problems. Children were randomly assigned to one of four experimental conditions: mastery goal with self-evaluation, teaming goal without self-evaluation, performance goal with self-evaluation, performance goal without self-evaluation. Children who were directed to work under a mastery learning goal orientation demonstrated greater task involvement and greater subsequent achievement than children who worked under a performance goal orientation.

"CHILDREN WHO WERE DIRECTED TO WORK UNDER A MASTERY LEARNING GOAL ORIENTATION DEMONSTRATED GREATER TASK INVOLVEMENT AND GREATER SUBSEQUENT ACHIEVEMENT THAN CHILDREN WHO WORKED UNDER A PERFORMANCE GOAL ORIENTATION."

These results strongly support the model proposed by Dweck and Leggett (1988), emphasising the importance of implicit theories of intelligence in terms of effort attributions, resilience and perseverance.

In terms of transition, there is further work. King (2012) studied implicit theories of intelligence and adjustment in high school students. The findings verified that entity theorists showed higher levels of maladaptive adjustment outcomes, while incremental theorists showed the opposite. Supporting this, Henderson and Dweck (1990) found that of students making the transition into junior high school, those holding an incremental theory of intelligence adjusted better and received significantly higher grades than entity theorists. These findings have key implications, demonstrating the value of holding an incremental theory on academic success (be that achievement or adjustment) successful.

When looking at attainment in relation to mindsets, there is good evidence of a relationship and an impact. Henderson and Dweck (1990) investigated whether children's theory of intelligence affected their academic results in their transition from infant school to junior school. It was found that due to the difficulties of the new setting, fixed theorists struggled and showed clear losses in their academic achievement compared to growth theorists.

Blackwell et al. (2007) followed American school children as they made the transition to seventh grade (equivalent to Year 8 in the UK) and found that pupils with an existing growth mindset outperformed those with a fixed mindset in maths and that – despite all pupils entering the seventh grade with similar past attainment – this gap continued to grow over the two-year period of the study.

"PUPILS WITH AN EXISTING GROWTH MINDSET OUTPERFORMED THOSE WITH A FIXED MINDSET IN MATHS AND – DESPITE ALL PUPILS ENTERING THE

> SEVENTH GRADE WITH SIMILAR PAST ATTAINMENT –
> THIS GAP CONTINUED TO GROW OVER THE TWO-
> YEAR PERIOD OF THE STUDY."

They also carried out an interventional study in which an incremental theory was taught to a group of students, leading to improved grades and classroom motivation in comparison to a control group. In another study, Good et al. (2003) demonstrate that pupils who received growth mindset training showed significant increases in their maths and verbal test scores (compared to a control group). Additionally, the girls in the growth mindset group not only improved their attainment, but also narrowed the gender gap in maths. Although this may suggest that growth mindset work is more effective with girls than boys, this isn't the case. This simply demonstrates that in relation to maths, the boys had less of an issue with fixed mindset and didn't have as far to move as the girls did. In other words, the transformation was smaller for boys because they were already positive and performing in this area. Furthermore, research has shown that the increased effort and persistence of a mastery goal orientation correlates with higher academic achievement (Elliot and Harackiewicz, 1996; Meece and Holt, 1993). A recent quasi-experimental study, for example, investigated the impact of brainology (a US online interactive program aimed at encouraging a growth mindset) on the mindset, resilience and sense of mastery of pupils aged 13–14 years (Donohoe et al., 2012). Findings indicated that the program led to a significant increase in these characteristics. These findings emphasise the importance of implicit theories of intelligence and the pivotal effects they can have, and the consistency of findings makes them extremely convincing.

Developing a growth theory of intelligence

Much research has explored whether we can change children's theory of intelligence. Blackwell and colleagues (2007) randomly placed seventh-grade students (age 12) in one of two weekly workshops for eight sessions. In the treatment group, students learned that intelligence is changeable and that the brain is like a muscle which grows with use. In the control group, students learned only study skills. After the eight-week intervention, the researchers tested the understanding of all students about how the brain works, as well as measured changes in their beliefs about the nature of intelligence. They found that students in the treatment group changed their understanding of the brain and their beliefs about intelligence such that they endorsed an incremental theory more strongly after participating in the intervention (4.36 pre-intervention vs. 4.95 post-intervention (d = .66)), but participants in the control group did not change their beliefs (4.62 pre-intervention vs. 4.68 post-intervention (d = .07)). Further research has shown that theories of intelligence are a dynamic concept, with a recent study showing that individuals can be manipulated to adopt a growth theory of intelligence. This was achieved through subjecting a year group of programming students to growth mindset workshops over a six-week period. The results revealed that there were significant changes, with students adopting a growth mindset, and through this learning-goal orientations were achieved. The limitation of this study was that only 89 out of 170 students completed the post-intervention questionnaires, with the potential for self-selection and distortion of results (Cutts et al., 2010). However, many other studies, including some already mentioned above, add credence to this finding by replicating the overarching conclusion that mindsets can be developed (Aronson et al., 2002; Blackwell et al., 2007; Cohen et al., 2006; Dweck, 2007; Good et al., 2003; Walton and Cohen, 2007).

Classroom behaviour

Finally, returning to laddishness in pupils: pupils with a growth mindset would have no reason to adopt self-protection strategies.

"PUPILS WITH A GROWTH MINDSET WOULD HAVE NO REASON TO ADOPT SELF-PROTECTION STRATEGIES."

Their learning orientation would already be mastery oriented where failure would not be attributed to self and a fixed ability (thus damaging self-esteem), but would be attributed to a need for more effort to a different strategy. In short, failure would be seen as a learning opportunity.

Thus, mindsets is the best approach from which to develop Growing Learners, defined here by engaged, enthusiastic learners who love a challenge, see mistakes and failure as a normal route to learning in which effort and strategy will enable you to achieve your goals.

In another US study, an experiment was performed to test a method of helping students resist responses to stereotypes about ability and ethnicity (Aronson et al., 2002) which is pertinent in our closing the gap agenda. Specifically, students in the experimental condition of the experiment were encouraged to see intelligence – the object of the stereotype – as a malleable rather than fixed capacity. This growth mindset was predicted to make students' performances less vulnerable to stereotype threat and help them maintain their psychological engagement with academics, both of which could help boost their college grades. Results were consistent with predictions. The African American students encouraged to view intelligence as malleable reported greater enjoyment of the academic process, greater academic engagement and obtained higher grade point averages than their counterparts in two control groups. These results are extremely promising. This supports the value of such interventions in that growth mindsets can be developed. In addition, the evidence presented suggests that these changes can be sustained without further intervention, can have long-term impacts on achievement and can close gender and ethnicity gaps in achievement.

Measurement

There is a wide variety of different instruments to measure learning orientation. The Patterns of Adaptive Learning Scale (PALS) examines the relation between the learning environment and students' motivation, affect (emotion) and behaviour. PALS has been shown to be reliable but it is a long tool to use, with items measuring many elements including 1) personal achievement goal orientations; 2) perceptions of teacher's goals; 3) perceptions of the goal structures in the classroom; 4) achievement-related beliefs, attitudes and strategies; and 5) perceptions of parents and home life. Dweck and her colleagues have developed an implicit theory of intelligence measure, a much easier tool to use that measures mindset rather than learning orientations. This measure includes six items: three statements measuring a fixed mindset. For example:

'You have a certain amount of intelligence, and you really can't do much to change it'; and three statements assessing a growth mindset, for example: 'You can always greatly change how intelligent you are'.

Respondents indicated their agreement with these statements on a six-point Likert scale from 1 (strongly agree) to 6 (strongly disagree). This measure has demonstrated high internal reliability and validity (Dweck et al., 1995). However, teachers often told us that they wanted a scale to measure no mindset but the resulting learning orientation (like PALs) but that was quick and easy to use. Therefore, we have developed our own tool to measure learning orientations (helpless or mastery oriented) – My Learning tested just under 2,000 junior school pupils (Years 4 and 5) in order that we can provide a way for you to assess your pupils quickly and easily.

In summary, many years of research has shown that:

• mindsets impact children's learning orientations and the way they approach their learning;

- children with a growth mindset are more engaged, resilient and persistent in their learning;
- children with a growth mindset do better at school;
- children can be taught a growth mindset;
- changes in mindset as a result of intervention have been maintained in up to eight weeks after intervention;
- teaching a growth mindset raises motivation and achievement, especially in traditionally difficult subjects (e.g. maths) and across difficult school transitions;
- these impacts on attainment occur as positive upward spirals via enhanced resilience to challenging tasks;
- different patterns in mindset (naturally occurring) in childhood persist into adulthood and have an impact beyond educational attainment.

The limitations of this work so far is that the studies tend to be small scale and often do not look at pupils across more than a couple of schools. They are largely based in the US, so results may not apply here in the UK and they do not follow up pupils much longer than 8–10 weeks after an intervention.

We have early results from our UK study, which are not published yet. We worked with just under 2,000 pupils from 36 schools. We pre-tested our pupils' attainment, mindsets and learning orientations with follow-up testing 6–10 weeks after the intervention and 10 months after the intervention. So far, early data analysis shows that initial mindset does relate to academic attainment and our intervention did improve growth mindset. We will be publishing a follow-up paper that explores this further.

Why train teachers?

Most of the work in the US has focused on educationalists from universities providing direct interventions with pupils. No one has yet tried or at least publicised an attempt to support mindset growth by working with teachers to support this growth in their pupils. There are many reasons why this is worth doing, among which:

- teachers know their pupils best and can adapt interventions for them;
- teachers can have a huge positive influence on pupils.

Teacher expectation has been shown to influence students' aspirations, expectations and achievement. There is a general consensus found in the literature that when teachers expect children to do well and show intellectual growth they do; when teachers do not have such expectations, performance and growth are not so encouraged and may, in fact, be discouraged in a variety of ways (Li, 2016). Eccles and Jussim (1992) also found that the expectations teachers have for their students whether positive or negative, and the theorisation they make about their potential, can greatly influence those children's academic achievement. Thus, if your expectation is that they can develop their ability, they should develop their ability. Our early work with teachers in a funded project with 30 schools shows us that training teachers can change changes pupils' mindsets. Training teachers is also a cost-effective way to influence pupils, so it is the type of intervention that the UK government and schools can invest in. Finally, training teachers in mindsets means that instead of a short-term intervention, we can support long-term legacy across UK schools.

In summary

We expect that your work with pupils can help to develop pupils as Growing Learners – more resilient, curious learners who are willing to take on a challenge and see this as part of the learning process. You should see the following improvements.

- Improved attendance.
- Gradual upward cycle of attainment.
- Better behaviour/more engagement in the classroom.
- More stable self-esteem of the pupils.
- Better relationships between children of different abilities.
- Lower impact of stereotypes on attainment.
- Teachers using feedback more confidently (positive or negative).

Hereafter, we provide an account of our critical exploration of these claims via an exploration of the existing research and literature, and our own classroom trials.

CHAPTER 2

A PRIMER ON CHILDREN'S PERSONALITY AND PERFORMANCE

LIAM SATCHELL

"NOT EVERYONE IS THE SAME."

Not everyone is the same. We all have different approaches to the world and people around us. Some people are more energetic in everyday life – they are more sensation-seeking and explorative. Others are calmer and need less information and busyness in their life. Some people are neat, tidy and ordered, and others less so. In this 'primer' chapter I will be introducing some of the key individual differences that educational psychologists discuss when studying school behaviour. Many of the concepts here are well-established areas of research with whole books dedicated to their individual influence. So, what follows is a gentle introduction to how we do individual differences science and our efforts to understand, predict and help pupils who are naturally different.

The naturally occurring differences between people is an ancient fascination. There are Norse myths that suggest that magic mead explains how some people prefer to write poetry while others are more practical. The ancient Greeks considered hypothetical bodily fluids ('humors') that might lead someone to be more dull or cheerful. Unfortunately, these humors did not exist, but the theory was based on the idea that we can look to biology and anatomy to explain differences between people's preferred behaviour. Individual differences in psychology has come a long way from these early roots and these days investigations into the variation between people is a largely scientific exercise. We study large numbers of people to work out what makes individuals unique when compared to the wider population. During our early work to understand uniqueness in individuals, we found that many features that made a person unique occurred together. Someone who is very 'energetic' is also likely to be 'sensation-seeking' and talkative. We started to realise that we can bring together collections of similar behaviours into *personality traits*.

"WE CAN BRING TOGETHER COLLECTIONS OF SIMILAR BEHAVIOURS INTO *PERSONALITY TRAITS*."

As individual differences psychologists, we aim to create as few as possible key terms that can efficiently summarise many features of a person. This is important as we can analyse and make predictions from these key packages of personality. For example, we know that people higher in the personality trait known as 'neuroticism' are more likely to develop mental health issues and people with a higher intelligence quotient (IQ) are also more likely to receive higher marks in educational assessment. In both of these cases, the relationship between individual difference and outcome exists, but importantly we also know how to identify and change (through therapy and education respectively) these individual differences. By learning how to package differences between people, we can predict behaviours and design ways to help them. So, individual differences are the psychologist's way of capturing why and how people are different so that we can use this information to improve life outcomes.

"THE STUDY OF INDIVIDUAL DIFFERENCES IS VERY IMPORTANT IN EDUCATION."

The study of individual differences is very important in education. In fact, the very process of assessment (SATs, GCSEs, etc.) is an attempt to identify individual differences in ability and memory of learned material. How individual pupils (and teachers) naturally vary affects classroom outcomes. The individual's personality, behaviours, abilities and beliefs in a classroom setting can lead to variations in classroom engagement and attainment. In this chapter, we will explore some of the most common theories of individual differences in psychology. We will talk about variation in the following.

- Personality: long-term consistent behavioural and thinking patterns.
- Intelligence: thinking speed and information processing.
- Learning styles: do individuals' 'preferred learning styles' affect educational outcome?
- Beliefs: what are our mindsets about how the world changes to us?

Personality

What is personality?

Personality has a specific meaning in psychology. A personality trait is a feature of behaviour or thought that is largely unchanging over a long period of time.

> "A PERSONALITY TRAIT IS A FEATURE OF BEHAVIOUR OR THOUGHT THAT IS LARGELY UNCHANGING OVER A LONG PERIOD OF TIME."

The study of personality draws a line between long-term personality *traits* and short-term emotional *states* of mind. For example, feeling happy or tired are temporary *states*. These states are thoughts and behaviours that are highly changeable and responsive to the world. They can be changed very easily, such as getting bad news (affecting happiness) or a good night's sleep (affecting tiredness).

Personality *traits*, however, are different. Personality traits are features that vary little over long periods of time.

> "PERSONALITY TRAITS ARE FEATURES THAT VARY LITTLE OVER LONG PERIODS OF TIME."

For example, someone who is highly talkative or organised is likely to be highly talkative or organised across many different contexts and across their lifetime. Importantly, when we describe a person's personality traits, we want to be efficient. There are many words you might use to describe a person's character, but personality psychology is interested in offering insight on as many behaviours and thoughts as possible from identifying a few key traits. For example, the data show us that someone who is outgoing and sociable is also likely to be enthusiastic about many things and be talkative. Someone who is organised is also likely to be persistent and careful in many other activities. With large data sets we can notice which features of behaviour most commonly co-occur and construct concise groupings of traits that detail variation between people. There are many different solutions to the ideal number of personality traits, but the most popular and widely used is the 'Big Five' personality theory.

The Big Five theory outlines five key traits that can summarise human personality. It is worth discussing as it is frequently used in educational contexts (see below). The five personality scales are:

- conscientiousness: tidiness in thought and behaviour;
- agreeableness: compassion, friendliness and trust;
- neuroticism: anxiety, worry and rumination;
- openness (to experience); curiosity about ideas and new experiences;
- extraversion: energetics and assertiveness.

It is important to note that personality does not inherently have a 'good' end. High scoring on conscientiousness is generally useful in office work environments; however, someone who is low on conscientiousness may be more flexible and spontaneous, and these are much needed skills in other settings. Scoring highly on neuroticism is related to mental health issues and difficulties; however, being fearless and having no anxiety can lead to social, occupational and well-being issues too.

Like many other aspects of modern individual differences psychology, we are coming to understand how an individual's personality is shaped by both their biological *nature* (genetics, body chemistry, etc.) and their *nurtured* environment (schooling, parenting, life events, etc.).

"AN INDIVIDUAL'S PERSONALITY IS SHAPED BY BOTH THEIR BIOLOGICAL *NATURE* AND THEIR *NURTURED* ENVIRONMENT"

Because of this, personality is heritable *and* naturally develops over a lifetime. Our traits are most flexible when we are younger and they 'solidify' as we get older.

> **"OUR TRAITS ARE MOST FLEXIBLE WHEN WE ARE YOUNGER AND THEY 'SOLIDIFY' AS WE GET OLDER."**

We can make personality change happen through intervention, therapy and schooling. In fact, many aims of mental health therapy are to change an individual's dispositional neuroticism and extraversion. Schooling is designed to train patience and self-control (conscientiousness), social skills (agreeableness) and expose us to new ideas (openness).

What does personality predict in schools?

Personality assessments can be relatively simple to administer (some personality tests are as short as ten questions). Further, many of the behaviours assessed in a personality questionnaire are easy to see by a teacher or parent (i.e. tidiness, chattiness). Because of this, personality traits can be easily assessed and related to performance and behaviour in classrooms. Below is an introductory conversation to how key personality traits (the Big Five) have been shown to relate to school behaviour and outcomes. The evidence presented below should be interpreted with caution.

Personality traits can be considered to be successful predictors of schooling outcomes, but that does not mean it is the only thing that matters.

> **"PERSONALITY TRAITS CAN BE CONSIDERED TO BE SUCCESSFUL PREDICTORS OF SCHOOLING OUTCOMES, BUT THAT DOES NOT MEAN IT IS THE ONLY THING THAT MATTERS."**

Very broadly, personality can explain approximately 10% of the differences between people in education. These traits are contributing findings and we should be aware of them, but they are far from the only explanation.

Conscientiousness

> **"CONSCIENTIOUSNESS IS THE MOST RELIABLE PERSONALITY PREDICTOR OF EDUCATIONAL OUTCOMES."**

Conscientiousness is the most reliable personality predictor of educational outcomes. Pupils who show more focus and persistence are those who tend to perform better in academic assessment. This effect is consistent from primary to secondary school, and persists into Further and Higher Education. Part of the profile of a conscientious person is to be more inclined to pursue long-term aims. Because of this, conscientious individuals understand challenge as part of the learning process and work harder when engaging with an unfamiliar topic. In our own research, we have found that conscientiousness is related to more 'growth' mindsets (which are discussed elsewhere in the book). Conscientiousness is also the opposite of impulsivity and restlessness traits. The challenges that low-conscientious individuals face with sitting still and focus, unsurprisingly, present challenges in the classroom. Many researchers (including some of our own research) have studied how low conscientiousness relates to more disruptive behaviour in the classroom and such individuals can create classroom management challenges for teachers. It is also worth noting that conscientiousness is an important trait to develop; it is related to occupational success and can predict healthy living (and even how long a person may live).

> **"IN THE CLASSROOM, THE CONSCIENTIOUS PUPIL IS THE ONE WHO WILL BE ABLE TO SIT STILL AND FOCUS FOR LONG PERIODS OF TIME. THEY WILL BE FOCUSED ON THE BIGGER PICTURE OF THEIR EDUCATION AND WILL WANT TO OVERCOME CHALLENGES TO GET THERE. THEY WILL BE THE TYPE OF PERSON WHO WILL CHECK THEIR OWN WORK AND WILL BE CAREFUL TO AVOID 'EASY' MISTAKES. THE CONSCIENTIOUS PUPIL WILL LIKELY FOLLOW INSTRUCTION BEST."**

In the classroom, the conscientious pupil is the one who will be able to sit still and focus for long periods of time. They will be focused on the bigger picture of their education and will want to overcome challenges to get there. They will be the type of person who will check their own work and will be careful to avoid 'easy' mistakes. The conscientious pupil will likely follow instruction best.

With this description, it is perhaps unsurprising that a conscientious disposition best helps a pupil adapt to the classroom environment.

Agreeableness

Agreeableness is reflective of an individual's pro-social tendency and, in general, does not relate to concrete academic outcomes. There's no evidence that agreeableness impacts on grades from primary school to university. However, elsewhere in the school, agreeableness can be important. When we look at the effects of low agreeableness (anti-social behaviour), we find that this personality trait can predict bullying behaviour and classroom disengagement. Lowly agreeable individuals can have impacts on classroom climate, and the performance of individuals in the class can falter as a consequence of this. Moreover, bullying and social hostility can create an unpleasant social environment, discouraging pupils from going to and enjoying school. As is often the way, it is the most friendly and pro-social students who can be targeted by the less friendly and the anti-social individuals.

The agreeable pupil will be a great participant in the classroom, being friendly and interactive in group tasks. The disagreeable pupil's behaviour in and out of class may pose challenges to the learning environment.

"THE AGREEABLE PUPIL WILL BE A GREAT PARTICIPANT IN THE CLASSROOM, BEING FRIENDLY AND INTERACTIVE IN GROUP TASKS. THE DISAGREEABLE PUPIL'S BEHAVIOUR IN AND OUT OF CLASS MAY POSE CHALLENGES TO THE LEARNING ENVIRONMENT."

Neuroticism

Neuroticism, the trait related to anxiety and stress, unsurprisingly relates to classroom stress and disengagement. At its strongest, neuroticism can manifest as mental health and social anxiety difficulties. In class, an individual who scores higher on neuroticism is likely to feel the pressure of having to do well (if a high-performing student) or disengage with a class where they are anxious that they do not measure up to their classmates (if not).

"IN CLASS, AN INDIVIDUAL WHO SCORES HIGHER ON NEUROTICISM IS LIKELY TO FEEL THE PRESSURE OF HAVING TO DO WELL OR DISENGAGE WITH A CLASS WHERE THEY ARE ANXIOUS THAT THEY DO NOT MEASURE UP TO THEIR CLASSMATES"

The interaction between neuroticism and performance is important, as it can have complex manifestations in the classroom. For example, while neurotic individuals are more likely to be stressed by exams or in-class deadlines, this stress can encourage more reflection and rumination on a topic. With this 'fear' of an upcoming deadline comes better preparation strategies for the assessment. In much the same way, an individual scoring very lowly in neuroticism will be confident and carefree about a deadline or exam, and thus be underprepared. In fact, there is some evidence that more neurotic individuals can perform better on exams. This productive rumination (having thoughts cycling around your head) can lead to heightened preparation, and preparation improves performance. While it is too simple to state that anxious people will always do better or worse in assessments, it is the manifestation of the neuroticism and the application of anxiety that can be of benefit in class. The neurotic pupil can develop stress and anxiety when faced with the challenges presented in the classroom. But rumination, and fear of going wrong, can be productive if it is tempered correctly.

We should give the neurotic pupil help with managing their likelihood to worry, but also help them recognise that their tendency to overthink can be directed into good revision.

"WE SHOULD GIVE THE NEUROTIC PUPIL HELP WITH MANAGING THEIR LIKELIHOOD TO WORRY, BUT ALSO HELP THEM RECOGNISE THAT THEIR TENDENCY TO OVERTHINK CAN BE DIRECTED INTO GOOD REVISION."

Openness

Openness to experience is often labelled 'intellect' in the Big Five models. This is due to the relationship that exists between openness and engagement with intellectual settings.

By their nature, individuals high in openness expose themselves to novel ideas and 'are curious about many things' (to quote a popular personality measure question).

"BY THEIR NATURE, INDIVIDUALS HIGH IN OPENNESS EXPOSE THEMSELVES TO NOVEL IDEAS AND 'ARE CURIOUS ABOUT MANY THINGS' (TO QUOTE A POPULAR PERSONALITY MEASURE QUESTION)."

Curiosity has its benefits, and an individual high in openness is motivated to learn more and accumulate new experiences. Unsurprisingly, this trait has been related to academic success (notably at university where student innovation is valued in formal assessment). There is also evidence of openness being related to IQ test performance (see below for more on IQ). The pupil who is less open to experience is likely to prefer to stick to their comfort zone and resist exploration into new areas. The often heard 'but when will I need this in the future?' comments are what one would expect from a student who is highly comfortable with their current knowledge set and not curiously seeking knowledge for knowledge's sake. Low and high scorers, like all personality traits, have their own benefits. The more measured engagement with wider knowledge can lead the student who scores lower on openness not to chase all tangents of the subject area. In turn, this may lead to better on-task behaviour. However, it is the more open pupil who performs better in class and assessment, and cultivating curiosity is desirable for improving schooling outcomes.

Extraversion

Finally, we have extraversion. This sensation-seeking and outgoing personality trait is one of the original traits studied in relation to success, with around 80 years of research into the effects of extraversion affecting education. Results are generally consistent: extraverts engage better with class, teachers and activities.

Ultimately, extraverts outperform introverts in academic environments. Introverts may well be more studious, as they are not distracted so easily, unlike the sensation-seeking and excitable nature of the extraverts, but assessments and the high-pressure nature of exams better suits the assertiveness of the extravert than the introvert. Elsewhere in the classroom, we find that extraverted teachers report better job satisfaction. Teacher confidence and self-assurance help with some of the difficult job demands that they face in day-to-day work. Overall, the extraverted pupil will engage more with class and have more 'presence' in the classroom. They may be a bit of a classroom 'joker' and be disruptive through chatter, but they will likely carry through their assertiveness to assessment in SATs, GCSEs and beyond.

"THE EXTRAVERTED PUPIL WILL ENGAGE MORE WITH CLASS AND HAVE MORE 'PRESENCE' IN THE CLASSROOM. THEY MAY BE A BIT OF A CLASSROOM 'JOKER' AND BE DISRUPTIVE THROUGH CHATTER, BUT THEY WILL LIKELY CARRY THROUGH THEIR ASSERTIVENESS TO ASSESSMENT IN SATS, GCSES AND BEYOND."

Personality research suggests that pupils high on conscientiousness, agreeableness, openness and extraversion and low on neuroticism will have the better experience of school. It is important to remember that personality, especially when young, is flexible and developable. While not all of these directly feed into academic performance, pupils should be encouraged to develop diligence, social skills, curiosity, assertiveness and resilience – as many schools already do.

Intelligence and IQ

What is intelligence?

Intelligence is one of the dominating topics in individual differences psychology. The development of the scientific approach to individual differences owes a lot to attempts at measuring intelligence. Intelligence research is a good example of the challenges that psychology has with terminology.

"IT IS EXCEPTIONALLY DIFFICULT TO DEFINE AND MEASURE 'INTELLIGENCE'."

It is exceptionally difficult to define and measure 'intelligence'. We could describe an esteemed scientist as highly intelligent. That person may have a high level of understanding of mathematics, philosophy and problem solving. These are all qualities that we could say make a person intelligent. However, we could also describe a famous author as intelligent. They can create worlds, play with language in enticing ways and communicate better than most. These qualities we could also consider intelligent. Intelligence can be many, non-overlapping things, and it can be hard to get a consistent definition of what we want to measure when we use the term. This is the work of individual differences psychologists who try to provide a working (scientific, measurable) definition of the term. Understandably, this is not easy.

Many countries have institutionalised 'intelligence' testing as part of the curriculum. In the UK, we have SATs, GCSEs and A Levels as standardised assessments that attempt to measure the intellectual capacity of young people. The results of these assessments are then used for later job applications and applying to universities, based on the assumption that the tests measure personal intellectual ability. It is often heard that such exams are just 'memory tests' and do not allow for creativity or 'real intelligence' to come through. However, even if it is 'simply' a memory test, we could easily include a good memory in a definition of intelligence. Moreover, many exams involve problem solving and the application of knowledge to a specific task, which again are characteristics we could easily include in a definition of intelligence.

On the other hand, in my examples of the intelligent scientist and the intelligent author, it is likely that these people are considered intelligent for their creativity and innovation. This is very hard to test and mass assessments (like SATs, GCSEs) cannot be easily constructed to recognise these skills. This is important because the goals of the state-designed exams define the context intelligence for pupils sitting these tests. In later chapters, we discuss pupils' beliefs about their intelligence, and we should be mindful that 1) we regularly try to measure the 'intelligence' of pupils (through exams) and 2) the mark schemes of such assessments set the tone for societal thinking about 'intelligence'.

In psychology, the most prominent evaluation of 'intelligence' is the intelligence quotient (IQ). There are many forms of IQ test, but they usually involve reasoning or logic activities in various forms. Across the varying formats, there are verbal, spatial and mathematical reasoning tasks. IQ tests are designed so that each test has known statistical qualities; the average person will score out of 100 points and the standard deviation of the population is 15 points. This tells us that the statistically normal IQ (where 68% of the population perform) is between 85 and 115. It is statistically unusual to have an IQ score less than 85 (16% of people) and above 115 (16% of people). IQ is the most dominant measure of intelligence we have, but few would argue that all IQ tests are a complete representation of 'intelligence' (in the general use of the term). One way to think about the relationship between IQ and intelligence is the model put forward by the eminent individual differences psychologist Hans Eysenck. He suggested three 'layers' of discussing intelligence.

- At the base layer, there is 'biological intelligence'; this is the brain functioning and biology (genes, hormones) that allow an individual to act intelligently in the world. It is the 'nature' component of intelligence and influences the later layers of intelligence.
- The next layer is 'psychometric intelligence'. This is the level where we can test general intelligence. These are generic problem-solving skills and thinking speed which can be applied to everyday problems. Psychometric intelligence is generated by biological intelligence, but is refined by cultural and environmental factors (this is where 'nurture' has an influence). Education, family, socioeconomic status and cultural norms all feed into the extent to which a person develops psychometric intelligence. A pupil's exam performance is a reflection of this psychometric intelligence.
- The further layer of intelligence is more common. Away from the abstract intelligence demonstrated in psychometric intelligence, is social intelligence. Social intelligence is reasoning and capacity in a practical

sense (similar to 'common sense'). It is influenced by many further factors such as personality traits (see above), physical and mental health, and life experience.

In Eysenck's model we can see two things. First, that psychometric intelligence (IQ) contributes to, but is not the whole picture for, everyday practical intelligence.

"PSYCHOMETRIC INTELLIGENCE (IQ) CONTRIBUTES TO, BUT IS NOT THE WHOLE PICTURE FOR, EVERYDAY PRACTICAL INTELLIGENCE."

Second, we can see how education and culture are essential throughout the latter stages of the model.

"EDUCATION AND CULTURE ARE ESSENTIAL THROUGHOUT THE LATTER STAGES OF THE MODEL."

This model provides a good framework for thinking about intelligence (and especially psychometric intelligence) as it highlights the known biological factors that relate to base intelligence, while recognising the importance of learned intelligence through education, society and culture.

Intelligence is hard to define as a concept. However, it is in the interest of individual differences that psychologists have a working definition of natural variation in ability – even more so in educational settings where, through standardised assessment of learning, the education systems of the world are making formal intelligence assessments of their own (in one form or another).

The context, origins and usefulness of IQ

The intelligence quotient and the use of IQ tests is controversial. IQ testing comes from a troubling period in psychometric testing with questionable motives. However, before discussing the limitations of IQ testing, it is important to know why IQ still has a place in scientific psychology.

We have two main criteria we expect of a good test of any psychology. First, a test must be *valid*.

"FIRST, A TEST MUST BE *VALID*."

This means that it must predict outcomes in some meaningful sense. For example, if I want to use the number of smiley faces in a text message as an indicator of how happy someone is feeling, I must first know that happiness is related to using smiley faces in texts. So, if an IQ test is valid, we would expect it to predict school grades, job success and economic benefits, achievements we would associate with more intelligent people (in general). This may seem obvious, but there are many cases of psychological measures that have not adequately demonstrated that they measure what they say they are measuring (see section on learning styles below). We do find good validity with IQ tests. In large, convincing samples, IQ does relate to academic, professional and financial life outcomes. IQ tests are valid.

"SECOND, WE WANT MEASURES TO BE *RELIABLE*."

Second, we want measures to be *reliable*. Reliability means consistency in findings and a result you can find time and time again. For example, if I can give a classroom of pupils a series of spelling tests drawn from the same bank of known words, I could find that the pupils perform very differently in each assessment, from 1/10 to 10/10, to 2/10 to 9/10. This would suggest that there is likely something unusual going on. Maybe my random selection of words for each test are from different ends of the difficulty spectrum and so some weeks pupils are asked to spell 'cat' and other weeks 'categorisation'. Or maybe I am not accurately testing 'spelling' and my test is measuring my pupils' willingness to engage with a test. This, logically, means that my test is not very helpful. Inconsistency (*unreliability*) of a test score can be a consequence of bad test design or not testing anything other than a temporary state in the people being tested (i.e. 'IQ is not a real thing'). However, IQ tests have been shown to be reliable. Response to IQ tests is consistent between testings and those who score higher in IQ tests when they are younger tend to score higher in IQ tests when they are older (when using age-relevant tests). IQ tests therefore are reliable.

So we see that IQ tests are psychometrically robust tools that predict useful life outcomes. However, there is public controversy about the research into working out how someone might have a high IQ. Many people are trying to research the 'nature' (biological precedents) versus 'nurture' (life experiences) drivers of IQ test performance. This is much like any type of research, but understandably we can have concerns about the implications of linking someone's intelligence with their genes. There is a growing body of research showing that IQ and educational outcomes are related to some genetic sequences. The advancement of genetic testing technology has allowed research using 'genome-wide polygenic scores' (GPS) to become cheaper and more efficient. This, combined with large commercial databases of DNA, led to a clearer understanding of how biology can lead to behaviour. These studies are advancing quickly, with understanding changing dramatically in the last two years. To quote the genetics and education experts Professor Robert Plomin and Dr Sophie von Stumm, 'until 2016, GPSs could only predict 1% of the variance in intelligence. Progress has been rapid since then, reaching our current ability [2017] to predict 10% of the variance in intelligence from DNA alone'. It is important to understand the terminology in this statement. When we discuss 'predicting variance' we are interested in how much the studied groups' IQ scores relate to their GPSs. We are not making predictions about individual people's scores.

> **"WE ARE SEEING CONVINCING EVIDENCE THAT EDUCATIONAL OUTCOMES AND INTELLIGENCE ARE RELATED IN SOME WAY TO GENETICS."**

There are two very important things to take away from this young body of research. First, we are seeing convincing evidence that educational outcomes and intelligence are related in some way to genetics.

Second, (and it cannot be emphasised enough), this is far from the complete picture.

The biggest predictors (that 90% unexplained variance) is the effect of variable life experiences, parenting, schooling and exposure to the world around us.

> **"THE BIGGEST PREDICTORS (THAT 90% UNEXPLAINED VARIANCE) IS THE EFFECT OF VARIABLE LIFE EXPERIENCES, PARENTING, SCHOOLING AND EXPOSURE TO THE WORLD AROUND US."**

In this sense we have not strayed too far from Eysenck's model mentioned above. GPS research is just another way of looking at how we are born with a set of tools (biological intelligence) that feed into the manifestation of our intelligence (psychometric and social intelligence). Genes are far from the whole picture of intelligence, but it is important not to ignore research that helps us understand why people behave the way they do.

Most prominent intelligence researchers would strongly emphasise that education and schooling are essential to improving IQ. Education does increase IQ.

"EDUCATION DOES INCREASE IQ."

The school process teaches pupils to think critically, problem solve and engage in complex thought – the hallmarks of intelligence and IQ. Intelligence, like any other skill, improves with practice. This is especially true in education where we have subject-specific knowledge – no genetic sequence provides a pupil with a working knowledge of history from birth. At best, the aforementioned genetics work explains how quickly a person may pick up a new skill, but biological priming does not explain subject-specific outcomes. For example, no child is born able to do complex statistics; they must train, learn and develop the specialised knowledge needed. Another great example is language. No child is genetically French-speaking or genetically English-speaking. However, human children are readily able to acquire language by their nature as a species – again, they are born with a toolkit that can be applied to life's challenges. No extreme opinions are needed here – we don't need to say 'everything is biology' or 'everything is school'.

"WE CAN SENSIBLY AND ACCURATELY SAY THAT BEHAVIOUR IS VERY MUCH INFLUENCED BY AN INDIVIDUAL'S NATURE AND THEIR NURTURE, BIOLOGY AND EXPERIENCES."

We can sensibly and accurately say that behaviour is very much influenced by an individual's nature and their nurture, biology and experiences. In fact, in my experience of talking to teachers, many say that their pupils do naturally vary in intelligence. The evidence-based position on IQ is that 1) IQ is important for academic performance and life outcomes, 2) is related to our genetics, and 3) is most improved through schooling and learning.

'Learning styles'

What is the current status of learning styles research?

Many people (including educational psychologists) have heard it suggested that we learn best when we match our learning style method to our learning preferences. Most typically, we hear people referring to the 'VARK' learning styles, where learning preference can be considered in terms of 'visual' (drawings, diagrams), 'acoustic' (listening, discussing), 'reading' (engaging with the written word) and 'kinaesthetic' (active, movement) approaches. This suggestion has been widely popular and is compelling; we do generally have preferences for how we receive information. However, there is exceptionally limited evidence, in scientific studies, that these learning styles improve academic outcomes. The question is, what evidence can there be to demonstrate a claim about human behaviour? What is the criteria where we can consider our research 'science'? It is our aim in the rest of this book to hold an evidence-based discussion about mindsets. So, briefly mentioning the issues with the VARK concept is a good way to demonstrate how we deem research scientific and the importance of scientific approaches to assessing educational psychology.

The evidence I have shared above on the topics of personality and IQ is all derived from scientific assessments of learning behaviour. To demonstrate a 'scientific' finding, one must meet important criteria. These criteria are assessed through the process of *peer review*. Before a piece of scientific research is published, it is reviewed by two to four other experts in the field. This anonymous process exists to prevent opinions being presented as facts. Peer review is far from perfect, but it has real advantages, in the form of assessing the following qualities of the scientific research.

- How well the paper acknowledges the previous research – to prevent ourselves 'reinventing the wheel', a good scientific paper discusses the new findings in the context of previous research. No knowledge occurs in a vacuum and no scientist should claim to discover something shown elsewhere. This is also an opportunity to cut down on bias and 'spin' in papers. If I wrote a paper saying, 'I have the secret to doing well in school, eat twelve chocolates a day and ignore everyone else's research', this would be very biased and misleading. Peer review stops a piece of research being solely the opinions of the researcher.
- How well the paper presents its statistics – in the modern world we are buffeted by statistics and projections constantly. These figures are often easy to interpret through our own points of view. If we find that 70% of a class is passing all their spelling tests, then that sounds great, but I could also stress that 30% of pupils are failing and that may not be acceptable to me. Peer review cleans the majority of overly biased presentations of statistics out of papers.

- How well the sample used in the research reflects the wider population – we should do research that meaningfully informs the world. There is good evidence that many of the methods used in educational psychology are not reliable until we study at least 200 people. There are many features of a person's performance on a personality, IQ or in-class test that can be attributable to random factors in the world. For example, some pupils may not have had any sleep the night before we conducted our study and thus do poorly. Or some pupils may have seen similar IQ tests before and thus do better. It's unlikely that these random factors would affect all pupils the same way at the same time. Collecting big samples lessens this 'noise' in our research. Further, large samples are more diverse. Collecting performance data from a private school in the countryside, where there are 12 pupils to a classroom, could look very different from performance data on an inner-city school with 40 pupils to a classroom (not to mention many gender, identity, race, cultural, disability, etc. features). We do not want to create national educational policy from a study of 10 pupils. Peer review works to make sure that published work is generalisable in sample size and nature.
- The other two key criteria have been mentioned above when describing IQ tests. Peer review ensures the publication of valid and reliable scientific research. If we are to use science to inform policy, then our measures must be predicting real phenomena (validity) – are we predicting educational outcomes? – and our studies must be reliably administered and described.

Much of the research advocating the 'VARK' approaches to understanding individual differences in learning has not been through peer review.

"MUCH OF THE RESEARCH ADVOCATING THE 'VARK' APPROACHES TO UNDERSTANDING INDIVIDUAL DIFFER-ENCES IN LEARNING HAS NOT BEEN THROUGH PEER REVIEW."

Because of this, many of the key checks applied to scientific research, such as generalisability, validity and reliability, have not been applied. When studied in scientific settings, we find that VARK styles are not predicting academic outcomes and inconsistently label individuals' styles.

"WHEN STUDIED IN SCIENTIFIC SETTINGS, WE FIND THAT VARK STYLES ARE NOT PREDICTING ACADEMIC OUTCOMES AND INCONSISTENTLY LABEL INDIVIDUALS' STYLES."

This more rigorous research does find that individuals have a VARK prefer-ence, and experiencing learning in a style that suits them improves their enjoyment of their learning. However, this is not the same as improving academic performance and the evidence suggests that academic success and academic enjoyment are not as related as one might expect.

Preferring evidence from peer-reviewed academic journals is not a case of elitism or snobbery by educational psychologists. As other people have argued, educational psychologists have a duty to do the best research that they can for the public. This research has a high standard, and so it should.

Lowering the burdens of proof for a successful intervention could lead to wasted investments and training which, while improving our pupils' satis-faction, does not help their topic understanding in the long run. It is for this reason that we have written this book. There is a debate about the impact of mindsets on academic performance and well-being.

"THERE IS A DEBATE ABOUT THE IMPACT OF MINDSETS ON ACADEMIC PERFORMANCE AND WELL-BEING."

There is a large and growing scientific literature on the topic of mindsets, but much of the evidence in its scientific format can be tough to under-stand. This evidence is of the most robust quality (large, generalisable samples, valid outcome measures and reliable designs) and it is our aim to share this with you here.

Going forward: beliefs and mindsets

In this very brief introduction to individual differences psychology, I have highlighted that people naturally vary in their character (personality) and their intelligence (such as with IQ). We know this from good quality (valid, reliable, generalisable) scientific research. Both personality and IQ seem to be strongly influenced by biology and society – and both can and do change over time. However, both are largely consistent: a pupil who is more extraverted and intelligent than their classmates on starting school is likely to perform in a similar way relative to their peers on leaving school.

To loosely categorise individual differences research, we can use catego-ries such as 'ability' for intelligence and other similar variations with a positive outcome (i.e. it is better to perform higher in an IQ test or a GCSE exam) and 'personality' for the Big Five and other similar variations where outcomes vary but are not inherently good or bad (i.e. highly and lowly neurotic people may both have strengths in school). We can also consider differences that do not so neatly fit into these categories. What about variations that can be unstable in the long run? Or features of a person that are highly dependent on the information we get from the world alone? 'Beliefs' about the world is a label that suits this group of behaviours. This includes our mindsets. Based on our experiences of learning and the world, we may come to believe that we cannot improve our academic performance, no matter how hard we try. Or perhaps we believe that every less than optimal performance on a test is just information and the challenge makes us stronger. These beliefs are related to personality and ability individual differences (as we have shown in our own research), but these are much easier to intervene on. An individual can be more readily inspired or motivated to change their beliefs about learning than their personality or ability. We will introduce mindsets with some focus in the next chapter.

In summary

This chapter highlights why we care about individual differences in our classrooms, how personality and ability matter to performance and why scientific approaches to understanding educational outcomes are important and needed. It is hoped that this toolkit of ideas can inform your understanding of mindsets as we talk about the good, the bad and the non-significant findings we have found in our mindsets research.

CHAPTER 3

THE DEVELOPMENT OF MINDSET BELIEFS

FRANCES WARREN

Introduction

Two of the most common questions we get asked by teachers are: 'How and why do the different mindsets develop?' and 'What factors might influence their development?'

Babies are born with a drive to learn, constantly soaking up new information; if you go into a Reception class and ask a question, you get 30 eager hands shooting up. However, after this point we start to see a real reluctance creeping into some classrooms, with certain pupils starting to disengage from learning altogether. So what happens? Why do some children 'choose' to become non-learners?

According to Dweck, there is a major shift at around 7 years of age when children suddenly become interested in ability, and it is around this age that our implicit beliefs about ability begin to develop, albeit in a more rudimentary fashion than the beliefs we see in older children. In fact, it is thought that our academic mindsets don't develop fully until the age of 10–12 years

(Dweck, 2002). Despite this, we know that children don't arrive in the Reception class (age 4–5 years) as a blank slate – already we see children who are more 'hardy' than others, resilient in the face of obstacles and more likely to give challenges a go. Other children are more vulnerable to helplessness, choosing to avoid challenges where possible and fear making mistakes. Even in children as young as 1–2½ years, we see differences in persistence and positive affect during frustrating tasks (e.g. Grolnick et al., 1984). So clearly, early experiences and beliefs are starting to affect behaviour in ways that look similar to those in older children. What is driving these differences in response patterns in young children? And how do these start to affect motivation and achievement? Throughout this chapter, we will attempt to answer these questions and identify any signs that children might exhibit in early childhood to indicate holding implicit beliefs about intelligence and ability.

Remarkably, there is a lack of research in the field with children of this age (it tends to be much more focused on older children). Attempting to identify the early precursors to later academic mindsets is important for a number of reasons:

- the achievement gap between certain groups of children is already present;
- it would allow us to target support before maladaptive patterns are established;
- the preschool period is associated with critical development in self-regulation (emotional and behavioural); furthering our understanding might tell us more about the mechanisms that underpin our ability beliefs.

Throughout this chapter, I will attempt to summarise what we already know about the development of mindsets/ability beliefs, and highlight some of the questions that still need to be answered.

The preschool and Key Stage 1 period: early signs

Traditionally, developmental research has suggested that young children (under 7 years of age) do not possess the cognitive prerequisites to have clear conceptions of ability or effort; they are unable to differentiate between them in terms of cause and effect (perceiving them as being one and the same) and do not have the capability to view either as a potentially enduring trait. As a result, it is believed that poor performance does not hold the same implications for them. It was widely assumed that children of this age do not suffer the same detrimental effects of failure that older children do, including decreased performance, negative self-evaluations, or negative affect during or after failure (e.g. Rholes et al.; Ruble et al., 1976).

However, perhaps we had previously underestimated young children's cognitive abilities.

"PERHAPS WE HAD PREVIOUSLY UNDERESTIMATED YOUNG CHILDREN'S COGNITIVE ABILITIES."

The use of more developmentally appropriate assessment procedures does seem to suggest that young children show at least some ability awareness. We know that from around the age of 3 years, children start to spontaneously compare themselves with others in speech. This suggests at least some knowledge that they have certain characteristics and traits that make them different from those around them. This insight and interest in self-appraisal appears to develop steadily from this point; Butler (1998) found that children as young as 4 and 5 years of age can use social comparison information to assess their relative performance on simple tasks. If they are able to compare their performance with others, then perhaps children are vulnerable to motivational deficits following failure much earlier than was previously thought.

"PERHAPS CHILDREN ARE VULNERABLE TO MOTIVATIONAL DEFICITS FOLLOWING FAILURE MUCH EARLIER THAN WAS PREVIOUSLY THOUGHT."

Indeed, Magid and Schulz (2015) found that 4- and 5-year-olds could spontaneously use evidence from social comparisons to make inferences about their abilities and that this affected their persistence at that task.

In his pioneering work on developmental changes, Nicholls (e.g. 1978) argued that although young children can make social comparisons, they still do not have normative conceptions of difficulty and ability, and therefore lack the ability to make accurate self-evaluations. The common notion is that younger children have a 'positivity bias' in their self-appraisals, holding unrealistically high perceptions of their own competence. However, this appears to depend on the setting. For example, Stipek and Daniels (1988) found that 5-year-olds in classrooms in which normative evaluation and comparisons were emphasised, were able to accurately assess their own competence, performance and class standing. Furthermore, Stipek et al. (1992) demonstrated that children as young as 3 years old are capable of engaging in autonomous self-evaluative judgements (without needing to look for adults' reactions), responding with pride (e.g. smiling) to success on a task and with shame (e.g. avoidance reactions) to failure. Heyman and colleagues (e.g. Heyman and Compton, 2006; Heyman et al., 2003) found that 3-year-olds were also able to draw inferences about others' ability if they were provided with some information about how hard they tried or how difficult the task was. In a more recent study, Cimpian et al. (2017) concluded that by the age of 4, children can conceive the self as possessing general traits and abilities, and, beyond that, also use these self-evaluations to judge their worth as individuals in flexible, nuanced and context-sensitive ways.

Finally, if it was the case that young children were not capable of viewing ability as an enduring trait, we would expect them not to blame failure on their abilities, and thus not to be negatively affected by failure (protected from the experience of helplessness). Indeed, the prevailing view in developmental research has suggested that these helpless-oriented responses do not occur until late childhood (around 10–12 years of age); before this age, children are believed to maintain positive emotions after failure, still assessing their flawed work positively, planning to fix their mistakes and seeking further opportunities for challenge (Nicholls, 1978, 1979; Rholes et al., 1980). However, considerable research exists to challenge this view, suggesting that although young children may not have a complete understanding of ability, individual differences do exist in the way that they react to failure, with some children responding with negative emotion and lowered evaluations of their work, showing pessimism for future efforts and avoidance of challenge (Heyman et al., 1992; Smiley et al., 2016).

A number of researchers studying children's responses to failure have found distinct motivational patterns. For example, Smiley and Dweck (1994) found that by 4 years of age, children begin to demonstrate differential learning and achievement goals, with these goal orientations predicting their cognitions, behaviours and emotions in response to failure.

"BY 4 YEARS OF AGE, CHILDREN BEGIN TO DEMONSTRATE DIFFERENTIAL LEARNING AND ACHIEVEMENT GOALS, WITH THESE GOAL ORIENTATIONS PREDICTING THEIR COGNITIONS, BEHAVIOURS AND EMOTIONS IN RESPONSE TO FAILURE."

They found that certain children responded to failure by showing more susceptibility to helplessness and lower confidence in future success. Specifically, these children were more vulnerable to performance worries, disengaging from the task, more negative emotion and harsher self-evaluations following failure. Similarly, Ziegert et al. (2001) found signs of helplessness in kindergarten children and evidence that these early individual differences remained stable across childhood, predicting their helplessness and approach to challenge 1 and 5 years later (over and above ability). More recently, Hicks et al. (2015) investigated young children's beliefs about self-disclosure of performance outcomes. They found that by 3 years of age, children reasoned that people are more likely to disclose successes than failures. It seems that by the age of 3, children are beginning to recognise people's reluctance to share certain performance information, realising that perhaps negative performance and failure are things to be ashamed of and that are best not to be disclosed to others.

Clearly in children of this age, individual differences are starting to emerge in how they respond to challenge and failure, and these motivational patterns appear to be similar to those seen in older children (mastery-oriented/'hardy' vs. helpless-oriented/'vulnerable'). However, Dweck and colleagues (e.g. Dweck, 2002; Heyman et al., 1992) hypothesise that these early motivational response patterns are built around children's conceptions of goodness and badness, rather than intelligence or ability. In line with this proposition, young children use their experience and knowledge from the social domain to explain outcomes in both academic and social tasks (Benenson and Dweck, 1986), having the tendency to link individuals' achievements to 'being good' or 'being bad' (rather than reflecting the domain of ability). These judgements of goodness and badness have been linked to children's vulnerability to helplessness following criticism (Heyman et al., 1992). It has been suggested that these types of judgements are early precursors to children's development of ability beliefs and trait explanations. There is longstanding evidence to suggest that children starting school are highly concerned with issues of people's goodness and badness (e.g. Frey and Ruble, 1985; Stipek and Daniels, 1990). Young children even appear to evaluate people on the basis of things that happen to them; by the age of 3 years, children judge lucky individuals to be nicer than unlucky individuals (see Olson and Dweck, 2009 for a review). It is hardly surprising that these social and moral judgements emerge so early on in development (even 6-month-olds appear to show a preference for 'good' actions over 'bad' actions; Hamlin et al., 2007); adults use rules regarding goodness and badness to socialise their young children into the rules and habits of a community. It would thus makes sense that trait explanations in the social domain should emerge before those in the academic domain given their increased familiarity and experience (e.g. Benenson and Dweck, 1986).

Taken together, the evidence presented here suggests that during the preschool years, children do show at least some understanding of ability as a trait that might be related to performance.

"DURING THE PRESCHOOL YEARS, CHILDREN DO SHOW AT LEAST SOME UNDERSTANDING OF ABILITY AS A TRAIT THAT MIGHT BE RELATED TO PERFORMANCE."

We start to see two distinct motivational response patterns developing, with some children showing more 'hardiness' and resilience in the face of challenge, and others showing more susceptibility to helplessness and vulnerability. However, as summarised above, it has been proposed that the motivational systems seen in children of this age are different from those seen in older children, being more focused on goodness and badness than effort and ability. Furthermore, Dweck (2002) has suggested that these young children still may not be as vulnerable as older children to failure and the difficulties associated with a fixed mindset for the following reasons.

1. Failure needs to be particularly obvious (or pointed out by adults) to impart a negative experience for young children.
2. While young children might react to failure, they do not appear to worry about failure before it occurs.
3. Overall, younger children still appear to be more resilient than older children and regain their optimism post-failure much more quickly.

In line with this view, Dweck surmises that after this early stage there are two important shifts in children's thinking about ability. The first of these occurs at around 7–8 years of age (coinciding with starting Key Stage 2), and then again at about 10–12 years of age (when transitioning into secondary school). The next part of this chapter will briefly review the changes that occur at each of these ages in turn as children become increasingly aware of ability and its implications.

The Key Stage 2 years: understanding ability

While younger children appear to show some signs of ability awareness, their interest in ability – their own and others – seems to grow considerably at around 7–8 years of age. They move from making social comparisons that generally focus on social and behavioural concerns to comparisons that include achievement and performance evaluations (Frey and Ruble, 1985). In this way, their conceptions of ability become more domain-specific, and they become able to separate academic outcomes from social and moral judgements (i.e. goodness and badness; Bempechat et al., 1991). Equally, while earlier social comparisons tend to be based on concrete and observable examples of performance on specific tasks, it is at around 7 or 8 years of age that children begin to show awareness that ability can be defined more normatively. In other words, they start to understand their own academic abilities in more relative terms to their peers.

> "THEY START TO UNDERSTAND THEIR OWN ACADEMIC ABILITIES IN MORE RELATIVE TERMS TO THEIR PEERS."

It is at around the same time that children really begin to consider ability as being a potentially stable personal trait. Before this, there appears to be little sense that some personal qualities, including ability, might have long-term stability or consistency that may affect future behaviour or performance. However, by 7–8 years, we see an increase in the belief that people's ability (and other traits) might persist over time and that past behaviour can be used to make inferences about likely future behaviour. This shift in children's ability conceptions also coincides with some fairly major changes in their educational journey. In the UK, children start school at the age of 5 and from this point forward, educational settings become increasingly more formal with regular high-stakes tests dominating the national curriculum. With schools facing progressively more emphasis on evidence, accountability and attainment (Turner-Bisset, 2007), classes are compelled to spend more and more time focusing on grades, performance and normative evaluation.

With these factors combined, as well as more general developmental changes in cognition (e.g. reasoning skills, wishful thinking, self-consciousness), children's spontaneous self-evaluations are affected. As a result of their new insights, it is at around this age that children become more accurate and realistic in their self-perceptions of academic ability. They also become more interested in performance feedback from others (about successes and failures), and their self-evaluations move more in line with teachers' ratings of competence (see Stipek and MacIver, 1989). It is from this age that we see children becoming considerably less positive in their outlook on their academic ability, showing more self-criticism and less optimism about their class standing and chances for future successes.

Clearly, across this educational stage (the Key Stage 2 years), there are important changes in children's conceptions of ability and self-awareness. In fact, these appear to be paving the way for more changes still to come, which have a greater impact on children's motivation. By 10–12 years of age, children's conceptions about ability, effort and their implications develop further, coming together into a more coherent 'meaning system', affecting motivation and achievement. It is also around this age that children transition into the next stage of their education. In the UK, the majority of children move to secondary school at age 11, which comes with a great many new challenges (both social and academic). The consequences of these changes will be discussed in the next section.

The secondary years: emerging academic mindsets

Many of the earlier trends we saw emerging continue to develop, and by the time children reach 10– 12 years of age, their reasoning skills have matured considerably. They are able to view effort and ability as separate concepts, and can use information about one to make inferences about the other when attempting to explain performance or attainment. They are now more likely than younger children to perceive that a pupil who tries harder to reach the same outcome as another pupil must have lower ability. (Although not all children choose to adopt this view, which will be discussed later.)

"THEY ARE NOW MORE LIKELY THAN YOUNGER CHILDREN TO PERCEIVE THAT A PUPIL WHO TRIES HARDER TO REACH THE SAME OUTCOME AS ANOTHER PUPIL MUST HAVE LOWER ABILITY."

Along with the aforementioned transition into secondary education comes a great many changes, including increasingly complex social concerns, differing educational pressures, new behavioural expectations and shifting societal demands. It is thus not surprising that this transition stage is often considered a catalyst for future problems, including increases in behavioural issues and declines in self-esteem, school engagement and academic grades (e.g. Blackwell et al., 2007; Eccles, 2004; Wigfield et al., 2006). As their preoccupation with grades and outcomes increases, we see self-evaluations of ability become even lower than before, moving further away from the positivity bias associated with the preschool years, with some children beginning to underestimate their ability and class standing (Benenson and Dweck, 1986). It is around this age that children really start to use academic grades as the yardstick of ability, becoming more sensitive to academic accomplishments and the implications that receiving lower grades might mean for their ability level.

If children have adopted the view that ability is a stable or fixed trait, these conclusions about ability can be very discouraging, and we see the resulting impact on their motivation. According to Dweck (2002), it is in this way that children's ability conceptions and beliefs start to come together into a 'meaning system' (or mindset), which in turn influences children's goals, values, motivation and achievement, creating the behavioural responses described in Chapter 1. Children holding this fixed view of ability start to value performance goals (which will validate intelligence or ability) rather than learning goals (which will increase intelligence or ability). It seems inevitable that facing challenge or failure while holding the belief that ability is fixed (and something that they have no control over) can cause children to feel the need to use (maladaptive) 'self-protection' strategies. These might include reducing their efforts in attempt to save face, devaluing the task in hand or avoiding the task altogether. At this stage of development, the effect of failure seems most profound, sapping children's intrinsic motivation and impairing their performance.

"AT THIS STAGE OF DEVELOPMENT, THE EFFECT OF FAILURE SEEMS MOST PROFOUND SAPPING CHILDREN'S INTRINSIC MOTIVATION AND IMPAIRING THEIR PERFORMANCE."

Although it is around this age that children reach the cognitive milestones that enable them to represent the view of ability as a stable trait which endures independent of effort, not all children choose to adopt this view. Indeed, one of the factors that makes intelligence so fascinating to study is the wealth of definitions, constructions and theories that exist. While some people and cultures might view intelligence as a set of 'hard skills' of cognitive ability (such as IQ), others also take into account non-cognitive skills such as persistence, motivation and self-discipline.

"WHILE SOME PEOPLE AND CULTURES MIGHT VIEW INTELLIGENCE AS A SET OF 'HARD SKILLS' OF COGNITIVE ABILITY (SUCH AS IQ), OTHERS ALSO TAKE INTO ACCOUNT NON-COGNITIVE SKILLS SUCH AS PERSISTENCE, MOTIVATION AND SELF-DISCIPLINE."

It appears that some children, while they are able to understand the perspective that intelligence and ability can be thought of as being stable traits, continue to view ability as a concept that can be developed through these non-cognitive skills. This incremental theory of intelligence, or growth mindset, is very similar to the resilience and optimism in the face of challenge that we saw in younger children. Both views are available to the mature reasoner, so what factors affect the likelihood of adopting a fixed or a growth view of ability? The next part of this chapter will explore this issue in more depth.

Factors influencing children's conceptions of beliefs

There are a multitude of factors that might influence the individual differences in the way that children view intelligence and ability. Some of these are likely to be intrapersonal factors (e.g. personality), while others are likely to be interpersonal factors (e.g. educational context).

"MUCH REMAINS TO BE LEARNED ABOUT HOW CHILDREN'S ABILITY BELIEFS ARE SHAPED,"

Much remains to be learned about how children's ability beliefs are shaped, and there are a variety of potential sources of information that might shape how children interpret failure, such as teachers, parents and the wider society. We will briefly review what is known about some of these factors in this section.

Gender

Discussing the role of gender in understanding individual differences in mindsets often strikes a hot debate. Parents and teachers seem to differ in their views, but from our experience, we find that more often than not, people expect that low-achieving boys are the most likely to demonstrate a fixed mindset. However, research evidence to support this idea is limited. In fact, while findings tend to be mixed, where gender differences are found in research, they tend to show that girls are more likely to hold a fixed mindset than boys (e.g. Dweck, 1986; Todor, 2014).

Indeed, in our most recent project with over 4,000 Year 6 pupils, we found that girls endorsed a fixed mindset more strongly than their male peers. To be specific, research suggests that it is high-achieving girls who are most vulnerable, being more likely to blame failure on a lack of ability, showing more performance impairment in response to failure and making more active attempts to avoid challenge (e.g. Seegers and Boekarts, 1996; Stipek and Gralinski, 1991; also see Dweck, 1999). It has been proposed that one reason for this difference might be the result of girls receiving more praise for their goodness and intelligence, while boys are more likely to receive praise for their efforts and strategy (more on praise later). Interestingly, these gender differences in mindsets seem to appear at a time when girls are outperforming boys academically; according to the Department for Education (2015), by the end of Key Stage 2, girls in the UK are generally outperforming boys in Reading, Writing and Maths. However, we see the impact of cultural stereotypes starting to creep in beyond this point, and by the time pupils come to choosing which subjects they wish to study, biases are obvious (Department for Education and Skills, 2007). Recently, one of the key strategies of trying to encourage girls to get involved with STEM subjects (Science, Technology, Engineering and Mathematics) has had its roots in mindsets theory and interventions.

Ethnicity

Research often shows that ethnicity impacts pupils' educational success. In the US, compared to white and Asian students, African-American students tend to earn lower grades and have higher dropout rates at practically every level of schooling (e.g. Good et al., 2003). In the UK, it has been reported that the ethnicity attainment gap during compulsory education has narrowed considerably in recent years (Strand, 2015), but the gap is still prominent in Higher Education (ECU, 2017). Despite this, some research points towards the suggestion that black students may be more likely to endorse a growth mindset than their white counterparts (e.g. Aronson et al., 2002), although research investigating this is too limited at this stage to draw firm conclusions. Within the existing literature, however, it has been found that encouraging students to develop a growth mindset can help to reduce the impact of stereotype threat and in turn have a positive influence on academic performance in minority groups (e.g. Aronson et al., 2002).

Our team at the University of Portsmouth are currently working to extend these finding by introducing black and minority ethnic students from a range of disciplines to a mindsets intervention targeted towards reducing stereotype threat, raising expectations and closing the attainment gap.

Culture

Cultural background inevitably plays an important role in children's approach to learning and school performance. Data consistently shows that East Asian countries (including Singapore, Japan, China and Korea) outperform other countries in the world in the core academic disciplines (OECD, 2016). Recent media attention has focused on the teaching styles used within these countries and trying to understand the lessons that could be learned from them. There are a number of explanations why the increased school performance might be, and many of these focus on how culture may influence the way that individuals view the world and process information. Nisbett and colleagues (e.g. Choi and Nisbett, 1998; Ji et al., 2000; Nisbett and Miyamoto, 2005; Nisbett et al., 2001) have concentrated their research on this, finding that, compared to Western societies, East Asian cultures pay greater attention to the relationship between situational factors, being more likely to endorse a holistic theory of causality. More specifically, in East Asian cultures, children are encouraged to adopt the belief that events are highly complex and determined by many factors, while children from more individualistic Western societies see the world in terms of objects as distinct entities.

"IN EAST ASIAN CULTURES, CHILDREN ARE ENCOURAGED TO ADOPT THE BELIEF THAT EVENTS ARE HIGHLY COMPLEX AND DETERMINED BY MANY FACTORS, WHILE CHILDREN FROM MORE INDIVIDUALISTIC WESTERN SOCIETIES SEE THE WORLD IN TERMS OF OBJECTS AS DISTINCT ENTITIES."

As a result, individuals from East Asian cultures are less likely than Westerners to explain behaviour and outcomes in terms of individual traits and dispositions (Choi and Nisbett, 1998; Wong-On-Wing and Lui, 2007). As a result, Asian cultures tend to be more effort-oriented than Western cultures, placing less emphasis on innate ability and more on the importance of hard work (Stevenson et al., 1990). However, as highlighted by Dweck (2002), just because individuals ascribe to these views does not mean they adopt all the behaviours and goals associated with a growth mindset – for example, they might orient towards performance goals over learning goals. There is a lack of research in this area and it would be an interesting avenue to pursue.

Personality

In Chapter 2, we were introduced to the relationship between mindsets and certain personality variables. Crucially, it seems that there are factors about a child's early psychological disposition that may affect the type of ability conceptions they adopt as they mature. As previously discussed in this chapter, while the majority of young children remain positive and resilient in the face of failure, some respond with negative emotion, harsh self-evaluation, lowered task engagement and poor expectations for future efforts (e.g. Heyman et al., 1992; Smiley and Dweck, 1994). A body of work has focused on the role of child temperament and self-regulation as predictors of these early response patterns, finding that both hold significant implications for children's development. For example, poor self-regulation during challenge has been linked to impaired task performance and lowered feelings of self-worth (e.g. Smiley et al., 2010), and has even been linked to later achievement outcomes in school (Belenky and Nokes-Malach, 2012). Equally, a recent study by Smiley and colleagues (2016) investigated temperament as a predictor of young children's response to failure while carrying out impossible puzzles. They found that lower levels of interest in response to novelty were associated with higher levels of helplessness during the task. Research into the role of psychological predictors of ability beliefs is limited, but clearly holds implications for early identification and targeted intervention. In the case of the findings of Smiley et al. (2016), showing signs of low interest may require early intervention to focus attention, encourage autonomy and boost competence in order to foster resilience in response to challenge.

Educational setting

"THERE IS CONSIDERABLE EVIDENCE TO SUGGEST THAT A CHILD'S EDUCATIONAL SETTING PLAYS AN IMPORTANT ROLE IN THE ABILITY BELIEFS AND LEARNING GOALS THAT THEY DEVELOP."

There is considerable evidence to suggest that a child's educational setting plays an important role in the ability beliefs and learning goals that they develop. Indeed, the majority of our projects have focused on developing school-level interventions. We believe that the most effective way to encourage growth mindsets in pupils is by adopting a whole-school approach, which involves a shift in school culture and ethos, as well as targeted lesson plans and activities.

> **"THE MOST EFFECTIVE WAY TO ENCOURAGE GROWTH MINDSETS IN PUPILS IS BY ADOPTING A WHOLE-SCHOOL APPROACH, WHICH INVOLVES A SHIFT IN SCHOOL CULTURE AND ETHOS, AS WELL AS TARGETED LESSON PLANS AND ACTIVITIES."**

Published research examining the effectiveness of mindset interventions shows that they can have a positive effect on academic achievement (e.g. Aronson et al., 2002; Blackwell et al., 2007; Good et al., 2003; Paunesku et al., 2015).

Even outside of tailored interventions, there are classroom processes that impact children's developing ability beliefs and how they interpret failure. For example, in some classrooms, mistakes are portrayed as a negative experience (of 'wrongness'), which reveal a lack of ability. This interpretation can be particularly intimidating for struggling pupils, inevitably making education something that is uncomfortable and debilitating, leading some children to disengage from learning altogether. Stipek and Daniels (1988) found that even children in preschools could be affected; in classrooms where relative performance feedback was obvious, encouraged and frequent, children rated their competency and predicted future attainment considerably lower than children who were in classes where the same kind of performance feedback was de-emphasised.

On the flipside, over 30 years ago, Dweck (1986) argued that one educational practice that was responsible for encouraging vulnerability to fixed beliefs was too much focus on the positive reinforcement movement. Specifically, she concluded that if we continue to frequently reward performance on short, easy tasks, we will not be promoting persistence in the face of failure or a desire for challenge.

> **"IF WE CONTINUE TO FREQUENTLY REWARD PERFORMANCE ON SHORT, EASY TASKS, WE WILL NOT BE PROMOTING PERSISTENCE IN THE FACE OF FAILURE OR A DESIRE FOR CHALLENGE."**

Instead, we will be encouraging performers with an over-inflated (but unstable) sense of confidence with a fear of making mistakes (and missing out on the reward) and thus a desire to avoid challenge. Rather than reinforcing attainment and seeing failure as something that should be avoided in order to gain a reward, we should be encouraging young children to view mistakes and failure as constructive and opportunistic. We urge the schools that we work with to reinforce the benefits of effort, struggle and persistence (many teachers do this already).

"WE URGE THE SCHOOLS THAT WE WORK WITH TO REINFORCE THE BENEFITS OF EFFORT, STRUGGLE, AND PERSISTENCE"

In fact, some schools have decided to remove external rewards altogether, arguing that they want their pupils to learn for the sense of achievement rather than the promise of a sticker. Longstanding research points towards the conclusion that the more extrinsic rewards we use to encourage a task, the lower the child's intrinsic motivation, enjoyment and interest in that task (e.g. Lepper and Greene, 1975).

Class teachers' perceptions and expectations can clearly have a powerful effect on student outcomes. Since Rosenthal and Jacobson's (1968) seminal work 'Pygmalion in the Classroom', the robust effect of teachers' expectations on student performance has been demonstrated time and time again; pupils with high-expectation teachers (who encourage challenge and focus on intellectual growth) do better than pupils with low-expectation teachers (see Jussim and Harber, 2005 for a review). Relatedly, Rattan et al. (2012) found that teachers who hold a fixed mindset themselves more readily judge a student to have low ability based on one instance of low performance, and are more likely to communicate this lowered expectation to the student, which in turn affects their motivation, expectations for grades and engagement in that subject.

Parental behaviour

Outside the school setting, we would expect considerable evidence to suggest a pivotal role for parent behaviour and perceptions in the development of children's ability beliefs. Everyone agrees that parents are key to children's motivation and success in school.

Interestingly, however, there is a real lack of research examining how parents influence children's ability conceptions and there has been no clear link established between children's mindsets and their parents'. However, in a recent series of studies by Haimovitz and Dweck (2016), parents' views about failure did appear to be related to children's mindsets. Specifically, they found that parenting practices were influenced by whether they viewed failure as an enhancing experience (that facilitates learning) or as a debilitating experience (that inhibits learning). Children could accurately perceive these differing views, and this in turn affected their beliefs about ability.

Within the existing literature, parenting style also seems to affect the failure response patterns that we see in very young children. Kelley et al. (2000) explored whether parents' behaviour while completing a difficult puzzle task with their 2-year-old children affected how those children responded to failure a year later. Children of mothers who used more negative evaluative feedback demonstrated more shame when they experienced failure. On the other hand, children of mothers who used more corrective feedback and positive affect during the difficult task demonstrated more persistence and task engagement. Gentle guidance from parents (as opposed to intrusive control) also promoted more autonomy and less challenge avoidance. Similarly, it has been found that maternal warmth (e.g. expressing high degrees of affection and positive emotions) during task-focused interactions is associated with more child mastery behaviours, including persistence and challenge seeking (e.g. Leerkes et al., 2011; Smiley et al., 2016; von Suchodoletz et al., 2011).

Praise

The majority of research that has examined why children might develop different mindsets has focused primarily on the praise they receive from others. Evidence from laboratory studies suggests that receiving process praise for effort and action (e.g. 'you worked hard') encourages more mastery-oriented behaviours, whereas person praise (e.g. 'you are clever') is associated with more helpless responses (e.g. Cimpian et al., 2007; Mueller and Dweck, 1998; Zentall and Morris, 2010). This has been shown to be the case in the messages communicated in the language that parents use with their children. For example, Pomerantz and Kempner (2013) found that the more parents used person praise, the more children held a fixed mindset and avoided challenge.

"THE MORE PARENTS USED PERSON PRAISE, THE MORE CHILDREN HELD A FIXED MINDSET AND AVOIDED CHALLENGE."

Furthermore, Gunderson and colleagues (2013) demonstrated the long-term impacts of very early praise, finding that the amount of process praise that parents used with their children aged 1–3 years predicted their motivation five years later. Children who received more process praise were more likely to believe that traits were malleable, seek challenge, and attribute success and failure to effort. These same children were followed up again two years later, with the results suggesting that the process praise they heard as toddlers predicted their academic achievement seven years later via these ability beliefs (Gunderson et al., 2018). Clearly, praise is an important means through which children become aware of the beliefs and values of the adults around them; unfortunately, however, recently some of these findings have been oversimplified and misrepresented in the media.

Goals for future research: what we still don't know

Understanding what makes individuals educationally successful is a key goal for researchers and practitioners alike. Since the 1980s, focus has moved beyond concentrating solely on existing intellectual strengths and cognitive abilities – i.e. the 'hard' skills – and has started to examine individual differences in the non-cognitive characteristics of learners as predictors of academic success (see Gutman and Schoon, 2013 for a review). It seems appropriate that individual differences such as persistence, motivation and self-discipline appear to influence academic success, but what is less clear, is where such attributes stem from. As we have seen already throughout this book, one dominant explanation that has gained considerable attention over the last three decades comes from the work of Dweck and colleagues who suggest that it is not the ability that predicts the resilience or perseverance of learners, but an individual's belief about the nature of ability.

This chapter has focused on reviewing existing literature on the development of ability beliefs. While researchers are starting to understand what the developmental trajectory of these beliefs might look like, we are clearly still limited in our understanding of how these beliefs develop. There are still many questions that we need to ask – here are just a few.

- Dweck postulates that the early differences we see in young children's responses to failure are governed more by their conceptions of goodness and badness, rather than of intelligence or ability. Whether these conceptions, which produce motivational responses that look very similar to those seen in older children, are predictive of later academic mindsets is not clear. Are these conceptions early precursors or are they qualitatively different? What determines the changes in motivation from early childhood to preadolescence, when academic mindsets emerge?

- **Is it ever too late to change someone's mindset?** Our team at the University of Portsmouth has worked with individuals from Nursery through to students in Higher Education (and even some staff). But is there a critical (or sensitive) period after which point it becomes much harder to intervene?
- **What determines differences between individuals within a certain developmental phase?** While developmental research has started to look at changes over time, we still need to look more at the factors that affect ability beliefs within time. Furthermore, researchers who have investigated individual differences have tended to focus on more conventional factors such as gender, ethnicity and culture. We now need to spend time focusing on other sociological factors and cognitive processes that might play a crucial role.
- **How do we successfully measure a child's mindset?** If we want to accurately track changes in academic mindsets across time – and understand differences within time – we need to create more developmentally appropriate assessment procedures. At present, the majority of mindsets research within the domain of education relies on Dweck's (1999) Implicit Theories of Intelligence Scale for Children. However, the use of these questions has come under criticism; they are intended for children over the age of 10 years, and it has been suggested that they elicit too much social desirability (children answering what they think the experimenter wants to hear). Other researchers have attempted to develop their own questionnaires, but these still fall victim to the inaccuracies associated with self-report measures. Developing an assessment procedure that would allow us to accurately capture a child's mindset – that can be used with children under the age of 10 years – would be an invaluable step for moving the field forward.

In summary

Reviewing the literature has revealed some notable findings about the development of children's academic mindsets, and the above are just a few broad questions for future research to tackle. What seems clear is that young children's understanding had been previously underestimated by developmental research.

"YOUNG CHILDREN'S UNDERSTANDING HAD BEEN PREVIOUSLY UNDERESTIMATED BY DEVELOPMENTAL RESEARCH."

We have seen multiple sources of evidence to suggest that preschool children do show at least some awareness of ability and, as a result, can be affected by failure. Early on, we see individual differences in children's self-evaluations and the way in which they respond to a challenge, and these responses look remarkably similar to those we see in older children. Beyond this point, children's beliefs about ability and preoccupation with grades, class standing and feedback appear to intensify and coalesce until academic mindsets begin to fully establish at around 10–12 years of age. If we focus our efforts on understanding more about the individual differences seen in very young children and identify early signs of maladaptive response patterns, then perhaps the preschool years would ultimately be the best time to target support. Children decide early on whether school is for them; whether they belong and whether it is worth investing in; and a number of children disengage from learning altogether from a very young age.

"CHILDREN DECIDE EARLY ON WHETHER SCHOOL IS FOR THEM; WHETHER THEY BELONG AND WHETHER IT IS WORTH INVESTING IN; AND A NUMBER OF CHILDREN DISENGAGE FROM LEARNING ALTOGETHER FROM A VERY YOUNG AGE."

Perhaps an intervention rooted in growth mindsets – presented early on in their educational journey – might prevent some of these maladaptive patterns from embedding.

CHAPTER 4

MINDSETS AND THE INTERPLAY WITH OTHER FACTORS

EMILY MASON–APPS

Introduction

This chapter will explore some of the other questions that teachers often ask us: 'Are there any links between mindsets and mental health?'; 'Is there any research looking at the mindsets of children with Special Educational Needs (SEN)?'; 'How do these children respond to mindset interventions?' We will also discuss some of the important nuances in the mindset theory that we like to explore with teachers: the case of high achievers with fixed mindsets, and the relationship between mindsets and socioeconomic status.

Are there any links between mindsets and mental health?

The reason this question is so often asked by teachers is because, theoretically, it absolutely makes sense that the cognitions and behaviours that have been shown to result from holding a fixed mindset could have a negative impact on mental health and well-being. Moreover, teachers are obviously very aware of the increasing rates of children and adolescents experiencing mental health difficulties.

"INCREASING RATES OF CHILDREN AND ADOLESCENTS EXPERIENCING MENTAL HEALTH DIFFICULTIES."

According to a recent report published by the Institute for Public Policy Research (Thorley and Cook, 2017), the rates of children with a diagnosable mental health condition is, on average, three in every classroom, which is twice as many as in the 1970s (Layard, 2011). The potential link between mindsets and mental health therefore leads to the next question: are mindset interventions a possible avenue not to only improve attainment, but also to improve mental well-being?

"ARE MINDSET INTERVENTIONS A POSSIBLE AVENUE NOT ONLY TO IMPROVE ATTAINMENT, BUT ALSO TO IMPROVE MENTAL WELL-BEING?"

When we first started developing our mindset interventions, there was actually very little research exploring the link between mindsets and mental health. However, there has been a wealth of research emerging over the last seven years, which does indeed offer support to the idea of the link between mindsets and mental health, as well as offering a promise that mindset interventions may be a useful avenue for improving well-being.

Research has shown that mindsets reliably predict how individuals approach challenges, as well as how they respond to success and failure. People with a growth mindset tend to adopt learning goals, meaning that they focus on developing their ability by mastering challenging tasks (Dweck, 1999; Robins and Pals, 2002). In the face of failure, they adopt a mastery-orientated response and increase their effort, or try another strategy. People with a fixed mindset, however, tend to adopt performance goals, where the focus is on demonstrating their fixed ability level and/or avoiding any negative evaluations of their ability. People with a fixed mindset therefore tend to attribute failures to a lack, or a limit, of ability (Cain and Dweck, 1995; Hong et al., 1999). Because people with a fixed mindset view performance as a direct indicator of unchangeable ability, not only are they more likely to disengage from a task following failure or avoid a challenge altogether in order to avoid revealing a lack of ability (Dweck and Legget, 1988; Heyman et al.,1992), research also shows that they experience greater negative affect and engage in more negative self-cognitions than people with a growth mindset theorist following failure or when facing challenging tasks (Aronson et al., 2002; Hong et al., 1999; Ruiselová and Prokopcáková, 2005; Dweck and Legget, 1988; Heyman et al., 1992; King, 2012; Plaks and Stecher, 2007). It is well known in the mental health literature that engaging in maladaptive cognitions and attributing failure or negative events to internal and unchangeable causes have been reliably shown to be a risk factor for developing mental health problems such as depression and anxiety (e.g. Seligman et al., 1995). Moreover, although experiential avoidance (such as avoiding a challenge or disengaging from a task) may be beneficial in the short term in terms of reducing negative emotions, it has actually been shown to contribute to and help perpetuate psychological problems such as depression, stress and anxiety (e.g. Tull et al., 2004).

As already mentioned, although much of the literature surrounding implicit theories has focused on the academic and motivational impacts, there is an emerging body of literature that is explicitly investigating the relationship between implicit theories and psychological factors such as well-being, depression and anxiety. Given the discussion above, it comes as no real surprise that research exploring these relationships in youths and adolescents does indeed show that compared to holding a growth mindset, holding a fixed mindset is associated with lower levels of well-being, higher levels of general distress, as well as greater levels of internalising problems such as anxiety and depression, and externalising problems such as conduct and behavioural difficulties (e.g. Cury et al., 2008).

"COMPARED TO HOLDING A GROWTH MINDSET, HOLDING A FIXED MINDSET IS ASSOCIATED WITH LOWER LEVELS OF WELL-BEING, HIGHER LEVELS OF GENERAL DISTRESS, AS WELL AS GREATER LEVELS OF INTERNALISING PROBLEMS SUCH AS ANXIETY AND DEPRESSION, AND EXTERNALISING PROBLEMS SUCH AS CONDUCT AND BEHAVIOURAL DIFFICULTIES"

Research has also shown that such negative internalising problems and externalising problems have also been shown to have a negative impact on later academic achievement (Deighton et al., 2017). As discussed by Deighton et al. (2017), this makes sense, given that externalising problems such as aggressive behaviour can have an adverse effect on factors such as peer acceptance and relationships with teachers, not to mention engagement in the classroom. It also makes sense that internalising problems would have a negative impact on academic performance, as these can alter cognitive functions and behaviours related to learning.

For example, research by Cury et al. (2008) showed that individuals with a fixed mindset are not only likely to worry more than people with a growth mindset before a test, but that this increased worry means that they procrastinate more when given time to practise before taking a test, which, of course, then leads to a poorer test performance. It is important to consider that some of this research looks at the mindset of emotions rather than the mindsets of intelligence. However, research by Schleider et al. (2015) has shown that there is consistency across domains (i.e. the difference measures of entity theories), which they suggest implies that it is likely the fixed beliefs, rather than the substantive content of the measure, that conveys a risk of mental health problems.

The most important finding to come out of the recent research is that mindset-based interventions have been shown to have benefits beyond academic outcomes.

"MINDSET-BASED INTERVENTIONS HAVE BEEN SHOWN TO HAVE BENEFITS BEYOND ACADEMIC OUTCOMES."

Even very short interventions that encourage youths and adolescents to adopt growth mindsets by promoting the malleability of personal traits such as emotions, personality and intelligence have been shown to reduce symptoms of psychological distress such as stress, depressive symptoms and anxiety (e.g. Miu and Yaeger, 2015; Schleider and Weisz, 2018; Yeager et al., 2014). This is perhaps unsurprising, given that encouraging someone with a fixed mindset to develop a growth mindset is somewhat akin to the very basic principles of Cognitive Behavioural Therapy (CBT). CBT is based on the notion that a person's thoughts, beliefs and attitudes (cognitions) affect their feelings and behaviours. If a person's negative interpretation of a situation goes unchallenged, then a negative cycle can begin. For example, if you think you are just not good at maths, you might feel especially anxious in a maths class. This anxiety may lead you to disengage with maths, meaning that your performance remains poor, which then reinforces your beliefs that you are not good at maths. A therapist utilising CBT would therefore help you to identify and challenge any negative cognitions and behaviours that you have about a situation. This in turn can help to change the way you feel about a situation, and therefore enable you to change your behaviour in the future, therefore breaking the vicious cycle. As we already know, this is essentially the very same process that we explore when encouraging someone to develop a growth mindset.

High achievers with a fixed mindset

Given that there is a plethora of research stating that having a growth mindset is associated with better academic attainment and educational outcomes, it is counterintuitive at first to even consider the idea that there might be high achievers with a fixed mindset. However, there are a few important points to consider.

First, research in science typically looks at trends, and these trends are based on what tends to be true of the majority. Of course, we often come across what we call 'outliers' in our data. This is data – which is often essentially people – who don't fit the norm. High achievers with fixed mindsets are our example of this in the mindset research. Second, when we talk about mindsets and their relationship to educational outcomes, what is more important is the longitudinal relationship – how mindsets predict educational outcomes over time, not just one point in time.

As discussed in Chapter 3, we know from the literature that the impact of a person's mindset matters most when they hit times of challenge, or going through transition periods, such as moving from primary to secondary school. Because our education system is set up in such a way that the high-achieving student is often overlooked in terms of intervention and extra support because they 'tick the right boxes', we therefore think it is particularly important to draw attention to these students. High-achieving students with a fixed mindset might comfortably coast along throughout primary school, and maybe even most of secondary school, but they will inevitably hit a challenge at some point in their educational journey. As we have already explored in this chapter, this has the potential to lead to poor outcomes both in terms of attainment and well-being, and there is evidence to suggest that there is potential for this to be even harder hitting for the high-achieving student.

The case of the high-achieving student with a fixed mindset is especially close to my heart, because when I started learning about mindsets, so much about myself suddenly made sense. On our training days, I would always tell a story about myself before we explored some of the research, and shall do so now. I was an extremely competitive child – I have two older brothers who I always wanted to keep up with. Before I even started at the tiny primary school in our village (with a grand total of 36 pupils), I had worked my way through the first few of my brothers' maths books. Therefore, from the day I started at school, I was labelled as a 'natural' at maths by my teachers, peers and parents. This continued throughout my education as I just found maths so easy. I found it so easy, in fact, that it was difficult for me to understand how other people struggled. I believed I was obviously just lucky – I had a natural talent at maths that most other people just didn't have. I won a scholarship to a boarding school where I sailed through, getting an A* at GCSE and then obviously chose to do maths at A Level. Then it all changed. Maths became hard and I was struggling. I had hit my first proper challenge and thought that my natural talent had just run out. My behaviour was exactly in line with that shown by the research of Cury et al. (2008). As the year went on and the exams came closer, I worried more and more, and completely avoided doing any revision for one of my three modules – the one I had found difficult. In the week before that exam, I was so distressed that I went to my housemistress one evening and she suggested that I sat the exam the following year. Instantly I felt better, of course, but essentially it just prolonged the stress, as I worried about it all summer. I never sat that exam. Instead, I sat a different module and settled with an AS Level. To this day, 16 years later, if ever I am feeling stressed, I will have the same recurring nightmare that I am sitting in a Pure 2 maths exam and I haven't done any revision.

Because of my personal interest in this topic, we ran our own research study looking at the relationship between prior achievement (A Level grades), mindsets and self-reported anxiety in undergraduate students. Not only did we also find that a fixed mindset was associated with increased levels of self-reported anxiety, but this relationship was mediated by previous achievement, meaning that it is significantly stronger in students who come to university with higher previous achievement.

Other than our own research, there is a lack of research looking specifically at high achievers with a fixed mindset. However, there has been a lot of research that is still of great relevance to understanding why supporting this group is important. Because people with a fixed mindset view performance as an indicator of ability, this can mean that high-achieving students set themselves very high, and sometimes unobtainable standards for success, and research has shown that holding an entity theory of intelligence is associated with higher levels of maladaptive (unhealthy) perfectionism (Dweck, 2006; Mofield and Parker Peters, 2018). Setting yourself such standards of performance when you have a fixed mindset obviously makes you more vulnerable to dissatisfaction with your performance and more likely to fear making even the tiniest of mistakes. High levels of maladaptive perfectionism has indeed been shown to be associated with lower levels of happiness and life-satisfaction, and increased levels of negative emotions, self-handicapping, anxiety and depression (Egan et al., 2011). As highlighted by Flett and Hewitt (2014, p. 899), 'perfectionism is pernicious and resistant to change'.

"PERFECTIONISM IS PERNICIOUS AND RESISTANT TO CHANGE'."

Within this paper, however, they suggest that promoting an incremental theory of intelligence may be an important factor in reducing perfectionism, as it encourages a more positive cognitive orientation regarding how individuals attribute failure and mistakes, thereby reducing negative feelings and rumination about the need to be perfect.

Although we know that it is likely to be beneficial in the long term to encourage high achievers with a fixed mindset to develop a growth mindset, it is important to consider that this group may be particularly resistant to this change at first. For a lower achieving student with a fixed mindset, growth mindset interventions offer hope that they can improve: with the right amount of effort and strategy, they won't always be a low achiever. However, for the high-achieving students who identify as 'talented' or 'naturally clever', growth mindset interventions may at first present as a threat. Essentially, these students are being told that without the right amount of effort and strategy, they won't always be a high achiever, which not only challenges their sense of self, but is also quite a scary concept if they have spent their academic life so far coasting along. I know that if I had been presented with a growth mindset intervention when I was at school, I would have dismissed it as nonsense and something that just didn't apply to me as I found school so easy. I think I might have re-evaluated this assessment, however, when I hit that big challenge in maths, and I genuinely believe that a growth mindset intervention would have helped me in many ways.

We therefore recommend that teachers keep these students in mind when starting a growth mindset intervention with their pupils. This is also why it can be really useful to try to measure your pupils' mindsets and approach to learning before you start any form of mindset intervention, as it is easy to assume that all your high-achieving pupils will have a growth mindset. When working with high achievers with a fixed mindset, one of the most important things you can do to help engage them with the programme is to ensure that they experience challenge and failure.

"WHEN WORKING WITH HIGH ACHIEVERS WITH A FIXED MINDSET, ONE OF THE MOST IMPORTANT THINGS YOU CAN DO TO HELP ENGAGE THEM WITH THE PROGRAMME IS TO ENSURE THAT THEY EXPERIENCE CHALLENGE AND FAILURE, WHILE THEY ARE IN A SAFE ENVIRONMENT

**SUCH AS SCHOOL, AND CAN BE SUPPORTED IN EXPERI-
ENCING AND OVERCOMING THE FEELINGS THAT RESULT."**

Experiencing challenge or failure, and overcoming it with effort and strategy, provides students with essential 'evidence' that the growth mindset
work might be worth paying attention to. It is also very important that you
try to encourage openness about your feelings during this process, as for
many high-achieving pupils, making mistakes or facing a real challenge
for the first time is likely to feel extremely uncomfortable. It is important
that such students understand that feeling that way with a new experience
is acceptable. The earlier school years are probably the safest time and
place to make mistakes and challenge yourself, so it is important that
students have a chance to do so, as this will help to foster the belief that
they can overcome challenges and learn from their mistakes in the future.

The mindsets of children with Special Educational Needs

Unfortunately, there has been very little research exploring beliefs about intelligence in children with Special Educational Needs (SEN) or learning
difficulties. To our knowledge, other than our own research (Warren et al.,
2019), there has been only one study that has examined the relationship
between SEN status and mindsets. Baird et al. (2009) found that students with
learning difficulties held significantly stronger fixed mindsets than students
without learning difficulties. As a result, students with learning difficulties
were also reported to have significantly lower self-efficacy, a greater prefer-
ence for performance over learning goals, and were more likely to regard
exerting effort as an indicator of reduced ability. In our own research, we also
found that pupils identified as having SEN were more likely to have a fixed
mindset than those without. The lack of research in this area means that it is
not possible to conclude why children with SEN are less likely to hold a
growth mindset, but we certainly have some hypotheses as to why this might
be the case. One reason, we suspect, is that the act of identifying a child as
having SEN is essentially 'labelling'. Although the purpose of labelling in this
case is to help such children get extra support for their learning, it is easy to
see that children with identified SEN may interpret this as a label that implies
they have limited intellectual ability or potential.

**"CHILDREN WITH IDENTIFIED SEN MAY INTERPRET THIS
AS A LABEL THAT IMPLIES THEY HAVE LIMITED INTEL-
LECTUAL ABILITY OR POTENTIAL."**

Moreover, a label of SEN may also have an impact on the attitudes of other people regarding a child's potential. In a recent paper (Enea-Drapeau et al., 2017), researchers explored people's beliefs about the intelligence of typical people and their beliefs about individuals with Down's syndrome. What was especially interesting about this research was that they explored the beliefs of adults from the general public as well as professionally qualified people who work with people with intellectual disabilities (such as Down's syndrome). The results showed that both groups (the adults from the typical population *and* the professionals who work with people with intellectual disabilities) conceived the intelligence of people with Down's syndrome to be less malleable than typical people. As we know from Chapter 3, teachers' expectations for children can have a significant impact on their outcomes. Research has also shown that beliefs in fixed intelligence are generally associated with negative teaching practices and lower student outcomes. As we also know from Chapter 3, very subtle differences in the language children hear, even when positive, can very easily influence their motivational framework and views about intelligence, as well as other factors such as self-esteem (e.g. Gunderson et al., 2013; Mueller and Dweck, 1998).

Some of the most difficult questions we have faced on our training days have been around children with SEN and what this research means for them. A few things we have therefore learnt to make clear: we are not saying that everyone can achieve whatever they want to achieve, or that every child will be the next Einstein if they and their teachers believe it to be true. We are also not purporting that learning difficulties and intellectual disabilities do not exist, or can simply be overcome through the power of positive thought. However, what we do firmly believe is something that Carol Dweck says in her book: 'a person's true potential is unknown (and unknowable) . . . it's impossible to foresee what can be accomplished with years of passion, toil, and training.'

Despite decades of research across numerous disciplines, there is still so much that we just don't understand about child development or intellectual development. On the whole, experts nowadays do agree that both nature (genetics) and nurture (environment) have an influence on development, but the debate is still very much ongoing as to as to *how much* of an influence these factors have, and whether one is more important than the other. For my PhD research, I ran a longitudinal study exploring early language development in typically developing infants and infants with Down's syndrome. What is particularly interesting about Down's syndrome is that it is a genetic disorder, and we know that it is caused by having an additional copy of chromosome 21. Research shows us that individuals with Down's syndrome have what we call a typical phenotypic profile, which is characterised by specific strengths and weaknesses, with one area of particular weakness tending to be language development, and especially expressive language development. On average, individuals with Down's syndrome have an average IQ of 50 – half that of a typically developing individual (Chapman and Hesketh, 2000). Therefore, when you want to recruit infants with Down's syndrome who are at the same stage of cognitive development as a typically developing infant (for my study this was 10 months), you look for infants who are twice the chronological age (20 months). Despite what the averages say, it is also well known that children with Down's syndrome present with a huge *range* of abilities. I didn't appreciate quite what a range of abilities this could be until I met one of my participants with Down's syndrome. On nearly every single one of my assessments, this infant not only performed better than any of the other infants in my study, but they performed in line with what would be expected of a typically developing infant at their age – proof that even in the face of genetic disorders, potential is most certainly unknowable.

Unfortunately, even after exploring these ideas in great depth on our training days, we have still come across a few cases where a teacher will say something like: 'I see your point, but I have a child in my class who I *know* will *never* achieve x, y or z.' Our response to this is still always to say that you just can't ever know that for sure.

"WE CARE ABOUT THE CHILD AS A WHOLE."

Furthermore, we will also point out that although the focus in education these days is on attainment, those of us who work in education care about the child as a whole. Therefore, even if encouraging a child to have a growth mindset doesn't have the desired outcome in terms of some children's attainment, the other potential benefits that come from instilling a growth mindset ethos in a classroom means that it is still worthwhile pursuing. What we therefore recommend to teachers regarding children with SEN is that they are mindful of the things we have discussed in the section. It is difficult, but vital that we try to monitor our own beliefs about the individuals we teach. Even if those who are not fully convinced can just get to a point where they accept that they *can't know* a child's potential, then this is progress.

"EVEN **IF THOSE WHO ARE NOT FULLY CONVINCED CAN JUST GET TO A POINT WHERE THEY ACCEPT THAT THEY *CAN'T KNOW* A CHILD'S POTENTIAL, THEN THIS IS PROGRESS.**"

In terms of children who are aware of their SEN status, we think it is important to make it clear that this doesn't mean they have a ceiling set for them. The status of SEN should be seen by children and educators as meaning that the child has been identified as needing extra support at a certain point in time. Just like any other child, the potential of a child with SEN is still unknowable; SEN status should be seen as a temporary signpost and not as a permanent label.

Mindsets and socioeconomic status

The final factor that we will explore in this chapter is the relationship between mindsets and socioeconomic status (SES). It is well known in the UK that there is an educational attainment gap between disadvantaged (low SES) and non-disadvantaged pupils, and we actually have one of the largest achievement gaps in the world (Laws, 2013). Figures from the Department for Education (DfE, 2014) show that between 2013 and 2014, only 67.4% of disadvantaged pupils achieved the expected standard (Level 4) in Maths and English at the end of Key Stage 2, compared to 83.5% of non-disadvantaged pupils.

By the time pupils reach the end of Key Stage 4, this gap appears to widen: between 2013 and 2014, only 36.5% of disadvantaged pupils reached the expected standard of 5 GCSEs (A*–C, including Maths and English) compared to 64% of non-disadvantaged pupils. Therefore, we have often been asked whether mindsets might have a role to play in this gap. Theoretically, we absolutely believe that mindsets might play a role in this attainment gap, but there has been very little research so far that has directly explored this. However, what little research there has been seems to suggest that mindsets might be a part of the puzzle, and we will explore why we think this might be.

Other than our own research, the only study we are aware of that has explicitly explored the links between SES and mindsets is recent research by Claro et al. (2016). In this study, they examined the relationship between SES (based on family income), mindsets and attainment in a nationwide sample of high-school pupils in Chile. First, they found that students from lower SES families were more likely to hold a fixed mindset than students from higher SES families. As would be expected, they found that mindsets and SES were both strong predictors of attainment; being from a higher SES family or having a growth mindset predicted higher levels of achievement. Further to this, though, they found a significant interaction between SES and mindsets in predicting academic achievement. What this interaction shows is that holding a growth mindset may actually reduce the negative effects of low SES on academic achievement, or equally, that being from a low SES family and holding a fixed mindset leads to even poorer achievement outcomes than one factor on its own.

We have also conducted our own research to explore the links between eligibility for free school meals (FSM), mindset and attainment (Warran et al., under review) in Year 5 pupils in the UK (although not a direct measure of SES, FSM status is often used as a proxy measure for SES status in the UK, and I shall use these terms interchangeably). We, too, found that holding a growth mindset was associated with higher achievement in both English and Maths. We also found that children eligible for FSM had lower levels of attainment, but more importantly (and in line with the study by Claro et al., 2016), we found that children who were eligible for FSM were also more likely to have a fixed mindset. Although the findings from both Claro et al. and our study show that children from lower SES are more likely to hold a fixed mindset, neither study was able to explain exactly *why* this might be the case. We certainly have some ideas, though.

As stated by Claro et al. (2016, pp. 866–7), we believe that *structural inequalities can give rise to psychological inequalities*. In other words, we know that there are environmental factors associated with being from a lower SES background that may have a direct negative impact on attainment, and these factors can lead to psychological differences that in turn also have a negative impact on attainment. For many years, there has been a focus on addressing the 'Poverty of Aspirations' associated with high levels of deprivation as a potential route to closing the attainment gap. However, we (and many others) believe that it isn't Poverty of Aspirations that leads to poor outcomes, but a Poverty of Expectations, and research has indeed shown that educational expectations are better predictors of attainment than aspirations (e.g. Goyette, 2008). The distinction between aspirations and expectations appears subtle at first, until you really unpick it. Aspirations are about wishing or hoping that your life will be different or better in the future, whereas expectations (as the word suggests) are about actually expecting or *believing* that your life will be different or better. It is important to consider that aspirations do not need to incorporate any self-assessments of ability or potential, whereas expectations do. It is in this self-assessment of ability or potential where we think mindsets might factor in, as having a belief that something is changeable or malleable is an essential factor in expecting something to get better (academic ability or otherwise). You can *wish* you could be better without believing that it is possible, but in order to truly *expect* to get better, you *have* to believe that you *can* get better.

"YOU CAN *WISH* YOU COULD BE BETTER WITHOUT BELIEVING THAT IT IS POSSIBLE, BUT IN ORDER TO TRULY *EXPECT* TO GET BETTER, YOU *HAVE* TO BELIEVE THAT YOU *CAN* GET BETTER."

As touched upon earlier in this chapter, our own beliefs and expectations can be easily influenced by those around us, including our teachers, our families and our peers. Research has indeed shown that both parents and teachers hold lower expectations for low SES and minority students in comparison to higher SES students.

"RESEARCH HAS INDEED SHOWN THAT BOTH PARENTS AND TEACHERS HOLD LOWER EXPECTATIONS FOR LOW SES AND MINORITY STUDENTS IN COMPARISON TO HIGHER SES STUDENTS."

These lowered expectations have then been shown to lead to poorer academic outcomes (e.g. Gershenson and Papageorge, 2018; Davis-Kean, 2005). We also know that other people's expectations for us also influence our own expectations for ourselves, and very recent research has shown that parents' mindsets influence their children's mindsets (Matthes and Stoeger, 2018). Therefore, it is very important to consider this when working with children from a low SES background.

- What are our own expectations for that child?
- Are those expectations at all influenced or biased based on the fact that we know they come from a certain area or a certain family?

More importantly for this chapter, though, even if we do maintain equal and high expectations for all the children that we teach, what do those children experience when they leave the classroom and go home?

Although the research is, of course, based on means and averages, it is well known that SES status is related to parental school involvement and that parents from lower SES backgrounds are less likely to be involved in schooling than parents of higher SES (Hill and Taylor, 2004). Studies have shown that increased parental school involvement can have a positive impact on behavioural outcomes, and academic success for pupils (e.g. Grolnick and Slowiaczek, 1994; Miedel and Reynolds, 2000). Of interest for this chapter is the fact that the factors affecting parental school involvement are also likely to have a direct impact on pupils' attainment, as well as having an impact on their expectations, how much they value education and the level of support available to them at home. These factors include increased parental stress, a lack of resources, parents' education level and parents' attitudes towards the importance of education (Hill and Taylor, 2004). How much children and their parents value education is an important factor to consider. The expectancy-value theory of motivation (Eccles et al., 1983) suggests that achievement motivation is predicted both by expectations for success, but also by a person's perceived value of a particular task. Eccles's theory defines different types of task value:

- attainment value: the personal importance placed on doing well at a certain task;
- intrinsic value: the enjoyment gained from a certain task;
- utility value: how useful the task is in achieving our own personal goals;
- cost: what an individual perceives must be sacrificed or given up to achieve a certain goal.

Research has shown that these values are influenced by those around us, and the values of those around us will, of course, vary depending on factors such as cultural norms. Ceballo et al. (2004), for example, found that adolescents from wealthier neighbourhoods were more likely to have higher educational values compared to those from poorer neighbourhoods. Of course, the value that we give to certain tasks is then related to the goals we set and therefore the effort we put in (Ceballo et al., 2004; Malka and Covington, 2005; Hulleman et al., 2008). We also know that a person's mindset is related to all of these factors. For example, we know that people with a growth mindset tend to set personal learning goals (rather than performance goals) and that this is associated with greater academic (or task) value and enjoyment (Rawsthorne and Elliot, 1999; Shim et al., 2013). We also know that when faced with a challenge, people with a fixed mindset are more likely to lose intrinsic interest, disengage from the task (actively or passively) and also devalue the task (Doron et al., 2009; Burnette et al., 2013; Ommundsen et al., 2005). As pointed out by Degol et al. (2018), those with fixed mindsets, therefore, may struggle to attribute high attainment and utility value to tasks they fear are too challenging or have a high risk of failure. What we don't know exactly is how this reciprocal relationship works over time: do mindsets influence values or do values influence mindsets?

"DO MINDSETS INFLUENCE VALUES, OR DO VALUES INFLUENCE MINDSETS?"

In whatever way this relationship works, what we do know is that mindsets, expectations and values are all related, and that they can be influenced by the mindsets, values and expectations of those around us.

It is also important to consider that for some groups, the potential benefits of having a growth mindset and high expectations and values may be more constrained than others due to the more circumstantial constraints that we mentioned, but did not discuss earlier in the chapter. Many children from lower SES backgrounds will experience a very different world outside of school from those from higher SES backgrounds. Think about a simple, everyday task, such as doing your homework. Children from lower SES backgrounds might not have their own quiet space to work at home; they might have limited resources, such as fewer books, no access to a computer or the internet. In addition, some children from low SES families or areas might also not have the support and encouragement to actually do their homework because of the attitudes and beliefs of those around them. This has the potential to mean that even if these children have the motivational framework and desire to do as well as they possibly can, they may find it very difficult to do when they step outside the school grounds.

In short, it is not just the mindset of the child that matters, but the mind-set of those around them, and it is essential that we remain conscious of this as educators.

CHAPTER 5

MINDSETS AND THE CURRICULUM

JOANNA NYE AND MATHILDE CHANVIN

Introduction

This chapter explores the use of mindsets across the curriculum and for specific subjects. Initially, the chapter discusses whether a general or a subject-specific approach is more effective. As teachers have requested subject-specific resources, examples of the effective use of mindsets in a range of curriculum subjects will follow; this includes maths, science, literacy, second language learning, sport and creativity, including music. Each section will look at the research that explores the relationship between mindset within that particular domain and describe any studies that have explored subject-specific mindset interventions. As there are limited published studies on school-aged populations, the review also draws on studies of college and university students.

Is a subject-specific approach required?

Carol Dweck and colleagues (Bempechat et al., 1991; Dweck et al., 1995) have asserted that people can have different mindsets for different abilities. However, there appears to be mixed evidence as to whether mindset interventions are best approached in a subject-general or subject-specific way. One of the questions that often arises when designing a growth mindset intervention is whether it need only address mindset in a general way (e.g. if you develop a growth mindset it will apply to all skills, abilities, topics, etc.) or if it needs to be targeted to a specific curriculum topic or lesson (e.g. mathematics). In turn, this gives us further questions to address – for example, do we as individuals have different mindsets for different skills, or do we have a general mindset that we apply to all topics or abilities?

> **"DO WE AS INDIVIDUALS HAVE DIFFERENT MINDSETS FOR DIFFERENT SKILLS, OR DO WE HAVE A GENERAL MIND-SET THAT WE APPLY TO ALL TOPICS OR ABILITIES?"**

If there is evidence that mindset can be subject specific, perhaps there is an argument that interventions should also be subject specific.

In addition, the interpretation of results may be complicated by how certain subjects are influenced by stereotypes (e.g. maths is hard), and this may vary depending on the value of a specific skill within a specific culture or community (e.g. school is a waste of time) or for certain individuals within in that community (e.g. girls are not good at science subjects).

Stipek and Gralinsky (1996) explored the relationship between mindsets and performance in maths and social science subjects in 8–12-year-olds in the US ($n = 319$), using two separate measures for fixed beliefs and growth beliefs. They predicted that maths performance would be less related to having a growth mindset than performance in social science subjects, with students seeing maths ability as more stable and less impacted by effort, and social science subjects requiring more verbal input. This stemmed from the evidence that maths and science are often seen by children as difficult subjects (e.g. Parsons et al., 1983; Stodolsky et al., 1991). However, they found no difference in the children's mindsets towards the two subjects, so children with a growth mindset for maths also had a growth mindset for social sciences. In addition, there was a positive relationship between their measure of growth mindset and academic performance, but not between their fixed mindset measure and academic performance (combined maths and social science grades). However, they did not look at the relationship between mindset and performance in the two academic subjects separately.

Similarly, no differences were found between specific mindsets for music, and general mindset measures or behaviour relating to general mindsets (Mullensieffen et al., 2018; Smith, 2005).

In contrast, Tarbestsky et al. (2016) found that in indigenous Australian high-school students, maths ability was more strongly mediated by maths-specific mindsets than by general mindset. There is a growing body of research from the second language learning field that specific mindsets are more useful for predicting outcomes than general mindset measures (Lou and Noels, 2017; Mercer and Ryan, 2009). In a meta-analysis of the mindset literature, Costa and Faria (2018) concluded that specific mindset measures result in a greater association with outcome measures than general mindset measures. However, as this was only based on ten studies that used a specific mindset measure, the results should be viewed with caution.

In addition, there is growing evidence that people can hold different mindsets within a domain, both with the sports domain (Jowett and Spray, 2013; Slater et al., 2012) and in second language learning (Lou and Noels, 2017; Mercer and Ryan, 2009; Molway and Mutton, 2019).

"IT IS POSSIBLE THAT INDIVIDUALS MAY EXPERIENCE VARIATIONS IN MINDSET AT DIFFERENT TIMES"

In terms of trying to make sense of how these different sets of evidence may co-exist, it is possible that individuals may experience variations in mindset at different times (e.g. Flanigan et al., 2017; Dai and Cromley, 2014), and experience setbacks and challenges at different times within different aspects of the curriculum (e.g. Dweck, 1999; Martin et al., 2015). In addition, pupils may be exposed to a range of values of their community for certain topics, and hence in some schools for some topics a general mindset will be more likely to be related to outcomes, whereas for other students in others schools the specific mindset will emerge (Dweck, 1986). Contributing to this may be societal views about how much natural talent contributes to particular subjects.

Specific curriculum subjects

We will now provide a review of subject-specific growth mindset interventions as 1) we have been asked by teachers for growth mindset interventions targeted at specific topics; 2) these may provide ideas of how to extend a general growth mindset intervention into subject-specific lessons, and 3) the evidence seems to be mounting that specific mindsets exist for specific topics.

Maths

"IT IS NOT UNCOMMON FOR ADULTS TO CLAIM THAT THEY DO NOT HAVE A HEAD FOR NUMBERS, EVEN BRAGGING ABOUT A LACK OF NUMERICAL ABILITY, WHICH CONTRASTS STRONGLY WITH THE SENSE OF SHAME THAT EXISTS FOR LACK OF READING ABILITY"

In Western society, maths is one subject that is seen to be associated with innate talent, and there is a pervading culture that believes that maths is difficult and not for everyone. It is not uncommon for adults to claim that they do not have a head for numbers, even bragging about a lack of numerical ability, which contrasts strongly with the sense of shame that exists for lack of reading ability (Du Sautoy, 2016). Therefore, mindset has the potential to have a significant impact on student achievement.

Mathematics seems to be one of the STEM (Science, Technology, Engineering and Mathematics) subjects in which UK pupils face issues in terms of attainment: UK pupils' numeracy attainment failed to make the world top 20 in maths, and no progress was made compared to previous tests (Gurria, 2016). The UK even reached its lowest rank since it began participating in the Pisa tests in 2000. Furthermore, there is a clear lack of interest in the topic, as demonstrated by the number of pupils taking A Level mathematics falling by two-thirds as a proportion of total A Level entries in the UK (Noyes, 2009).

Nussbaum and Dweck (2008) suggested that implicit theories of intelligence (mindsets) can affect how pupils cope with challenging tasks, such as maths. Some children are convinced that they are bad at maths, which can prevent them from enjoying and succeeding in it, and lead to disengagement.

"ONE WAY TO ENHANCE PUPILS' NUMERACY ATTAINMENT, LOVE OF MATHS AND ENGAGEMENT IS TO DEVELOP A GROWTH MATHS MINDSET CULTURE IN THE CLASSROOM"

Therefore, one way to enhance pupils' numeracy attainment, love of maths and engagement is to develop a growth maths mindset culture in the classroom (Boaler, 2009; 2015). This approach would also help to reduce the number of students from dropping challenging topics when they have a choice (Blackwell et al., 2007).

In 273 secondary school students, Luo et al. (2014) found a positive association between a growth maths mindset and maths enjoyment and pride, and negativity with maths boredom and anxiety. In addition, maths mindset was mediated by achievement emotions (maths enjoyment, pride, boredom and anxiety) to impact on classroom engagement and maths achievement. Similar results have been found in the US with 163 ninth-grade students, whereby maths mindset was found to relate to maths ability, mediated by mastery goals, positive strategies, effort beliefs and helpless attributions (Jones et al., 2012).

Maths mindsets interventions are being promoted both in the US and more widely, and Jo Boaler is the key author in this regard (Boaler, 2015). Boaler has drawn on her experiences as a teacher to adapt the growth mindset approach to maths, including a case study of two UK schools, with a total of 288 pupils (Boaler and Selling, 2017). One school (107 students) had a particularly open approach to learning maths, with mixed ability groups and project-based teaching, and there were significant benefits for the students in terms of GCSE results. In addition, when the pupils were followed up eight years later ($n = 63$), those who had attended the 'open approach' school were employed in jobs that gave significantly higher socioeconomic status ratings, and had more positive attitudes towards maths at school and in work. However, there are limitations to this study as it is not clear how much these differences were due to the maths teaching specifically or the overall approach of each school.

Stronger evidence has come from a randomised control trial with undergraduate students using a 'massive online learning course' (or MOOC), which integrated growth mindset messages with mathematics teaching (Boaler et al., 2018). Results show that the treatment group ($n = 459$) that took the MOOC (6 units each taking 15–20 minutes) reported more positive beliefs about maths, engaged more deeply in maths lessons and achieved at significantly higher levels on standardised mathematics assessments than the control group ($n = 651$).

Daly et al. (2019) have provided some compelling neuropsychological evidence to support the use of mathematical mindset interventions. Undergraduate mathematics students ($n = 16$) were either presented with problems presented in a traditional way or in a maths mindset way: e.g an open task with multiple methods, pathways and representations; inclusion of enquiry opportunities; ask the problem before teaching the method; include a visual component and ask students how they see the maths; 'lower floor and higher ceiling' – making it accessible to all, but also challenging, and ask students to convince and reason (based on Boaler, 2015). The problems presented in the maths mindset way were concluded to be more motivating, both in terms of the students' self-reports and in different brain activity in prefrontal EEG asymmetry, which has been widely reported to correlate with motivation (Coan and Allen, 2004; Schmidt and Trainor, 2001). In contrast to many mindset interventions, the students were not told explicitly about mindset theory, yet the difference in the way the tasks were presented was enough to result in these significant differences.

Some schools in the UK are also developing specific Maths Mindset programs (see www.growthmindsetmaths.com/). However, there is not yet a specific Maths Mindset topic attached to the National Curriculum. Nevertheless, a specific approach to teaching and learning maths in the UK, which can be linked to the growth mindset theory, has been developed recently. Called the mastery approach in maths, it aims to have pupils succeed at maths, and build confidence and a positive attitude through setting them in mixed ability grouping, with a depth of understanding, developing cross-objectives and multi-modal teaching (Boyd and Ash, 2018). Inspired by leading performers in South Asia, the mastery approach in maths became a priority for the Department for Education (DfE) as it is now part of the 2014 English National Curriculum for mathematics in primary schools. The aim is that eventually *any pupils considered to have attained the 'Mastery standard' are expected to explore the curriculum in greater depth and build on the breadth of their knowledge and skills within that key stage* (p. 7) and hence score higher on the new SATs test, even if they know the same content (Department for Education, 2014). Although one case study has been tested, empirical results have yet to be published to prove the effectiveness of this approach (Boylan et al., 2018). Some schools have adopted this approach independently or as part of pilot projects called Maths Hubs (www.mathshubs.org.uk), led by the National Centre for Excellence in the Teaching of Mathematics (NCETM).

Our Growing Learners team at the University of Portsmouth has led a small study as part of the Solent Maths Hub (https://solentmathshub.org.uk/), and while the results are limited by small numbers, there is an indication that students who were least able at the start of the project gained most in terms of maths ability by taking part in the Maths Mindset intervention.

Science

Reduced performance and engagement in science beyond compulsory education for females and ethnic minorities, compared to non-STEM subjects, has been well documented (e.g. Broome, 2001; Fink et al., 2018; Stoet and Geary, 2018). Growth mindset interventions have been suggested as one way to improve academic gaps and increase engagement in these subjects (Aguilar et al., 2014; Broome, 2001; Fink et al., 2018).

Broome (2001) studied a group of 13–14-year-olds (268 girls and 327 boys, across 5 schools) in Germany and found a clear relationship between physics mindset and both interest in physics and confidence in their own ability for physics. He also found an interaction between physics mindset and gender on academic outcome in physics. Despite there being no difference in physical knowledge at the start of the study, after a year of physics instruction, the girls with a fixed mindset performed worst out of all the groups.

Chen and Pajares (2010) investigated the relationship between science mindset, motivation and epistemological beliefs in sixth-grade science students (n = 508) in the US, along with gender and ethnic group. Epistemological beliefs focus on how knowledge about a domain (e.g. science) is arrived at, how certain we can be about that knowledge, how simple that knowledge is and how we can evaluate sources of that knowledge (Hofer and Printrich, 1997), and hence these beliefs may be related in some way to a student's mindset. For example, if we believe that scientific facts never change and are given to us by scientists, then we might also have a fixed mindset. The study found that students' science mindsets were mediated by their epistemological beliefs to determine science achievement (along with achievement goal orientations and self-efficacy). The only gender difference found was that boys reported significantly higher views about the incremental (e.g. growth) nature of science ability than girls. In terms of ethnic differences, both Asian and Hispanic students reported higher scores on the source of the scientific knowledge element of epistemological beliefs, which means that they were more likely to believe that scientific knowledge is handed down from authorities. One possible recommendation from this study would be that science teaching may benefit from both a science growth mindset intervention in combination with discussion of the nature of scientific knowledge (Lederman, 1999).

Fink et al. (2018) evaluated a chemistry mindset intervention with 565 first-year American undergraduate chemistry students in an attempt to reduce academic attainment gaps for female and ethnic minority students. Students were randomly assigned to either a mindset intervention group or a control group (receiving general study skills advice). Both groups received three online homework tasks across the first semester. The first task was to read an article – either 'You can grow your brain' based on Yeager et al. (2016), or 'Transition tips' with general guidance on study skills and time management. The second and third tasks asked the students to write a reflection on how the information in the previous article would help them prepare for forthcoming course exams, and to outline the main ideas of the approach. The growth mindset tasks asked the students to focus on domain-specific views of chemistry intelligence (rather than general intelligence). The tasks were deliberately presented just before exams took place, as students often make the best use of such study skill techniques at these times (Chen et al., 2017).

No sex differences were found in the exam results, and the authors comment that this may be because there was a fairly equal balance of genders on the course. Therefore, the impact of the mindset intervention could not be investigated for gender. However, differences were found between the ethnic minority and white students, and this gap was successfully removed for those students engaged in the growth mindset intervention at the end of the first semester exam. The longevity of the intervention was also tested by looking at the end of the second semester exam, and there is some evidence that the reduction in attainment gap was maintained. However, the results are less clear at this point. The students received their main chemistry course together, and the authors acknowledge there may have been some cross-contamination of the intervention ideas if students compared notes, and this was evident in their written task responses. There may therefore be some underestimate of the impact of the growth mindset intervention. The authors suggest that as the intervention focuses on writing reflection tasks, they can easily be adapted to other subjects.

Language learning

Learning an additional language is another subject area where having a growth mindset is likely to have significant benefits, as it is often characterised as being the kind of skill that people often have a 'talent' for (Horwitz, 1999). It has been debated in the language learning literature whether beliefs about the malleability of language learning are stable from early in life (e.g. Wenden, 1998; Peacock, 2001) or are more dynamic (e.g. Kalaja et al., 2015; Mystowska, 2014), and it is likely that this will depend on the learning environment and messages received about the nature of language learning. In addition, it is often seen as a subject with a high level of challenge and failure as part of the learning process (Lou and Noels, 2017), there are low levels of KS4 students taking languages at GCSE (Coleman et al., 2007), and there is often a low retention rate of the language learnt (e.g. Snow et al., 1988). This suggests that language learning may be a particularly challenging skill to acquire and would benefit from learning strategies that would promote motivation, persistence and resilience – i.e. a growth mindset. There is little research on language mindset in primary or secondary aged children, with literature searches only identifying one study based in a UK secondary school (Molway and Mutton, 2019). However, the research that has been done with university-level students can still provide useful indicators for guiding language learning at Key Stages 1, 2 and 3.

Mercer and Ryan (2009) have drawn a clear parallel between mindset theory and the attitudes that people have towards learning an additional language – e.g. that either language is an innate talent or something that can be achieved by anyone through effort. In a small exploratory study, they conducted qualitative interviews with second language learners in Austria ($n = 5$) and Japan ($n = 4$). Students made statements that suggested a clear growth or fixed mindset about learning language. However, most students expressed a mixture of beliefs, and they therefore supported the continuum model of mindset, with individuals residing at some point along that continuum rather than at the extreme ends of the scale. They also found evidence of students having different mindsets for different aspects of language learning (e.g. writing vs. speaking, prepositions vs. pronunciation), and this was more pronounced in the Austrian group than in the Japanese group. It was also noted that the Japanese group appeared to have a more general growth mindset overall when they commented on approaching learning in all topics (e.g. needing effort), highlighting the need for awareness of cultural differences in mindset (Horwitz, 2001).

Lou and Noels (2016) investigated whether it was possible to manipulate language mindsets with 150 Canadian university students who had enrolled in a second language course. The intervention involved reading a two-page article that was written to promote either a fixed or growth mindset view of language learning (this is a common technique used in previous research for manipulating mindset in the short term – e.g. Hong et al., 1999). They were successful in changing mindsets within the experimental session, with the students reading the fixed language mindset article developing a significantly more fixed mindset and those reading the growth article developing a significantly more growth mindset. There was no long-term follow-up of the students and, as the authors acknowledge, it is possible that this change was just a temporary one with their language mindset in the long term depending on the messages that the students were receiving in their language classes. However, it clearly demonstrates that even a brief specific language mindset intervention can have a significant effect and supports the suggestion that it would be worth including growth mindset messages and feedback in standard language classes.

In addition, Lou and Noels (2017) developed a specific measure to assess language mindsets – the Language Mindsets Inventory (LMI). This was found to be a better predictor of language motivation and outcomes than a general mindset measure in North American university students who had chosen to study a second language. Further, using this measure they found there were three specific mindsets for within the language domain: 1) general language intelligence beliefs – e.g. is general language skill fixed or malleable?; 2) second language aptitude – e.g. can it be improved with practice or not?, and 3) beliefs relating to age sensitivity and language learning – e.g. are children more adept at learning second languages up to a certain age or can you learn at any age? These three subdomains provide useful information on what to include in a specific language mindset intervention. The key difference this reveals is that in addition to framing the usual general growth mindset messages with a language context, the message that languages *can* be learnt at any age should be included.

"LANGUAGES *CAN* BE LEARNT AT ANY AGE"

Although this research has stemmed from university-level students, these messages would be worth primary and secondary schools integrating into language lessons, as these mindsets could have a huge impact on whether students even choose to learn additional languages beyond the compulsory curriculum.

Finally, we should return to the only study found investigating the use of a growth mindset intervention in a secondary school. Molway and Mutton (2019) included all Year 9 children in a UK comprehensive school who were studying German as a compulsory subject (n = 127 across five classes). They allocated classes to one of three conditions: 1) a growth mindset plus 'reading strategies' intervention; 2) the 'reading strategies' intervention only, and 3) a non-intervention control group. The growth mindset intervention was based on Blackwell et al.'s (2007) intervention, with two hour-long sessions early in the term, followed by a further one-hour session later in the term. The growth mindset sessions introduced them to the general principles of mindset with additional exercises applying this to learning languages. The reading strategies intervention was designed to give the students extra knowledge of techniques and strategies to enable progressions in learning German, following Blackwell et al.'s (2007) suggestion that these are needed in addition to developing a growth mindset, otherwise learning might stall due to a lack of skills. The reading strategies sessions involved asking students about the reading strategies they already used, and introducing them to new strategies, followed by activities using 'code-switched' texts (those alternating between two languages) of increasing complexity and which required one strategy at a time.

The intervention was successful in terms of significantly increasing the number of students who had a growth mindset. Interestingly, 64% of those with a growth mindset at the final data collection point also agreed with the statement that 'Some people are naturally good at languages', with Molway and Mutton concluding that you can simultaneously believe both that language skills can be improved by effort *and* that some people are naturally good at languages. This could be taken as further evidence that different mindsets can be held about different abilities, or even different aspects of the same ability. The combined mindset and reading strategies intervention group also displayed a more positive shift in self-reported classroom behaviours – e.g. 'When I have a problem understanding something in my German class I am more likely to ask my teacher for help'. In contrast, the control group displayed increasingly maladaptive behaviours – e.g. they were more likely to give up, or feel depressed – possibly due to the building frustrations of trying to cope with a challenging topic without the coping mechanisms that the two intervention groups had been provided with. In terms of academic outcomes, while there was only a weak correlation between mindset status at the last test point and National Curriculum attainment levels, there was an observable, but non-significant trend that those in both intervention groups made more academic progress overall than the controls. However, when looking at ability at the start of the year, those who were least able and took part in the combined intervention made greater progress than their counterparts in the two other groups, adding to a growing body of evidence that it is the least able students who benefit most from mindset interventions – e.g. Grenfell and Harris (2013) and the Portsmouth team. The researchers also asked the students during the final testing point if they intended to take GCSE German the next year, and later also checked to see if they actually did so. Interestingly, the students who were in the reading strategies only group had the highest rate of interest and actual take-up of German GCSE. However, that group was also found to have a slightly higher ability level at the start of the year, which may have influenced their choice of GCSE subject. Overall, 22% of the students chose GCSE German, in comparison with 12% in the previous year, so the intervention could be considered a success in terms of maintaining engagement in learning German. Overall, this study provides some evidence that a targeted mindset intervention supported by topic-relevant strategies is an effective way of improving language skills attainment and engagement, and provides a useful model for how schools can include these interventions within the curriculum.

Sports and physical education

> **"SPORTS ARE ANOTHER AREA IN WHICH TOP ATHLETES ARE OFTEN CHARACTERISED AS HAVING 'NATURAL TALENTS', SUGGESTING WE MAY FIND A FIXED MINDSET TO DOMINATE."**

Sports are another area in which top athletes are often characterised as having 'natural talents', suggesting that we may find a fixed mindset to dominate. However, sports scientists and coaches are now working together to maximise the potential of their athletes (Brady and Grenville-Cleave,

2018), and the importance of having a growth mindset is starting to have an impact. Carol Dweck in her 2006 book, *Mindset: How You Can Fulfil Your Potential*, devotes an entire chapter to case studies of high-profile athletes and teams in the USA. She suggests that mindsets have made a significant difference to the careers of these athletes, with a fixed mindset limiting the success of some – e.g. John McEnroe – and developing a growth mindset helping to break through to the next level of competition – e.g. Michael Jordan. Setbacks and failures are integral in progression in sport and so are perfect for growth (Crust and Clough, 2011), including developing resilience and a growth mindset, and this can apply to physical education in schools.

There is a growing body of research that has explored the role of mindset in sports and related psychological phenomena (Biddle et al., 2003; Brady and Alleyne, 2018). This research in sport and physical education (PE) has found that a growth mindset is positively associated with positive affect, higher self-efficacy and enjoyment of physical activity, skill acquisition, performance, task orientation, interest, motivation to engage, increased participation and persistence (Biddle, et al., 2003; Jourden et al., 1991; Kasimatis et al., 1996; Ommundsen, 2001, 2003; Van Yperen and Duda, 1999; Wang and Biddle, 2001).

There is also evidence that there are separate mindsets for subdomains within sports, so that a fixed belief can be held for one aspect and a growth mindset for another. For example, Jowett and Spray (2013) found that in a small sample ($n = 4$) of British Olympic hopefuls, to be successful an aspect of talent was preferable, with some specific physiological factors being important for some sports, but that working hard through practice was far more important for achieving success. Similar results were found by Slater et al. (2012) with golfers.

Several studies have demonstrated successful short-term manipulation of mindset related to sports (Kasimatis et al., 1996; Spray et al., 2010) and motorskills (Jourden et al., 1991). These studies use similar techniques to those within previous studies manipulating general mindset by presenting an instruction or an article that either explains sports excellence in terms of natural ability (fixed mindset) or in terms of training, practice and experience (growth mindset), and hence suggest that sports-related mindset interventions across repeated sessions are also likely to be useful. For example, Spray et al. (2010) manipulated sports mindset in 123 secondary school pupils (aged 11–15) using a brief article that described the skills involved in golf and how a professional golf player had achieved success using either fixed mindset language – e.g. Tiger Woods is naturally gifted – or growth mindset language – e.g. Nick Faldo's rigorous training routine. After the mindset manipulation, pupils were asked to take part in a golf-putting task. They were all told they had performed badly and to look at the combined effect of failure and mindset. Those with a fixed mindset were more likely to select performance goals – e.g. 'I like levels that are hard enough to show that I am good in golf' – and to attribute failure to a lack of ability rather than to a lack of effort. In contrast, students with a growth mindset were more likely to set learning goals – e.g. 'I like to try difficult and challenging levels so that I can try to learn from the task, even if I won't do well'.

For specific ideas and guidance on how to apply the growth mindset approach to sports and PE, Vella et al. (2014) outlined six key areas:

- focus on effort and persistence;
- challenge;
- value of failure;
- perceptions of success;
- promote learning;
- high expectations.

These are based on a review of previous literature and draw on elements of general growth mindset interventions applied to the sports domain. In addition, see Brady and Grenville-Cleave (2018) and the Growth Mindset Coaching Kit by Frith and Sykes (2016) – a team of sports coaches and psychologists who have used the techniques with schools, sports teams and elite athletes.

Reading

While there is a large amount of research on how children learn to read, there has been very little specific research looking at the role of mindsets in reading.

Law (2009) tested a group of 120 Chinese children (mean age 12.2 years) attending a Hong Kong primary school and found an association between implicit beliefs about intelligence and reading comprehension. This population was of particular interest as they were particularly good readers; the Chinese children in Hong Kong Primary 4 schools were found to outperform 45 countries or provinces.

In an interesting study, Anderson and Nielsen (2016) conducted a large-scale classroom-randomised intervention ($n = 1,587$ children) in Denmark, with parents given information and instructions on how to deliver reading support with a growth mindset approach. They concluded that this intervention significantly improved the children's reading skills in three domains (language comprehension, decoding and text comprehension) after three months and seven months (though with smaller effects at seven months). As predicted by the researchers, there were great improvements for children whose parents had a more fixed mindset before the intervention. However, there are some confounds to this study as there were various 'reading' elements to the intervention; as well as parents being given instructions on how to support reading in a growth mindset way, the children were also given three books, information on how to access more at the library and school, and there were rewards for reading regularly at home. In contrast, the control group were not given any books, or encouragement for accessing further books, or reading regularly, so it could be that these factors have caused the reading improvements rather than the specific growth mindset approach delivered by parents, and the authors do acknowledge this. It would be worth repeating this study with a more comparable control condition to identify the important variables, because if parental involvement can be sustained through support from schools, it is a very low-cost way of improving reading skills.

Growth mindset messages have been starting to appear in various non-fiction and fictional books for children, and these include a set that have been published by the Growing Learners Team at Portsmouth with the aim of providing teachers and parents with resources for discussing growth mindset. Each book includes a set of questions for discussion, and there is a range of books appropriate for pre-schoolers (*My Hero and George: A True Story of His Early Years*), through to KS2 (*The Mystery of Mrs Raven*).

Arts, creativity and music

The application of the growth mindset model has started to appear in discussions of the arts and creativity, including small-scale master's projects – e.g. case studies in online teaching resources – and blogs – e.g. The Art of Education University, US. Warren et al. (2019) found that holding an incremental theory of intelligence (or growth mindset) was related to higher performance on a divergent thinking task – e.g. a measure of creativity – in both 4–7-year-olds and in university students, suggesting that including a growth mindset approach to teaching arts would be beneficial. However, little experimental research has explored its application in the classroom, neither in terms of a general mindset intervention, nor as an arts-specific mindset intervention. Where experimental research has taken place in this area is within the field of music.

Music education varies hugely around the world, with most Western schools including its teaching at some level. In the UK, music has been generally taught in schools and is part of the National Curriculum. Teachers therefore have an opportunity to engage children in the enjoyment of playing music (including singing) from a young age (Cogdill, 2015). However, for an instrument to be learnt in depth it usually becomes an additional activity, with students often withdrawing from other lessons or taking instruction outside of school (Patston and Waters, 2015), and hence motivation to continue to learn an instrument becomes crucial to continued engagement. Cogdill (2015) and Patston and Waters (2015) provide a summary of psychological research that would be useful for all teachers to use in music lessons, and both include growth mindset. Davis (2016) highlights the importance of applying growth mindset feedback when students make mistakes in music practice. If a growth mindset is promoted within music teaching, it may be possible to reduce the perception of music as an innate talent (Sloboda, 1996), enable students to deal with the difficulties involved in learning a musical instrument, and encourage students to engage in the deliberate practice required to improve musical skill (Hallam, 1997; Ericsson et al., 1993). However, as yet there are no studies evaluating the effectiveness of promoting a growth mindset specifically for music, but studies have looked at the relationship between music mindset and other variables.

Mullensieffen et al. (2018) report on the first set of data from a five-year longitudinal study of an all-girls secondary school (n = 313, age range: 10–18 years), looking at musical ability, a range of ability and personality measures, plus both a general growth mindset measure and a specific music mindset measure. They found that general mindset and specific music mindset were closely related. In terms of musical ability, music mindset was related to the melodic memory test given to each student. There was no relationship between musical mindset, concurrent musical activities, musical training and beat perception. The authors concluded that the relationship between musical mindsets and involvement in musical activities must be mediated by at least one musical skill (melodic memory). Smith (2005) surveyed 344 university students majoring in music across the US to investigate the relationship between music mindset, and motivation and musical practice. A positive correlation was found between growth mindset for music and both ego-approach goals (goals that demonstrate high ability) and ego-avoid goals (goals that avoid demonstrating lack of ability).

Conclusion

At present, very few published studies have investigated subject-specific mindset interventions. Studies suggest that the longer the growth mindset intervention can be maintained, the greater the impact on outcomes.

"STUDIES SUGGEST THAT THE LONGER THE GROWTH MINDSET INTERVENTION CAN BE MAINTAINED, THE GREATER THE IMPACT ON OUTCOMES."

In addition, providing subject-specific strategies is important as having a growth mindset is not always enough without something to apply it to. Overall, the evidence seems to point to subject-specific mindsets, and even subdomain mindsets, which for educators is important to keep in mind, so just because students have a growth or fixed mindset for many of areas of schooling, it does not mean that they have the same mindset for all domains.

PART TWO

MINDSETS IN THE CLASSROOM

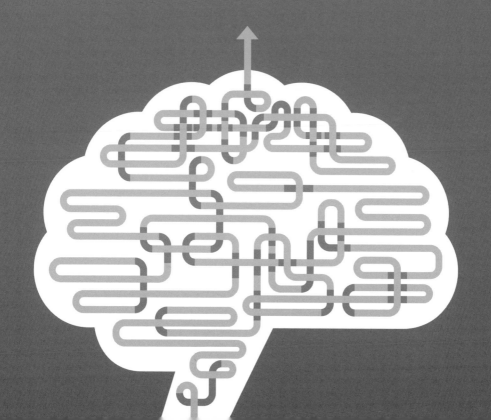

Key information

The following sections of the book will describe the activities and exercises that make up the Changing Mindsets intervention programmes. For ease of use, these have been divided into three age groups:

- Early Years Foundation Stage and Key Stage 1;
- Key Stage 2;
- Secondary and Further Education.

You will see that there is an overlap across the three age groups. We wanted to include all the activities in a format that would allow teachers to be able to refer quickly and easily to lesson plans designed for the relevant year group. However, you know your pupils best, so feel free to pick and choose activities from all the programmes if you think this would be helpful.

Timings

In previous versions of these lesson plans we had suggested timings for each activity. However, we are aware that teachers will vary in their delivery of the lesson plans and how long they want to focus on each activity.

CHAPTER 6

EARLY YEARS FOUNDATION STAGE AND KEY STAGE 1

SHERRIA HOSKINS, VICTORIA DEVONSHIRE, EMILY MASON-APPS AND FRANCES WARREN

Notes on using the lesson plans

These activities have been divided into six sessions, which each last approximately 1.5 hours. The sessions are as follows.

1. Introduction to the main concepts and exploration of pupils' mindsets.
2. Responses to challenges and 'internal voices'.
3. Use of feedback for improvement and a growth mindset approach to problem-solving.
4. The importance of hard work and responding positively to mistakes.
5. Reflection on how different responses can lead to different outcomes.
6. Consolidation of key themes.

We have suggested that you carry out a session once a week, so that the intervention lasts for six weeks. However, we have designed the programme to be flexible, so that the way you administer the intervention can be adapted to suit the needs of your class. We understand that for younger children, a 90-minute session might be too long, but you could easily break up each lesson plan into shorter sessions to be implemented more regularly. Likewise, you may want to devote a few days to mindsets, and therefore work through the activities more intensively.

Given the variability in age and ability of pupils across Early Years Foundation Stage and Key Stage 1, we have suggested adaptations to certain activities to either simplify or extend the exercise for you to choose as appropriate. You know your pupils best, so please feel free to adapt and modify the materials and activities yourself; what's important is that the Learning Outcomes for each session are achieved by the children.

Throughout the lesson plans, you will see that we have also included additional ideas.

Materials and resources to accompany these lesson plans are available online at **https://study.sagepub.com/education/education-all-phases/ hoskins-growth-mindset-for-teachers**. If they are available online, these are indicated by a ⌖ symbol.

6.1 Week 1

KEY THEME

Introduction to main concepts and exploration of pupils' mindsets.

LEARNING OUTCOMES

1. To understand the connection between feelings and challenges.
2. To discover that the brain is like a muscle and that we can all 'grow our brains' through hard work, learning and practice.
3. For pupils to begin to think of themselves as 'Growing Learners'.

ACTIVITIES

1. Class discussion: 'The things we find hard' and associated emotions.
2. The brain as a muscle (facts and demonstration).
3. Cartoon and introduction to growth and fixed mindsets.
4. Assignment of statements.

MATERIALS REQUIRED

- 'Mindsters' poster (available online).
- 'Mindsters' Cartoon (available online).
- Mindl and Teezle posters.
- Mindl and Teezle pre-written statements.
- Optional: sunflower seeds/materials for making sunflower hats.

ACTIVITY DESCRIPTIONS

1. Activity: Class discussion: 'The things we find hard' and associated emotions.

   Using a circle time set-up, ask children about the things they find hard and what it's like to try something new, and how this makes them feel. More articulate responses might range from 'It makes me angry' and 'It makes me want to not do it any more' to 'It makes me want to try harder' and 'It makes me feel proud'. Suggestions might need to be modelled by teachers. This will help children identify the relationship between feelings and challenging situations, and provides a good opportunity for staff to explore pupils' mindsets. (For younger children, this may need to be done in smaller groups.)

   You might like to link this to the following activity saying something like: 'We've all now talked about some of the things we find difficult and sometimes we feel like we will never be good at these things. This means that sometimes we feel like just giving up, but . . .'

2. **Activity: The brain as a muscle**

   From this point, introduce the idea that challenges provide an opportunity to 'grow our brains'. To begin this topic, you might like to provide children with some facts about the brain (perhaps in a quiz format). For example:

   - The brain controls everything we do.
   - The brain sends messages to the body.
   - The brain controls how we feel (e.g. happy, sad, angry).
   - The brain is protected by our skull.

   (Continued)

(Continued)

- The brain stores all of our memories.
- The brain helps us to remember things like how to play a game or ride a bike.
- The brain is in charge of our reading, writing and spelling.

Finish this discussion by explaining to children that the *brain is like a muscle*. Ask children how they would build up other muscles, and get them to mime their responses (e.g. lift weights to build arm muscles, lunges for leg muscles, etc.). Explain that, like all other muscles, we can build up our brains. 'The more we practise something, the easier it gets because parts of the brain grow stronger – it's like we are stretching our thinking muscle!'

To illustrate this point, get children to stand in a circle holding hands. Explain that this is how the brain works when we're not working very hard. Still holding hands, get the children to then spread out as far as they can, and explain that this is what happens to our brains when we are working really hard on something. You might like to say something like: 'The circle is like our brains! See how much bigger it gets when we work hard. When we're "stretching ourselves" and working really hard on something, our brains are growing stronger!'

NB: The point of this discussion is to inspire children to believe in themselves; even when they find something hard to begin with, they can always improve as the brain grows stronger. It is important to highlight that there is no reason why we can't all improve at anything – we just need to put our minds to it and work hard. You could point out at this stage that the brains of babies and toddlers are growing all the time; they are always learning new things, so their brains develop rapidly.

Additional activity: To illustrate the point of 'growth' further, you might like to plant sunflower seeds as a class. As these start to grow, you could relate these to the growth of our brains. You could go even further by planting seeds in different environments (e.g. one in soil, one in pebbles, one in water, etc.) so that children can see the difference in growth rate – you can use this demonstration to highlight the point that the sunflower seed alone is not enough; the environment in which it is planted makes a difference to its growth.

3. **Activity: Cartoon and introduction to growth and fixed mindsets**

Introduce children to the 'Mindsters' by showing them the Mindsters poster. Then go on to show the animated cartoon. Highlight the two different approaches to learning. For example, you could say:

> Mindi and Teezle have two very different ways of thinking about learning. This means that they have two different *mindsets*. One of them, Teezle, wants to give up. He's found playing the guitar very difficult so doesn't want to try any more. This is called a 'fixed mindset' because he thinks he's never going to be any good. We're going to call these sorts of learners 'fixed learners' because they feel they can never improve; once they get stuck on something, they don't want to try any more. Rather than try to find a way around the problem, they give up or try to find something easier to do.

> On the other hand, Mindi knows that it's important to work even harder if you find something difficult. She learnt to play the guitar because she practised lots and didn't give up. This is called a 'growth mindset'. People with a growth mindset know that they can grow their brains and get better at things; they know that they just need to work hard and find the right way to do it. We're going to call these sorts of learners 'Growing Learners' because they carry on going, even when things seem hard – they are very brave. They love a challenge because they feel proud when they succeed. They don't give up, no matter what!

4. **Activity: Assignment of statements**

Put the posters of Mindi and Teezle on the board and go through the fixed and growth statements one by one. Ask children which Mindster they think each statement relates to and get them to stick it on to the correct Mindster.

Some further discussion questions are:

- Which Mindster (Mindi or Teezle) loves a challenge? Why do you think this?
- What would Mindi do if she was finding something difficult?

(Continued)

(Continued)

- What do you do if you find something difficult?
- How can *you* be a Growing Learner?

PLENARY

Recap with the children what you have talked about during the session. Explain that we all want to be Growing Learners and have a growth mindset. Teachers might like to give an example of when they have been a Growing Learner themselves.

Additional activity: Being a Growing Learner could be a class goal and involve making a behavioural reward chart display for reinforcement.

6.2 Week 2

KEY THEME

Response to challenges and 'internal voices'.

LEARNING OUTCOMES

1. To introduce and understand the concept of resilience.
2. To consider and adjust 'internal voices'.
3. To set personal targets/challenges and view the effect of practice and effort.

ACTIVITIES

1. Recap from previous week.
2. Class discussion about resilience (with demonstration).
3. Internal voices (encouraging pupils to adapt their own internal voices).
4. Target setting – making personal challenge boards.

MATERIALS REQUIRED

- Bouncy ball/stone/jug of water.
- Mindi and Teezle posters.
- Materials for making a Challenge Board (available online).
- Optional: *Little Red Hen* story book (not included).

ACTIVITY DESCRIPTIONS

1. Activity: Recap from previous week.

   Remind children about what the class had discussed previously. The important points to mention are as follows.

   - The brain is a muscle and gets stronger when we work hard.
   - The difference in approaches to learning between growth (Mindi) and fixed (Teezle) mindsets.
   - The whole class are aiming to be Growing Learners.

2. **Activity: Class discussion about resilience (with demonstration)**

   Talk to children about the concept of resilience – describing the difference between being a 'bouncy ball' or a 'sinking stone'. (You could demonstrate these metaphors using a bouncy ball and a stone in a jug of water.) You might like to say something along the lines of:

   When we find something difficult, we sometimes feel sad or cross, and we can respond to that in different ways. We can either be a 'bouncy ball' or a 'sinking stone'. Being a sinking stone [drop stone into water] means that we don't think we can do it and can't help ourselves, so we don't bother trying and give up. This means that we never improve and don't get any better at it. However, being a bouncy ball [bounce ball] means that we keep bouncing back, even when something seems hard. We know that there are usually different things we can try to succeed – we just have to keep trying until we find the right way.

   (Continued)

(Continued)

Using these metaphors and/or demonstrations will help children to understand the difference between rebounding from set-backs as opposed to giving up and not trying any more. Remind children about the importance of being a Growing Learner; even if we find things hard to start with, we can always improve. You might like to link these words to other related mindset terms, including perseverance and determination.

3. **Activity: Internal voices**

Encourage children to use 'self-talk' in a growth mindset way by referring to the Mindi and Teezle posters used in the previous week. Remind children about the two characters and get them to think about what each would say to them when they are facing a challenge – e.g. trying to write their name, riding a bike or a spelling test. For example, ask children to imagine that Mindi and Teezle are sitting on each shoulder and think about what they would tell them to do. (Alternatively, you could do this activity using puppets from your classroom.) Examples of what Mindi would say might include:

'You can get better, you just need to practise and try your hardest!'

'Challenges help you grow your brain!'

'Don't give up; you will get there in the end!'

'Keep going – you can do it!'

Finish the activity by getting children to think about what they would say to themselves next time they find something difficult.

Additional or alternative activity: It would be easy to emphasise this point further by including a game at this stage. For example, you could get the pupils to line up, one in front of the other. To the right of the line, put up the picture of Teezle and to the left of the line, put up the picture of Mindi. You could then read aloud some examples of the 'internal voices' that we might hear, and after a few moments of reflection, ask children to run to the Mindster that best represents the statement. After each decision, ask pupils to give their reasons and think about ways to deal with it next time they might come across that thought.

4. **Activity: Target setting – making personal challenge boards**

The final activity in this session is intended to change the way that children think about challenges and help them to want to seek out their own challenges.

As a group, brainstorm things that are difficult for some children to do and then ask them to create their own 'challenge board' on which they write one challenge (or add a pre-made picture depending on age) that they would like to work on. It might be useful to think up some 'stock' challenges as some children might not be able to think up their own challenge. Ask the children to decorate these, either by drawing or cutting out pictures. When the children have finished, display their challenges on the wall and explain that for the next two weeks at school, the children will practise this activity for a short while every day. This will then be reviewed in Week 4 so that they can look at their own improvement. Teachers might also want to make their own challenge board with the children.

We feel that focusing on physical challenges is a good idea as these will be easy to see the improvement, for example:

- throwing;
- catching;
- skipping;
- kicking a football;
- balancing.

Other, non-physical challenges might be:

- handwriting;
- spelling name;
- number bonds;
- times tables;
- colouring;
- drawing.

PLENARY

Discuss the key points of the session with the class. Remind them about the difference between being a sinking stone and a bouncy ball, and that next time we face a challenge, we are going to listen to our Growing Learner voice and keep practising.

6.3 Week 3

KEY THEME

Using feedback for improvement and problem-solving.

LEARNING OUTCOMES

1. To think about the use of feedback when trying to improve on a challenge.
2. To learn how to solve problems independently in a growth mindset way.

ACTIVITIES

1. Recap from the previous week.
2. Peer mentoring and feedback (see 'Austin's butterfly' on the video link page online for more information).
3. Growing Learners problem-solving routine.
4. Role play.

MATERIALS REQUIRED

- Pictures for peer mentoring activity.
- Paper and pencils.
- Optional: puppets.

ACTIVITY DESCRIPTIONS

1. **Activity: Recap from previous week**

   Remind children about discussions in the previous week. The important points to mention are as follows.

   - Responding with resilience when facing challenging situations.
   - Thinking about the internal voices we listen to.
   - Target setting and the importance of practice.

2. **Activity: Peer mentoring and feedback**

Based on the Austin's butterfly activity, put children into pairs and give each child a picture (examples can be found online) and ask them to draw it. After they have finished, ask them to provide each other with feedback on how they could make their drawing look more like the picture. Suggestions might include:

- 'You could make your petals a bit more pointy.'
- 'The car in the picture is longer than yours.'
- 'The front door is on the side, not in the middle.'

Then, ask them to have another go at drawing the picture on a new piece of paper, using the feedback they have just received to help them improve. Keep repeating this process of draft and feedback until the children are happy with their own drawings and each other's. The aim of this task is to help children view their improvement and realise that the more effort you put into something, the more you improve. It should also highlight that getting advice from others is a good strategy to use to improve and that they shouldn't be frightened to ask for help. Keep each draft copy of the drawing so that they can see how they got to their finished result and emphasise the 'journey' that got them there.

3. **Activity: Growing Learners problem-solving routine**

Learning to solve problems independently is a key stage in development. Introduce children to the Growing Learners problem-solving routine. Explain that, as a class, this will be the new approach to solving all sorts of different problems and challenges, in lessons and

GROWING LEARNERS PROBLEM-SOLVING ROUTINE

A challenge is a chance to grow my brain!

1. What is the problem?
2. How can I solve the problem?
3. Solving the problem.
4. Did my solution work?

(Continued)

(Continued)

in social situations – e.g. sharing, taking turns and interacting with others. To begin with, remind children that nothing is insurmountable and that challenges are not something to be frightened of – they are opportunities to grow our brains.

1. Work out what the problem is.

   Encourage the child to identify the problem. This might require support from teachers, especially if the child is particularly upset. While doing so, you can introduce children to words that describe feelings that they might not already be familiar with (e.g. frustrated, disappointed, fed-up).

2. Think about different ways to deal with the problem.

   Once the child has identified the problem, encourage them to come up with as many possible solutions for solving the problem as they can. If the child finds this difficult, teachers should suggest some ideas. It is important not to dismiss any ideas if the child has come up with them independently – even if it includes 'I could hit him over the head!' – because the next step will involve selecting the most appropriate strategy.

3. Try the solution.

   From all the possible solutions, ask the child to choose which one they want to try first. Get them to consider whether the solution would be appropriate (e.g. fair, safe, the impact on the other children). If you both agree that it would be appropriate, select this idea. Before trying it out, ask the child to choose a back-up plan in case the first solution doesn't work.

   Encourage the child to try the first solution. If that doesn't work, get the child to implement the back-up plan. If necessary, you might like to say something such as: 'Hm, that solution didn't seem to work as well as you thought it might. It looks like you might need to try your back-up plan to solve your problem.'

4. Evaluate how well the solution works.

   It's important to revisit the issue afterwards where possible, as this routine can become a cycle and inform pupils' decisions and behaviour the next time a similar situation arises. When short of time, this might just be a simple comment from the teacher: 'You worked hard to find a way to solve your problem. Your brain must be growing!' It is also good to ask the child to reflect on whether the strategy had been effective, why that might be, or what they might do next time.

As an example: if two children are arguing over one toy, stop them, remind them that this could be an opportunity to grow their brains and find out what the problem is. Then ask them to brainstorm ways in which they could solve the problem. Ideas might include: taking turns, trying to see if there is another toy, or playing with the toy together. Ask them to choose which solution they are going to try first, and then ask them to choose a second option in case the first idea doesn't work. Finally, evaluate how well the strategy worked; this might come from teachers or from pupils. (When it is not possible to employ this routine immediately, discussion after the event can still follow this format.)

Try setting simple problem-solving activities for the children to solve in this way. Some examples might include the following.

- Missing shoes: ask children to take off their shoes and place them in a pile in the middle of the room. Hide another pair of shoes among the pile and ask the children how to go about being 'shoe detectives' – i.e. helping you to find the shoes. This could involve asking for clues and sorting through the shoes until they find the correct pair (e.g. 'my shoes are brown' and then 'my shoes have red laces').
- Cleaning up: how can we make sure all the toys fit on the trolley without falling off?

4. **Activity: Role play**

As a class, talk about some more situations when people could use the Growing Learners problem-solving routine. Some examples might be:

- sharing in the classroom;
- struggling with spellings;
- imaginary play with everybody wanting to be the same part;
- feeling nervous about an upcoming event.

In small groups, get children to role play different scenarios using the Growing Learners problem-solving routine to deal with the

(Continued)

(Continued)

imaginary situation. These can be self-selected situations or ones previously discussed (these could be distributed at random to the groups). Depending on what you feel is appropriate for your class, you could get the children to show each other their role plays and use this to form the basis of a discussion about the various solutions and strategies that we can find. (An alternative would be for pupils to use puppets, or for each group to receive the same scenario in order to come up with, and compare, different solutions.)

PLENARY

As a class, discuss the main points of the session. Referring back to the progress they made with their drawings, reiterate the importance of hard work, effort and persistence. Remind children that everyone is going to try to use the Growing Learners problem-solving routine from now on in order to try to solve challenges and problems independently, thinking of them as opportunities to grow their brains.

6.4 Week 4

KEY THEME

The importance of hard work and responding positively to mistakes.

LEARNING OUTCOMES

1. To appreciate the importance of hard work and practice.
2. To re-evaluate responses to mistakes.
3. To identify the 'journeys' of inspirational people and characters.

ACTIVITIES

1. Recap from previous week.
2. Revisit challenge boards and demonstration of skills.

3. Mistakes board.
4. Case studies of inspirational people.
5. Read Growing Learners story: *George*.

MATERIALS REQUIRED

- Challenge board (made in Week 2).
- Mistakes board (available online).
- Case Studies of Inspirational People some suggested videos (available online).
- Optional: 'journey' storyboards for chosen inspirational people (not included).
- Growing Learners story book *George* (available online).

ACTIVITY DESCRIPTIONS

1. **Activity: Recap from previous week**

    Remind children of what you had discussed previously. The important points to mention are as follows.

    - Everyone can improve at everything, we just need to keep trying (to be reinforced in this session).
    - The Growing Learners problem-solving routine and how to deal with problems using a growth mindset approach.

2. **Activity: Revisit challenge boards and demonstration of skills**

    Refer back to challenge boards and ask each child to demonstrate the skill they have been practising. Emphasise the improvement they have made using growth mindset language. For example:

    'You really tried hard.'

    'You found a really good way to do that.'

    'Keep trying and you will get there.'

    'Your skipping is getting better and better.'

    (Continued)

(Continued)

> 'Your catching has really improved; remember how many you could catch before?'
>
> 'There were hardly any mistakes this time.'

Get them to think about other things they might have been practising – e.g. How are they practising being a better friend? How are they practising being a Growing Learner?

3. **Activity: Mistakes board**

Emphasise to children that *learning* is the most important thing and knowing that you have tried your hardest; making mistakes doesn't matter – it's how you deal with them that's important. Mistakes are all part of the learning process – you can learn from them and get better next time. Often the fear of making mistakes – and associated embarrassment – can be the biggest factor that stops children from trying in the first place. Highlight that making mistakes is a fact of life and that we shouldn't be scared to 'give something a go' just because we are worried about getting it wrong. You could say something along the lines of:

> Another important thing about Growing Learners is that they don't mind making mistakes. They understand that mistakes are all part of the learning process and will help them get better next time. Mistakes don't mean you are stupid. You don't look at babies and think they are stupid when they fall over – they just haven't learnt how to walk yet. We all understand that they are still learning how to do it. It's OK to make mistakes; it's how we deal with them that's important. We shouldn't be scared to give something a go, and we mustn't give up, or stop trying, just because we've made a mistake.

Ask each child to describe a mistake that they have made recently and how they can learn from it and what they would do differently. Once they have done this, write their name on the mistakes board. This should help children to understand that we all make mistakes and they shouldn't feel embarrassed or ashamed.

Additional activity: If you would like to do something more active to bring home the point that we all make mistakes – and that it's OK – you could try the following game with your class. Seat children on chairs in a circle, with one pupil standing in the middle. The pupil in the middle of the circle tells the others about a mistake they have made. If some of the other pupils have made the same mistake, they all have to stand up and swap seats as quickly as possible. During this swap, the child in the middle has to find a seat in the circle. If they succeed, then there should be one child left without a seat, so that child becomes the next person to stand up in the middle and tell the others about a mistake. If the child in the middle does not manage to find a seat, then they have another go. The idea is for the children to share some mistakes in the knowledge that they are not alone in making them.

4. **Activity: Case studies of inspirational people**

The aim of this activity is to emphasise that even the people we most admire had to work really hard to be successful. Discuss case studies of inspirational people, relating them to the children to make them engaging. (If you prefer, you could discuss one each day in the days leading up to the session.) For example, you could use the following.

WALT DISNEY

Ask children if they have seen various Disney films (and/or show them Disney characters that they might be familiar with). Tell them that they were drawn by Walt Disney and then tell them all about him and his 'journey'. You might like to say something like:

Do you want to hear something interesting about Walt Disney? He really struggled with his reading and writing, but when he was at school (over 100 years ago) his teachers could not understand why. That meant that he found school very difficult and had to work even harder to learn to read. Sometimes his marks at school weren't very good. But Walt Disney worked really hard and didn't give up, and ended up going to a special academy to practise his

(Continued)

(Continued)

artwork. He carried on working hard and looked for extra challenges to grow his brain. He is now one of the most famous artists in the world and everybody recognises his cartoons. What can we learn from Walt Disney's journey? Even though he found things difficult, he carried on going and didn't give up. He must have been a Growing Learner!

Other examples might include the following.

GRACE DARLING

- Daughter of a lighthouse keeper.
- One night, looking through the window, she spotted a shipwreck with survivors.
- She rowed out with her father in stormy conditions to rescue the survivors.

  There is a useful video on the BBC website that you might like to show (NB: it's quite long, so you might not want to show all of it. A link to this can be found on the video link page online.)

DAVID BECKHAM

- Played for Manchester United and England.
- In 1998, he got a red card in the World Cup.
- Many people were very angry with him and he was subject to lots of abuse.
- He didn't give up or let it get to him, and carried on working hard.
- At the following World Cup, he scored an important goal.
- He went on to become one of the world's most famous/adored footballers and was Captain for England.

  (For your information, there is a video suggested on the video link page, but we don't recommend that you show it to children of this age.)

J.K. ROWLING

- Wrote the *Harry Potter* books.

- Sold over 400 million copies and the books are written in many different languages.
- Books have been the basis for the highest-grossing film series in history.
- It wasn't always easy, though: she had a tough family life, was very poor and suffered ill health (depression).
- First book (*Harry Potter and the Philosopher's Stone*) was rejected by 12 publishing houses before somebody finally agreed to publish it.

JESSICA ENNIS–HILL

- Famous athlete.
- Rigorous training regime which involves lots of different strategies and exercises.
- Has experienced injuries that meant she had to pull out of competitions in the past, but worked even harder and managed to regain her competition titles.
- Won a gold medal in the heptathlon at the London Olympics in 2012, silver at the Rio Olympics in 2016 and was three times world champion.

HELEN KELLER

- Contracted an illness at 19 months of age which left her deaf and blind.
- Left with almost no language, but managed to learn signs to communicate with her family.
- Taught to communicate by Anne Sullivan, who arrived with the family when Helen was 7 years old, and started by spelling words into Helen's hand.
- Learned to speak and 'hear' people by reading their lips with her hands and was able to read Braille.
- At the age of 24, Helen graduated from college, becoming the first deaf blind person to earn a Bachelor of Arts degree.
- Spent much of her life giving speeches and lectures, and travelled the world raising money for the blind.
- She was also an author, publishing 12 books, and a political activist, meeting lots of famous people including many US presidents.

(Continued)

(Continued)

If you go through more than one case study, ask the children which role model is their favourite, and then talk to them more about their 'journey' and the Growing Learner characteristics that they might possess. Some example questions to promote discussion might be:

- Do you think [name of role model] had to work hard?
- Do you think everything was easy?
- Do you think they ever made mistakes?
- What do you think they did after making the mistake or finding something difficult – i.e. give up or pick themselves up and carry on?

5. **Activity: Read Growing Learners story: *George***

Read children the story of George the puppy (a copy is provided online). The story describes the life of a young puppy that feels very nervous about playing with other dogs. However, with some encouragement, he manages to overcome this fear. (You can either read the story in one go, or read it over a few days and incorporate it into your literacy hour.) When discussing the story, refer to the questions at the end of the book to help guide children towards understanding the key messages. The older the children in your class, the more you might like to focus on these questions and associated themes.

PLENARY

Summarise the main points of the session with your class. Emphasise the importance of hard work and not giving up, with reference to case studies. Remind children that everyone makes mistakes; they are not something to be ashamed of. What's important is not being afraid to give things a go and persevering even if it doesn't always go right the first time.

6.5 Week 5

KEY THEME

Different responses lead to different outcomes.

LEARNING OUTCOMES

1. To think about how to deal with situations as a Growing Learner.
2. To recognise the importance of practice and hard work.
3. To consolidate the idea that making mistakes doesn't matter; it's how you deal with them that does.

ACTIVITIES

1. Recap from previous week.
2. Read *Oh, the Places You'll Go!* (by Dr Seuss).
3. Static mindster cartoons.
4. Class creative writing.
5. Discussion about hypothetical scenarios.

MATERIALS REQUIRED

- *Oh, the Places You'll Go!* by Dr Seuss (link to audiotape online).
- Static cartoon Humphrey.
- Static cartoon Willow.
- Pre-written hypothetical scenarios (available online).
- Puppets (optional).

ACTIVITY DESCRIPTIONS

1. **Recap: Recap from previous week**

   Remind children of what you discussed previously. The important points are as follows.

   - The improvement made in a given skill through practice and hard work.
   - Mistakes are something to be learnt from, not something to be ashamed of.
   - Even the people we most admire have had to face challenges and work hard.

   (Continued)

(Continued)

2. **Activity: Read *Oh, the Places You'll Go!***

Play the audio version of *Oh, the Places You'll Go!* by Dr Seuss (or alternatively, you might prefer to read the book to the children yourself). The story emphasises that we can all be what we want to be and reach our goals. We just need to work hard and believe in ourselves. It also reminds the reader that we might come across obstacles and life may not always be easy, but highlights the importance of being motivated and 'giving things a go'. This provides a good start for a discussion about resilience in that we might come across stumbling blocks, but we can overcome these if we are Growing Learners.

(Note that there is some fixed mindset language in the book; depending on the age of the children, this could provide a source for further discussion. Refer to training day slides for more information on the implications of different types of language.)

3. **Activity: Static Mindster cartoons**

The cartoon is designed to emphasise the importance of hard work, practice and not giving up. Introduce the characters to the children and read through the cartoons, discussing the two different scenarios.

> This is Willow and this is Humphrey, and they are going to tell us their story. Let's see what happened to them.

This could then lead on to a discussion about the different ways we can react when we find things difficult. Example questions to ask might include 'What do you think happens when you keep trying hard like Willow did?' and 'What happens when you give up like Humphrey did?'

4. **Activity: Class creative writing**

As a class, write your own story to emphasise the growth mindset approach to dealing with situations. To do this, provide children with a starting sentence and then ask each child to add their own sentence in turn. This story could be based on the cartoons you have just read with the children. Alternative suggestions are as follows.

- 'It's Willow's and Humphrey's first day at school and they are feeling a bit nervous.'
- 'Teezle is struggling with his times tables and doesn't know what to do.'

- 'Humphrey and Willow are about to go on holiday but can't find their suitcase.'

As the story builds up, discuss each child's addition, especially if a child offers a sentence that doesn't 'fit' with the story's overriding theme. When the story is finished, type it up and give each child a copy to decorate with their own drawings to stick in their literacy books. Once again, for older children, you might prefer to use this activity as an opportunity for independent writing.

5. **Activity: Hypothetical scenarios**

   Read children the hypothetical scenarios provided online and talk about the different ways that people could deal with each of these. To make this more engaging for younger children, you could introduce children to two puppets that you have in the classroom; assign one with a growth mindset and one with a fixed mindset. Use these to demonstrate, compare and contrast a growth mindset response with a fixed mindset response.

PLENARY

Remind children that the way we respond to challenges and hard work affects the outcome. It's important to think about what will happen if we give up, versus what will happen if we persevere. If we come across stumbling blocks or challenges, we need to deal with these in a growth mindset way to make the most of every situation.

6.6 Week 6

KEY THEME

Consolidation.

LEARNING OUTCOMES

1. Recap and consolidate the key points from each of the weeks.

(Continued)

(Continued)
ACTIVITIES

1. Recap from all the previous weeks.
2. Mind map/spider diagram: 'How to be a Growing Learner'.
3. Make posters on 'How to be a Growing Learner'.
4. Consolidation game.
5. Prepare 'expert-led' workshop for parents/other classes.

MATERIALS REQUIRED

- Large sheets of paper for mind maps.
- Materials for making posters.
- Items for consolidation game (most relevant to your pupils; suggestions outlined but not provided).
- Workshop materials (e.g. posters, mind maps and things created in previous weeks).

ACTIVITY DESCRIPTIONS

1. **Activity: Recap from all previous weeks**

   The most important points from the sessions are as follows.

   - The difference between growth and fixed mindsets, and associated approaches to learning.
   - The brain is a muscle and can be strengthened/developed.
   - The importance of resilience and not giving up when we face challenges.
   - The importance of hard work, practice and effort.
   - The importance of learning from mistakes.

2. **Activity: Spider diagram: 'How to be a Growing Learner'**

   After reminding children of the key themes from each week, make a big spider diagram with the class about 'How to be a Growing Learner'. Write this in the middle of the 'spider' and ask children to volunteer ways to be a Growing Learner and add this to the diagram.

3. **Activity: Make posters on 'How to be a Growing Learner'**

    Based on the discussion, ask children to make their own posters about how to be a Growing Learner, potentially to display at the workshop (Activity 5, below). Depending on the age and ability of your class, this might require pictures or pre-written words/ sentences for children to stick onto the poster. Ask them to imagine that these posters are to help other children to know how to be a Growing Learner.

4. **Activity: Consolidation game**

    In a large space – perhaps a sports field or school hall – divide children into two equal teams. Give each child in both teams a number (so that children in both groups have the same designated numbers). Spread out the groups and in the middle (equal in distance from both teams) place some large laminated pictures or objects on the floor. Choose items or pictures that reflect discussions or activities that you feel are most relevant to your pupils.

    The teacher then reads out statements relating to one of the items. At this stage, give both teams a couple of moments for reflection to decide as a team which item the statement relates to. When you feel that both teams have decided, shout a number to indicate which children should play. As an example, you could say, 'It is like a muscle and grows when we work hard'. After a couple of moments, tell the 'number 2s' from both teams that it's their go. Then both children who had been given '2' at the beginning, race to the middle to take the correct item that corresponds to the statement (in this case, the brain). When a pupil takes it, they have to run back to their team without being caught by the 'number 2' from the other team. If the child manages to get back to their team without getting caught, then this team wins a point. (For younger children, you might prefer for them just to race to the object, and the winner is the child who gets there first.)

    Using the above items, other example statements might be as follows.

    *   When we find something difficult, we all want to bounce like a . . .
    *   Next time we face a problem, we are going to think about the . . .

    (Continued)

(Continued)

- The Mindster who wanted to give up playing the guitar because it was too hard.

5. **Activity: Prepare 'expert-led' workshop for parents/other classes**

   Based on the activities in previous weeks, organise things for children to do in an 'expert-led workshop'. This workshop should be for children to show parents or other classes what they have learnt over the sessions. Either way, begin the workshop by telling the parents/children a bit about what you have been doing, and ask them to go and talk to the children about what they have learnt. You could choose children to show their role plays, challenge boards, stories or posters.

WHAT HAPPENS NEXT

It is important that pupils are encouraged to continue using what they have learned over these sessions. The following section in your manual details some suggestions for what to do next and other activities that you can use to continue and reinforce the growth mindset approach.

6.7 Other ideas for the Early Years Foundation Stage and Key Stage 1

Where to go from here

Where possible, we recommend a 'whole-school approach'. Perhaps run a training day for the rest of the staff at your school based on your experiences from running the intervention. From this point, you could designate some time during regular staff meetings (perhaps once a month) to focus on how, as a whole school, you can change the school's culture to a growth mindset culture and, just as importantly, how you can maintain this change. This might also be a good time to share good classroom practice and have discussions about the school motto, reward systems, assembly content, corridor displays, etc. We also recommend using the intervention provided here throughout the school, so feel free to copy the materials you have been given and distribute them to each teacher within the school.

If you haven't already done so, work through the additional activities described throughout the lesson plans, as well as the other ideas in this section to extend your six weeks. Be open with the pupils about what you are doing with them; it has to be their choice to change their beliefs about intelligence and their approach to learning. The quicker they familiarise themselves with these concepts about beliefs and associated language, the better. Once all pupils have been introduced to the idea of mindsets, we recommend setting up a mindset peer-mentoring scheme – perhaps older pupils mentoring younger ones, or pupils you notice who have a particularly strong growth mindset becoming 'mindsets champions' to mentor those who might be more fixed. Another option, where possible, is to bring parents on board. This could be implemented by running whole-school events around mindsets to show parents – e.g. plays, workshops, etc. – or you could run a series of family learning sessions with pupils and their parents.

The key thing is to make sure that the sessions with pupils are repeated each academic year (we have materials for all age groups) and to ensure that everyone in the school is using growth mindset language and praise. It is important, therefore, to run refresher staff training and consider using this during new staff induction.

The following pages outline some other activities that you might like to implement with your pupils, but by now we are sure that you have lots of your own ideas about what would work with your classes. Keep a look-out on our website for other activities and products because we are always updating our ideas. For example, we are currently in the process of developing a series of Mindset books for pupils which could be integrated into classroom activities.

Other ideas

- **Growth time**

    At the end of a given piece of work (this can be in every lesson or just selected subjects), ask *all* children to spend 5–10 minutes improving their work. Refer to this as 'growth time' to help children realise that they can all improve their work. This should also help children view this time as rewarding, not as a punishment for those who are less able or less willing to engage with learning.

- **Caterpillar**

    Use the caterpillar wall display (an e-version can be found online) to help pupils understand the 'steps to success'. Through

    (Continued)

(Continued)

discussion with each child, set a target that has some clear steps for progression until the goal is reached. Explain that each child's name will be stuck to the end of the caterpillar (number 1) and that their aim is to reach the face. As the child progresses towards their goal, move their name along the caterpillar to illustrate this journey.

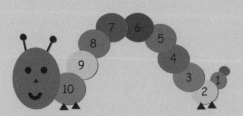

- **Teacher–pupil reversal**

This activity encourages children to really understand fixed and growth mindsets in a learning setting, and particularly from the teacher's perspective.

- One teacher plays the role of a fixed mindset pupil and one teacher plays the role of a growth mindset pupil.
- One or more pupils play the role of a teacher trying to teach a specific teaching point – schools have used a maths problem for this activity.
- The fixed mindset teacher (in pupil role) responds by saying things like: 'I can't do it', 'It's too hard', 'Can I do an easier problem?', and so on. In contrast, the growth mindset teacher (in pupil role) responds by asking questions, working on different strategies and making mistakes without being embarrassed, etc.
- The rest of the class watches and discusses the activity and different responses.

- **My Growing Learner book**

Provide each child with their own Growing Learner book. Within this book, allow children to do whatever they wish to help inspire a 'joy of learning'. You could use this book once a week and allow children to select a topic that they would like to write about, a picture that they would like to draw, or something that they would like to think about.

- **Cooking with a deliberate mistake**

Introduce a cooking activity with the class, where children are able to participate in the process. During the demonstration, make a deliberate mistake (dependent on the recipe you are using). From this point, discuss how you could deal with it to highlight that making mistakes doesn't matter. (This method could be applied to other activities, including clay modelling or intentional spelling mistakes by the teacher.)

- **Class Thinking Journal**

As a class, keep a 'Thinking Journal' to keep a record of the growth mindset journey that the class go through. You can jot down whenever a child finds something difficult, how this made them feel, and what strategies they used to overcome the difficulty. You can also note down when a child is proud of something that they have responded to in a growth mindset way or when they have supported others using a growth mindset. Encourage all children to contribute, and teachers may also wish to add their own contribution. This activity encourages self-reflection in a positive way.

- **School behaviour and reward policies**

After starting on their growth mindsets journey, many schools decide to change their behaviour and reward policies in line with characteristics of a Growing Learners' approach. In particular, schools have focused rewards on effort, hard work and improvement, rather than 'absolute' ability. For example, a Learning Award certificate can be awarded to a child whenever they learn something new; this doesn't necessarily have to be academic, but can be anything that the child is proud of.

CHAPTER 7
KEY STAGE 2

Notes on using the lesson plans

You will see that the activities have been divided into eight sessions, with each lasting approximately two hours. Each lesson plan includes learning outcomes, an activity overview, a list of materials required and detailed descriptions of each activity. The sessions are as follows.

1. Introducing key concepts; exploring pupils' mindsets.
2. Dealing with mistakes and emotions.
3. Understanding the brain and encouraging challenge.
4. Appreciating the importance of effort and persistence in improvement and progression.
5. Reflecting on the language we hear.
6. Understanding the impact of stereotypes and strategies (maths challenges).

7. Unravelling talent and luck myths: the journeys of inspirational people.
8. Consolidating key concepts.

The intervention is designed to last for eight weeks. Although we suggest that you carry out a session once a week, we have designed the programme to be flexible. For example, if it is preferable, split them into more regular, shorter sessions. You know your pupils best, so please feel free to adapt and modify the materials and activities yourself; what's important is that the learning outcomes for each session are achieved by the children. Equally, we have designed activities to be set as homework, but you may adapt these activities to be run as in-class activities instead.

You will see the 'Mindster' characters crop up throughout the learning materials. Teezle, Mindi, Willow and Humphrey are all featured in activities and each have their own characteristics and beliefs about learning. We have purposefully not used Fred and Frankie; we thought it would be nice for children to come up with their own ideas for these characters.

7.1 Week 1

KEY THEME

Introducing key concepts; exploring pupils' mindsets.

LEARNING OUTCOMES

1. To think about what 'intelligence' is.
2. To identify barriers to learning and how these can be overcome.

(Continued)

(Continued)

3. To consider an individual's ability to adapt and change.
4. To understand the difference between growth and fixed mindsets.

ACTIVITIES OVERVIEW

1. Discussion and mind-maps: 'What is intelligence?' 'What makes you intelligent?'
2. Discussion and class list: 'Barriers to learning'.
3. Introduction to growth and fixed mindsets and Mindsters cartoon.
4. Assigning statements.
5. Homework activity: Myself as a learner.

MATERIALS REQUIRED

- A3 paper and pens for mind-maps.
- Mindster poster (available online).
- Mindster cartoon (available online).
- Mindl and Teezle posters (available online).
- Lists of growth and fixed mindset statements (available online).

ACTIVITY DESCRIPTIONS

1. Activity: Discussion and mind-maps: 'What is intelligence?' 'What makes you intelligent?'

Begin this activity with a general class discussion about pupils' perceptions of the nature of intelligence and what makes people intelligent. Then get the children into smaller groups so that they can come up with ideas themselves. The aim is to get pupils to think about what intelligence (or being 'clever') actually is. It will also give you some insight into which mindset pupils exhibit more strongly. Each small group will need a large piece of paper so that they can make a mind-map of their ideas.

The sorts of things that pupils might say in response to the question 'What is intelligence?' are:

- Something you are born with.
- How 'smart' you are.
- There are different types of intelligence.

Some examples of things pupils might say in response to the question 'What makes you intelligent?':

- Being a girl.
- Being in a certain set (e.g. the red group for maths).
- Having clever parents.
- Being able to read.
- Being good at maths.
- Teachers.
- Listening in class.
- Working hard.

Ask each group to feed back to the rest of the class by giving an example or two from their mind-maps. Once pupils have shared their thoughts, summarise the key points given. You might like to discuss the *Oxford Dictionary* definition of 'intelligence', relating and comparing this to pupils' answers: *Intelligence: The ability to* **acquire** *and apply knowledge and skills.*

You can conclude the activity by explaining to pupils that you are going to be learning a lot about intelligence over the next few weeks and that this might change some of the answers and views that they have today. (It would be interesting to get pupils to keep their minds-maps from this activity as you could get pupils to redo this activity at the end of the intervention and compare their responses.)

2. **Activity: Discussion and class list: 'barriers to learning'**

The aim of the activity is to get pupils to think about the barriers to their learning – i.e. the things they find difficult and why this might be. Start by asking children to spend a few moments thinking about what they think might get in the way of their learning, and the subjects and hobbies they find hard. Ask what makes these things hard and whether they think they will always find them hard. (If you hear some fixed answers, you will be able to correct this view later.)

(Continued)

(Continued)

Get them to then start thinking about what they could do to overcome these barriers and problems.

Split the class into groups, if possible, and give them some questions to get the discussion started. For example:

- 'What do you find hard?' and 'Why?'
- 'How do you think you can overcome this?'
- 'Do you think you will always be bad at it?'

Examples of things that get in the way of learning (and solutions) that you might hear are:

- Distractions/noisy children (move seats).
- Computer games (allocate time that you are allowed to play).
- Watching what others are doing instead of focusing on own work (focus).

Examples of subjects that they find hard:

- Maths/art/writing (we find these often crop up).

After the children have had time to discuss these topics, ask the groups to feed back their ideas and make a class list which could be used as a wall display with the headings 'Barriers to learning' and 'Solutions'.

3. Activity: Introduction to growth and fixed mindsets and Mindsters cartoon

Introduce children to the 'Mindsters' by showing them the Mindster poster. The aim of this activity is to introduce children to Dweck's theories of intelligence (information can be taken from the training day slides). Watch the Mindster cartoon and discuss the main message – i.e. do not give up trying even when something seems difficult at first. The video should allow discussion about the two different approaches to learning. Key points are as follows.

- Mindi and Teezle have two very different approaches to learning (two different mindsets).
- Teezle has a *fixed mindset*; he's finding learning the guitar very difficult and wants to give up because he thinks he's never going to be any good – he doesn't want to try any more. He thinks his ability is fixed.

- These sorts of learners are called 'fixed learners' because once they get stuck on something, they don't want to try any more. Rather than try to find a way around the problem, they give up or try to find an easier task to do instead.
- Mindi has a *growth mindset*; she knows that it's important to work even harder if you find something difficult. She learned to play the guitar because she practised lots and didn't give up. She knows that she can 'grow' her skills and develop her ability.
- People with a growth mindset believe that they can always improve and develop, they just need to find the right strategy/ way to learn.
- These sorts of learners are called 'growing learners' because they persevere even when things get hard – they are very brave! They love a challenge because they feel good when they succeed. They don't give up no matter what.

4. Activity: Assigning statements

Put the posters of Mindi and Teezle on the board and give children a mixture of fixed and growth mindset statements. Ask children to read out their statement(s), think about which Mindster their statement relates to and then stick it onto the correct Mindster. Some further discussion questions are:

- Which Mindster (Mindi or Teezle) loves a challenge? Why do you think this is?

(Continued)

(Continued)

- What would Mindi do if she was finding something difficult?
- What sorts of strategies could you use to be a Growing Learner?
- What do you do if you find something difficult?
- How can *you* be a growing learner?

5. Homework activity: Myself as a learner

To build on this session, ask children to write a short reflective essay, presentation or poster based on what they have learned about mindsets today. Ask children to think about themselves and honestly consider their approach to learning, addressing the following questions.

- Do you have a growth or a fixed mindset?
- Is this different in different areas of your life? Why do you think that is?

PLENARY

Recap with children what you have talked about during the session. Explain that we all want to be 'Growing Learners' and have a growth mindset. Teachers might like to give an example of when they have been a Growing Learner themselves.

7.2 Week 2

KEY THEME

Dealing with mistakes and emotions.

LEARNING OUTCOMES

1. To begin to reflect on the connection between feelings and challenges.
2. To think about the role of fear and other emotions in learning.
3. To re-evaluate responses to mistakes.

ACTIVITIES OVERVIEW

1. Homework recap.
2. Class discussion: Learning likes and dislikes, and associated emotions.
3. Posters: How to combat negative emotions.
4. Class discussion: Mistakes and mistakes board.
5. Homework activity: What I know about my brain worksheet.

MATERIALS REQUIRED

- Michael Jordan video (YouTube link online).
- Mistake board (printed in A3) (available online).
- Homework: What I know about my brain worksheet (available online).

ACTIVITY DESCRIPTIONS

1. **Activity: Homework recap**

   To start the session and remind pupils of the work covered in the previous week, ask children to discuss their homework. If they chose to do posters or presentations, you could ask them to show these to the rest of the class. If they wrote an essay, they could summarise the key points. NB: some pupils may not feel comfortable doing this, so if you feel that this is not an appropriate activity, feel free to skip to the next activity.

2. **Activity: Class discussion: Learning likes and dislikes, and associated emotions**

   Ask pupils to spend a few moments thinking of one thing that they really enjoy learning and one thing they don't enjoy learning. These can be academic or non-academic. Then ask them to think about *why* they do or do not enjoy learning whatever they have selected. For the things that they say they don't enjoy learning, ask pupils to think about what would make these more enjoyable.

   (Continued)

(Continued)

Using a circle time set-up, start by talking about the things they do enjoy learning. Examples of the 'whys' pupils might give and potential follow-up questions are as follows.

- It's fun. (Why?)
- I'm good at it. (Do you spend lots of time doing it?)
- I find it easy. (Is this because of transferable skills from other similar hobbies?)

Examples of the 'whys' pupils might give for things they don't enjoy learning and potential follow-up questions:

- It's boring. (Why? Self-protection strategy?)
- I'm not very good at it. (Is it something you might avoid?)
- It's pointless. (Is it really? What impact might that have in the future?)
- It's too hard. (Why do you think that is? How does that make you feel?)

Ask children to expand on their 'whys' – especially when they say they don't enjoy things they find hard. The idea is to encourage children to identify the relationship between feelings and challenging situations. It will also provide another opportunity to explore pupils' mindsets. Some children will realise that sometimes challenges might seem scary. The aim of the next few sessions is then to unpick this view and encourage children to change how they view challenges; they should be seen as exciting opportunities to develop.

3. **Activity: Posters: How to combat negative emotions**

   Based on the previous discussion, ask children to create posters full of ways in which to combat these negative emotions associated with challenge and strategies they could use to turn challenging situations into opportunities for learning. Ideally, these could be put up on the wall so that children can be encouraged to look at them if they are feeling frustrated or nervous when embarking on something new or difficult.

4. **Activity: Class discussion: Mistakes and mistakes board**

   Another role of fear in learning is avoidance of mistakes. Often the fear of making mistakes – and associated embarrassment – can be the biggest factor that stops children from trying in the first place. The aim is to emphasise to children that *learning* is the most important thing and knowing that you have tried your hardest; making mistakes doesn't matter; it's how you deal with them that's important.

To introduce pupils to the idea, show the Michael Jordan video. Talk to the class about the video and explain the implications of the message he is making about the mistakes he made throughout his career.

Mistakes are all part of the learning process – you can learn from them and get better next time. Highlight that making mistakes is a fact of life and that we shouldn't be scared to 'give something a go' just because we are worried about getting it wrong. You could say something along the lines of:

> Another important thing about Growing Learners is that they don't mind making mistakes. They understand that mistakes are all part of the learning process and will help them get better next time. Mistakes don't mean you are stupid. You don't look at babies and think they are stupid when they fall over – they just haven't learnt how to walk yet. We all understand that they are still learning how to do it. It's OK to make mistakes; it's how we deal with them that's important. We shouldn't be scared to give something a go, and we mustn't give up, or stop trying, just because we've made a mistake.

Introduce the mistakes board and ask each child to describe a mistake that they have made recently, and how they can learn from it/what they would do differently next time. Once they have done this, write their name on the mistakes board. This should help children to understand that we all make mistakes and shouldn't feel embarrassed or ashamed. Emphasise the importance of *celebrating mistakes*, rather than being afraid of making them.

This activity can be ongoing in the classroom; it doesn't have to be used exclusively in this lesson.

5. **Homework activity: What I know about my brain worksheet**

The main aim of the following session is to encourage children to view the brain as a thinking muscle – i.e. that it can be developed

(Continued)

(Continued)

through hard work and exercise (challenge). Use this worksheet for homework to find out children's pre-existing understanding of the brain. You can recap their answers at the beginning of the next session and follow up after completing Activity 3.

PLENARY

Recap on the main themes of the session. Remind children that everyone makes mistakes; they are not something to be ashamed of. What's important is not being afraid to give things a go and persevering even if it doesn't always go right the first time.

7.3 Week 3

KEY THEME

Understanding the brain and encouraging challenge.

LEARNING OUTCOMES

1. To learn about the brain (appreciating the similarities with muscles).
2. To understand that we can all 'grow our brains'.
3. To reflect on the importance of challenges.

ACTIVITIES OVERVIEW

1. Homework recap.
2. Brain article.
3. Taxi driver study (video).
4. Target setting – making personal challenge boards.
5. Homework activity: Practising skill.

MATERIALS REQUIRED

🖱 Brain article (available online).

🖰 Taxi driver study (YouTube link on video link list).
🖰 Challenge Board (available online).

ACTIVITY DESCRIPTIONS

1. **Activity: Homework recap**

   To start the session, talk about pupils' homework from the previous week. Discuss the main things that pupils included on their worksheets about the brain. You might like to say that you will be focusing a lot more about the way the brain works when we are learning and that they might have a lot more to add to the worksheet later on.

2. **Activity: Brain article**

   Give pupils a copy of the brain article and read through it as a class. Once you have finished reading the article, discuss it with the class. Ask them questions like 'How do you build up your arm muscles?' and 'How do you make your legs stronger?' Then link back to the brain and emphasise that it is hard work that leads to its development and growth.

3. **Activity: Taxi driver study (video)**

   Watch the video about taxi drivers learning 'The Knowledge' and the impact this has on the brain. The aim of this video is to provide scientific and concrete evidence that working hard and practising really can improve our skills and intelligence. The video shows a clear demonstration of the processes that take place in the brain when we are engaged in learning. Discuss how practice strengthens the connections in the brain – taxi drivers learn all about the streets of London and the more they drive around, the better their brain gets at storing this information. Go on to explain how this relates to them and their learning at school, as well as what they think they should do when something seems difficult.

   Ideas of what you could discuss include:

   (Continued)

(Continued)

- If you find maths difficult, you can practise to get better. What types of things could you do?
- If you are learning an instrument and you find it hard to remember the notes, going over it will help you remember more and more.
- If you don't find reading very easy, don't use this as a reason not to do it – find books you really enjoy and read them at night before you go to bed, etc.

NB: The point of these discussions is to inspire children to believe in themselves; even when they find something hard to begin with, they can always improve as the brain grows stronger. It is important to highlight that there is no reason why we can't all improve at anything – we just need to put our minds to it, find the right strategy and work hard. You could refer back to the worksheet they completed for homework and ask children if they would change what they had written before.

4. **Activity: Target setting: making personal challenge boards**

   The final activity in this session is intended to change the way children think about challenges and help them to want to seek out their own challenges. As a group, brainstorm things that are difficult for some children to do and then ask them to create their own challenge board (template available online), on which they write one challenge that they would like to work on. When children have finished, display them on the wall and explain that for the next few weeks, they are going to practise this activity for a short while every day. This will then be reviewed in week 7 so that they can look at their own improvement. Teachers might also want to make their own challenge board with the children.

   We feel that focusing on physical challenges is a good idea as these are an easy way to view improvement, for example:

   - throwing;
   - catching;
   - skipping;
   - kicking a football;
   - balancing.

   Other, non-physical challenges might be:

- handwriting;
- number bonds;
- times tables;
- colouring;
- drawing.

5. **Homework activity: Practising skill**

   For this week's homework, ask pupils to start practising the skill they have chosen for their personal challenge boards (to be ongoing until week 7).

PLENARY

Recap the key points of the session with the class. The main goal is to encourage children to be enthusiastic about the prospect of challenge – see it as an opportunity and not something to shy away from. Plenty of evidence exists to suggest that the brain adapts to challenges by building new connections – we can grow our brains.

7.4 Week 4

KEY THEME

Appreciating the importance of effort and persistence in improvement and progression.

LEARNING OUTCOMES

1. To consolidate previous week's learning about the brain.
2. To think about the importance of persistence and effort.
3. To appreciate the use of feedback and understand that everyone can improve, no matter what their ability.

ACTIVITIES OVERVIEW

1. Homework recap.
2. Peer mentoring and feedback.

(Continued)

(Continued)

3.   Static cartoon.
4.   Homework activity: Action plan quiz.

MATERIALS REQUIRED

- Pictures for peer mentoring activity (available online).
- Paper and pencils.
- Static cartoon Humphrey.
- Static cartoon Willow.

ACTIVITY DESCRIPTIONS

1.   Activity: Homework recap

To begin this session, check in with pupils about how their skill practising is going. Encourage them to keep practising so that they really get a sense of their improvement by week 7. If it is feasible, you might like to give them a few minutes to practise their skill in this session.

2.   Activity: Peer mentoring and feedback

Based on the activity shown in the Austin's Butterfly video (YouTube link on video link list), put pupils into pairs and give each child a picture (examples can be found online) and ask them to draw it. After they have finished, ask them to provide each other with feedback on how they could make their drawing look more like the picture. Suggestions might include:

- 'You could make your petals a bit more pointy.'
- 'The car in the picture is longer than yours.'
- 'The front door is on the side, not in the middle.'

Then, ask them to have another go at drawing the picture on a new piece of paper, using the feedback that they have just received to help them improve. Keep repeating this process of draft and feedback until children are happy with their own drawings and each other's. The aim of this task is to help children view their improvement and realise that the more effort you put into something, the more you improve. It should also highlight that getting advice from others is a good strategy to use to improve and that they shouldn't be frightened to ask for help. Keep each draft copy of the drawing so that they can see how they got to their finished result and emphasise the 'journey' that got them there.

3. **Activity: Static cartoon**

This activity builds on the previous exercise and emphasises the importance of hard work, practice and not giving up. Remind children of the Mindsters; in this case, the characters are Willow and Humphrey. There are two different cartoon strips for this activity, which show different responses to the same problem. Read through these with the class and ask questions such as:

- What do you think would happen if you kept trying hard like Willow did?
- What happens when you give up like Humphrey did?

The main point is that the decisions we make and the ways we choose to deal with situations can have long-term implications. This idea of having control of our learning will be picked up in the next activity.

4. **Homework activity: Action plan quiz**

It is important for pupils to also realise that having a growth mindset is only half the battle, as working hard is hard work. The aim of the quiz is to get pupils to honestly and independently evaluate their approach to learning and challenges, and to highlight where they may need to put in more effort. This quiz is also designed to encourage pupils to come up with a Growing Learner's action plan to help them recognise how they can take control of their own learning.

- Give each child a copy of the quiz and ask them to fill it in individually.
- This is an activity that you may want to get pupils to complete again at a point later in time to see if they have achieved any of the goals they have set in the action plan.

PLENARY

Discuss with pupils the ideas covered this week. The key points are to highlight that it is within pupils' control to improve. Everyone can keep

(Continued)

(Continued)

developing; it might take hard work, practice and finding the right strategy, but we all have the ability to do that. The aim is to help children appreciate the importance of taking ownership of learning opportunities.

7.5 Week 5

KEY THEME

Reflecting on the language we hear.

LEARNING OUTCOMES

1. To think about the language that people use to describe success and failure.
2. To reflect on language associated with fixed and growth mindsets.
3. To understand helpful and unhelpful language associated with learning and to think about ways of counteracting unhelpful language by using their 'internal growth mindset voices'.
4. To appreciate that decisions and actions have consequences.

ACTIVITIES OVERVIEW

1. Homework recap.
2. Class discussion: the comments people use to describe success and failure.
3. Traffic lights game.
4. Journey to Success board game.
5. Homework activity: Mindset language in action.

MATERIALS REQUIRED

- Traffic lights and statements (available online).
- Journey to Success board game (available online).

ACTIVITY DESCRIPTIONS

1. **Activity: Homework recap**

   To start this session, talk about the action plan quizzes that pupils completed for homework. It would be fantastic if you could discuss them in full with each child, but you could also ask pupils to share examples with the class of what they have written and ways they can help themselves improve at 'x'.

2. **Activity: Class discussion: The comments people use to describe success and failure**

   The aim of this task is to illustrate that both positive and negative comments can be phrased in fixed mindset language. Ask children about the comments we hear when people talk about success and failure. For example, 'What do people say when you do well on a task?' Make a column on the board (titled 'Success') and write up children's answers. Then ask 'What do people say when you fail, or not do very well on a task?' Create a second column (titled 'Failure') and write up children's answers on the board.

   Try to get a mixture of both fixed and growth mindset statements. If pupils are stuck, the following are some more examples that you can use.

   - You got a great score on your maths test. You are so smart.
   - You are really clever.
   - You are really good at maths.
   - This is definitely one of your talents.
   - You're so lucky – you can do it so easily.
   - This is an excellent piece of work; you must have spent lots of time on it.
   - You worked so hard on that – well done.
   - You've really improved.
   - You are just not good at this.
   - You don't have a natural talent for this.
   - Never mind, you are good at other things.
   - Let's try an easier one.
   - Don't give up – keep trying.
   - It looks like you haven't put much effort into this.
   - Why don't you try that again?

   (Continued)

(Continued)

After pupils have given you their ideas, recap. It is important to highlight that the messages we hear might affect how we *feel* about learning. For example, we might hear messages that make us feel good temporarily, but they might not be very helpful in the long term. Take the example (or something similar) and discuss with the pupils: 'You did really well in your last test, Emily. You're so clever.'

This comment might convey the message that the reason Emily did well in her test is just down to talent, something innate that she was born with. If this is the case, then these sorts of messages can lead to holding a fixed mindset. For instance, it might cause Emily to want to give up as soon as she finds something difficult; if doing well is the result of being clever, then finding something difficult must be due to a lack of intelligence. Emily might also feel embarrassed because she had actually worked really hard – does that mean she's not really clever? Alternatively, if we are told that we do *not* have a talent for something, we may believe that there is no point in trying at all. Recast this belief by referring to what they learned about the brain in previous weeks.

In order to inspire learning, the 'helpful' messages that we want to convey are that individuals are in control of their own learning and that we can *all* always improve. We will hear people (teachers, parents, friends, siblings) using fixed mindset language all of the time, and the way to deal with this is not to challenge who we hear the language from, but to use our own 'internal growth mindset voices' to remind ourselves what is important – i.e. how much effort we have put in, how hard we have worked, what we have learned, etc. For more information about the effect of language and praise, refer to the slides in the training day presentation.

3. **Activity: Traffic lights game**

Give out traffic lights to the children (they can each have their own set or work as a group). Read out the statements and ask children to hold up the corresponding traffic light.

There are two versions of the traffic lights game, which are as follows.

1. Simple: Green (GO) and Red (STOP).

   Read out the statements and ask pupils to hold up the green light for growth mindset statements and the red light for fixed mindset statements.

2. Advanced: Green (GO), Amber (WARNING/BE CAREFUL) and Red (STOP).

If you want to make this game a bit more complex, you can include the amber traffic light. The green light remains the same; pupils hold this up in response to a growth mindset statement. The amber traffic light should be held up for statements that are positive, but not very helpful – i.e. when the statement is something that might make them feel good at the time, but is actually a fixed mindset statement. The red light should then be held up for negative fixed mindset statements.

Read out the following examples, and ask children to hold up the appropriate traffic light.

- You tried really hard on that task, well done (GREEN).
- You have a real talent for that, keep it up (AMBER or RED).
- Football just isn't your thing (RED).

Discuss their answers in more detail and recast if necessary. Explain that the first example should be green as it's a growth mindset statement; it appreciates hard work and effort. The second example should be amber (because although it is positive, it is not very helpful) or red (because it is fixed and might make you believe that you don't need to practise). The third statement is red because it is fixed; it suggests that you just cannot do it, thus it is pointless for you to even bother trying. The amber traffic light tends to stimulate discussion and debate, and pupils automatically assume that because the statement is positive, it must be green. Work through the examples provided online or feel free to come with your own.

4. **Activity: Journey to Success board game**

The children will need to be in groups of six. Each table/group needs a board game and children choose a character and a counter. Make sure that each group has a set of question cards for each character. Explain that they roll the dice and move forward the corresponding number of spaces. If they land on a question circle, they pick up a question card for their character. The player then reads out the question card and all players discuss whether the statement is growth or fixed. If the statement is fixed, the player should miss a go; if the statement is growth, the player moves forward two places. The winner of the game is the player who reaches the end ('Success!') first.

(Continued)

(Continued)

You could ask the pupils what messages the game is sending about how we should respond to setbacks and what sorts of thing we need to do to make progress. Here you can also mention the importance of being resilient. Get some feedback from the pupils and reflect on their suggestions. You want to emphasise the point that even famous 'role models' experience failures and will have heard comments that are unhelpful, but because they believed in the importance of effort and persistence, they kept trying again and again, and as a result became really successful.

5. **Homework activity: Mindset language in action**

Tell pupils that you would like them to practise using growth mindset language – both with other people and in their own heads when they encounter fixed language. Also tell them that you want them to listen out for the language that other people use, and to try to remember some examples of people using either fixed or growth language so that they can share examples with the rest of the class next time. It might be useful for them to keep a log.

NB: Make it clear to the pupils that the point of this is *not* to challenge what other people say to them, but to practise using their 'internal growth mindset voices' to counteract the fixed language that they hear people using.

PLENARY

Summarise the session; emphasise to pupils that some of the things they might hear people say can send out messages, which can be helpful or unhelpful. When they hear unhelpful comments, it's important to think like a Growing Learner and remember that everybody can improve at anything; it's hard work, persistence and resilience that are important.

7.6 Week 6

KEY THEME

Understanding the impact of stereotypes and strategies (maths challenges).

LEARNING OUTCOMES

1. To learn about the effects of stereotypes.
2. To consider a stereotype we might encounter regarding maths, and how a growth mindset can help us overcome/challenge this.
3. To understand that different strategies and tricks can not only help us to be more accurate, but can also make maths fun.

ACTIVITIES OVERVIEW

1. Homework recap.
2. Discussion and worksheets: what are stereotypes?
3. Class discussion: the effect of stereotypes: gender and maths.
4. Posters: how to overcome stereotypes.
5. Strategies: multiplication tricks.
6. Strategies: divisibility tricks.
7. Racing the calculator.
8. Homework activity: Multiplication and divisibility booklets.

MATERIALS REQUIRED

- Stereotype Worksheet 1 and 2 (available online).
- Paper and pens for working through examples.
- Sums for Racing the Calculator (available online).
- Calculators.
- Homework: Multiplication and divisibility booklets (available online).

ACTIVITY DESCRIPTIONS

1. **Activity: Homework recap**

   Talk to the class about their mindset language in action homework. Ask them to share some of the examples of growth and fixed mindset language that they heard, and how they might have used their 'internal growth mindset voices' to counteract the fixed language that they heard people using.

   (Continued)

(Continued)

2. **Activity: Discussion and worksheets: what are stereotypes?**

The purpose of this activity (and session as a whole) is to get pupils to appreciate that they will encounter stereotypes all the time, but that they should remember that these are too general to be true. There are cases when the stereotypes are true, but they are not always true. It's also important to encourage pupils to realise that these are more examples of fixed mindset language and that it is unfair to make such sweeping statements.

Start by giving children Stereotype Worksheet 1, which contains pictures of different people (a French person, an old person, a girl and a boy). Ask the children to write a sentence about each of the people. Next, give out Stereotype Worksheet 2, and ask children in small groups to match the photographs of people to the jobs they think each person would do. Once this has been completed, discuss the children's decisions – i.e. why did they choose a certain person for a certain occupation? Set their worksheets aside (to review after Activity 3).

Discuss with the class the meaning of the word 'stereotype'. Write any answers that are suitable on the board. If no pupils have responded, or once all willing pupils have given an answer, write the definition of 'stereotype' up at the top of the board: Stereotype: an overly simple picture or opinion of a person, group or thing.

Write a few examples of stereotypes up on the board, for example:

STEREOTYPE IDEAS

- All old people are forgetful.
- People who wear glasses are smart.
- Women are better cooks than men.
- Men are better drivers than women.

As you go through each statement, ask pupils to say what they think about them. Encourage them to challenge the beliefs – e.g. pupils might say their dad always cooks dinner or their mum is a much better driver.

NB: You want to encourage pupils to come up with examples of how they aren't true (obviously they will also come up with supporting examples, too; you want to show that they can be true in some cases, but they aren't *always* true).

3. **Activity: Class discussion: The effect of stereotypes: gender and maths**

Leaving the definition of stereotype on the board, write up the following statement: Boys are better at maths than girls.

Ask the class if they think that this statement is true or not. By this stage, some pupils will probably realise that this is another example of a stereotype, so should believe it isn't true. Whatever happens, ask the pupils to say why they think the way they do, leading them to the conclusion that this is a wide overgeneralisation that is not true.

Key point: We want to get the message across that this isn't true, and in fact, any differences in maths ability may be caused by people believing this stereotype.

Leave the maths stereotype sentence on the board and ask the pupils how this belief might make boys and girls feel differently about maths. You want to highlight the point that this may cause girls to have a *fixed* mindset about maths, and therefore not want to try as hard at the subject. (In the long term, this belief can have an equally unhelpful impact on boys, too.)

Write these notes on the board. You want to aim to produce a flow chart that shows that this belief reinforces a circular effect.

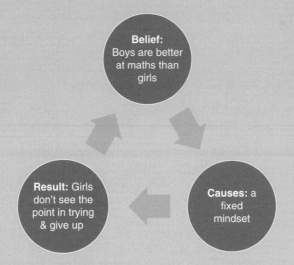

Key point: You want the pupils to understand that believing stereotypes can lead to a *fixed* mindset. Beliefs can become

(Continued)

(Continued)

self-fulfilling prophecies that can limit performance – which in turn reinforces the belief.

4. **Activity: Posters: How to overcome stereotypes**

Write 'What would a Growing Learner say about stereotypes' on the board and ask pupils what they think. Get pupils to make posters or banners outlining their ideas. You want to encourage comments like:

- They aren't true.
- Don't believe them as anyone can improve.
- Don't let them stop you from trying.
- Anyone can be improve at maths; they just have to try hard at it.

Key point: For the maths example: you want to make the point that a growing learner wouldn't let such stereotypes stop them from trying, as they know that it doesn't matter if you are a boy or girl. What helps you improve at maths is trying hard and everyone can try hard, so there is no reason why girls should not be as good as boys at maths if they want to be. (Of course, there are a number of stereotypes around subjects that affect boys and girls differently, so feel free to pick up on more of these.)

Once you are confident that your class understand what a stereotype is, revisit the sentences written in Worksheet 1 and the decisions made in Worksheet 2, and see whether pupils' perceptions, and answers, have changed.

5. **Activity: Strategies: multiplication tricks**

Recap the key points from the first half. Then tell the class that you are now going to move on to learning some different multiplication strategies that will make quite hard maths problems much easier.

NB: The point of the following activities is not to teach maths per se, but to demonstrate how using different strategies can have a big impact.

MULTIPLICATION RULE FOR 10

- Write the number '223' on the board.
- Present the following problem to the class:

    o   223 children went on a school trip to the theatre to see *The Lion King*. Each ticket cost £10. How much did it cost for them all to go?

- Some pupils may know straight away. Even so, work through the following steps on the board:
  - Ask the pupils what sum we need to do to work this out and write it on the board (223 × 10).
  - Then ask the class if anyone knows the answer to this sum. Either way, make it explicit that the rule for multiplying a number by 10 is to add a 0 to the end (this is technically moving the decimal point one place to the right, which will need to be explained especially if multiplying a decimal number).
  - This means that it cost £2,230 for the theatre trip.

Key point: Explain to children that this is a simple example of a multiplication rule and that there are many more for different numbers, but most people just don't know about them.

MULTIPLICATION RULE FOR 11 (DIGITS 1–9)

- Write the number '9' on the board.
- Present the following problem to the class:
  - 9 football teams take part in a county tournament (none take any substitutes). How many players were there in total?

- Again, work through the following steps:
  - Ask the pupils what sum we need to do to work this out and write it on the board. The answer is that we need to do 9 × 11 since there are 11 people on a football team.
  - If anyone knows the answer, ask them to explain how they know.
  - Again, talk the class through the rule, which is that to multiply any 1 digit number by 11, you just repeat the number.
  - So 9 × 11 = 99.
  - Therefore, 99 players took part in the tournament.
  - You can do some more examples.
  - Again, explain that this is another example of a rule.

MULTIPLICATION RULE FOR 11 (2-DIGIT NUMBERS)

- Write '17' on the board.

(Continued)

(Continued)

- Present the following problem to the class:

  o   17 football teams from the county rounds then take part in a bigger tournament. How many players are there in total? (Again, no team took any substitutes.)

- Again, some may know this rule, but it is less likely. (NB: Some may say that they know the rule to times by 10 and then add the number, which is also correct. Say that this is another example of a rule, and that we are going to learn a new one, and they can use whichever they find easier.)
- Work through the following steps:

  o   Ask the pupils what sum we need to do to work this out. Write the answer on the board (17 × 11).
  o   As before, talk the class through the rule for multiplying 2-digit numbers by 11:
  o   You write down the number you want to multiply by 11, leaving a space between the two digits.
  o   1 . . . 7
  o   You then add the two digits together and write the answer in the space.
  o   1 + 7 = 8. So, 187 is the answer.
  o   Therefore, 187 players took part in this tournament.

- Work through another example board '15 × 11 = ?' and ask pupils to tell you the answers as you go through each of the steps (**165**).
- Work through as many examples as you need to in order to be sure that the pupils know what to do.
- Once you are sure the pupils understand, explain that this works with all 2-digit numbers, but if you get a 2-digit number when you add the numbers together, then you need to do something slightly different.

MULTIPLICATION RULE FOR 11 (2-DIGIT NUMBERS WHERE THE SUM OF THE DIGITS IS 2 DIGITS LONG)

- Write the following example on the board: '88 × 11 = ?'. Explain that you need to do one more step here. Work through this with the pupils, encouraging them to work through it with you on their sheets of paper.

- ○ Again, write down the number you want to multiply by 11, leaving a space: 8 . . . 8.
- ○ Add the two digits together: 8 + 8 = 16. Make it clear that the difference here is that *you have a 2-digit number* this time, so you need to do something slightly different, as 'the space' is only big enough for 1 digit.
- ○ If you get a 2-digit answer, all you need to do is to put the second digit in the space and then add the 1 to the first digit.
- ○ So you put the 6 in the space – 868 – and then add 1 to the first digit. That gives you an answer of **968**.

- Work through another example with the pupils – e.g. 66 × 11– again asking pupils questions about what they need to do at each step.

6. **Activity: Strategies: divisibility tricks**

   Tell the children that they are now going to look at some divisibility rules.

DIVISIBILITY RULE FOR 2

- Write the number '432' on the board.
- Explain the following problem to the class:

  Two girls called Frances and Emily are given a *huge* bag of sweeties. They count them out and there are 432 sweeties. Can they split them evenly between them? (The answer is yes, they can.)

- Some pupils may know straight away (and even calculate the actual answer), in which case, ask them if they know the rule for whether a number is divisible by 2.
- Either way, work through the following steps with the class:

  - ○ Ask the pupils what sum is needed to work this out. The answer is that we need to know if 432 is divisible by 2. Once this has been discussed with the class, write it on the board (432 ÷ 2).
  - ○ Then ask the class how they would work this out.
  - ○ The answer is 'because it ends in 2, which is an even number'.

(Continued)

(Continued)

  o   You can then write up the numbers '0, 2, 4, 6, 8' and explain that this is a simple division rule: if any number, however long, ends in an even number (or a 0), then it is divisible by 2.
  o   Conclude by answering the question – i.e. by saying that yes, Frances and Emily can split the sweets evenly between them.

•   Work through some more examples with the class. For example, ask if 91872 is divisible by 2, and why? Then try one that isn't divisible by 2. So ask if 871623 is divisible by 2, and why not?

Key point: Explain that there are many rules like this for lots of different numbers; it's just that people don't know about them.

DIVISIBILITY RULE FOR 3

•   Leave '432' on the board and present the following problem that leads on from the previous problem:

  o   Just as Frances and Emily are about to divide the sweeties, their friend Victoria comes along, so they decide to split the sweets between the three of them. Can they split the sweets evenly between the three of them?

•   If any pupils know the answer, ask them if they can explain how they know. Either way, you want to work through the following steps with the class:

  o   Ask the pupils what sum they would need to do to work this out. The answer is that we need to know if 432 is divisible by 3.
  o   Explain that there is a simple rule for testing if a number is divisible by 3 *before* you work through an example.
  o   To do this, you add up all the digits in a number until you get down to a 1-digit number. If this number is divisible by 3 (i.e. a 3 a 6 or a 9), then you know the original number is divisible by 3.
  o   Work though the example on the board.
  o $4 + 3 + 2 = 9$
  o   9 is divisible by 3.
  o   Therefore, 432 is divisible by 3.
  o   This means that Frances, Emily and Victoria can split the sweets evenly between them.

•   Work through more examples on the board, getting the class to tell you what to do at each stage. Do some examples that are divisible by 3 (909, 213, 300) and also some that aren't (871, 403), until you are happy that the pupils understand this rule.

Key point: Even problems that may seem hard can actually be really easy once you find the right *strategy* and then practise it. People who are good at maths tend to be good because they have worked hard to find different strategies and practise using them. Anyone can improve at maths if they are prepared to work hard and practise different strategies.

7. **Activity: Racing the Calculator**

To demonstrate how effective these strategies can be, get pupils into groups of three, and tell them that they can now put their new skills to the test by playing a game called 'Racing the Calculator'. After explaining the rules, hand out the problems (there is a sheet of sums to be cut out online), calculators and pieces of scrap paper. You don't need to spend very long on this, but it is often a fun activity.

- First, ask the class who they think would be quicker working out sums – someone with a calculator or someone just using the new tricks we have learnt?
- Tell the pupils that one of them is to choose a problem. They should then show this problem to the other two members of the team. One *has* to use a calculator to work out the sum – i.e. cannot use the rules – and the other one *has* to work it out using what they know from the rules and tricks (they can also use scrap paper).
- Once they have the answer, they must put their hand up. Whoever gets the answer first is the winner.
- Get the pupils to take it in turns so that they each have a go picking out a problem, using the calculator, and not using the calculator.

Key point: You want to make it clear that the point of this game is to show that finding the right strategy can sometimes be even better than a calculator. The more we practise these strategies, the quicker we become, and that is the same with everything – hard work + practice = success.

8. **Homework activity: Multiplication and divisibility booklets**

Give pupils the multiplication and divisibility booklets and tell pupils to work through these on their own at home. NB: if you have time, pupils could start working through these in the session.

(Continued)

(Continued)

PLENARY

Summarise the session, focusing on what the class have learned about stereotypes – i.e. not really true. Recap on the link between stereotypes and having a growth mindset (to avoid falling into the trap of self-fulfilling prophecies). Highlight the importance of finding the right strategy and *practising* that strategy; in doing so, even really hard problems can be much easier for us to do.

7.7 Week 7

KEY THEME

Unravelling talent and luck myths: the journeys of inspirational people.

LEARNING OUTCOMES

- To challenge pre-held beliefs about talent and luck.
- To identify the journeys of inspirational people.
- To link role models to mindsets and reflect on responses to failure and challenge.

ACTIVITIES OVERVIEW

1. Class discussion and PowerPoint presentation (with video): talent and luck myths.
2. Revisit challenge boards and demonstration of skills (from week 3).
3. Inspirational people.
4. Character development.
5. Homework activity: People's Journeys to Success worksheet.

MATERIALS REQUIRED

🖱 Presentation: Talent and luck myths (available online).

Case studies of inspirational people (available online).

Homework: Journeys to Success worksheet (available online).

ACTIVITY DESCRIPTIONS

1. **Activity: Class discussion and PowerPoint presentation (with video): Talent and luck myths**

   The aim of this activity is to challenge pupils' beliefs about talent and luck. For this activity, you can either just use the activity description here to guide discussion, or you can use the PowerPoint presentation available online as well.

   Write the words 'talent' and 'luck' on the board. Ask the class to define each of these words and, once you have reached a consensus, write the agreed definition on the board. For your reference, here are the *Oxford Dictionary* definitions:

   - Talent: 'natural aptitude or skill'.
   - Luck: 'success and failure apparently brought by chance rather than through one's own actions'.

   Using the questions and quotes provided below, the point of this activity is to lead pupils towards seeing talent and luck in a growth mindset way:

   - Talent: from a growth mindset point of view, talent is considered to be 'the beginnings of an opportunity, and not a ticket to success'. We want pupils to realise that talent does not automatically lead to success, and that even people born with a natural affinity for something have to work hard.
   - Luck: from a growth mindset point of view, luck is considered to be 'preparation meeting opportunity'. We want pupils to understand that being prepared for opportunity is a way of increasing your own luck.

   Possible questions to ask and discussions to have about talent are as follows:

- Is talent enough to ensure success?

(Continued)

(Continued)

- o   How can you develop a talent?
- o   If you don't have a natural talent for something, does that mean you won't ever be able to do it?

You could also ask the class if they have ever been told that they are talented at something, or if they have ever found that they picked up a skill much more quickly than other people. Ask them why they thought that was. Often, this happens when the new skill involves using skills that we have gained from other aspects of life.

- People who have a 'natural talent' for certain sports tend to play a lot of other sports, meaning that the skills that are required to be 'naturally good' at a new sport (such as fitness, stamina, hand–eye coordination) have been developed from practising other sports.
- Also, people who are considered 'talented' are often just more passionate about that particular activity, and this passion is what motivates them to keep practising and improving. (For example, a young child who enjoys playing football with their parents from an early age might be perceived as 'naturally talented' when they first start playing at school with other children who have never played, but this is actually just the result of previous experience.)

Possible questions to ask and discussions to have about luck are as follows:

- Is luck the same for everyone?

    - o   Can you think of any examples where a situation might be lucky for someone but not for someone else? Was this really luck?
    - o   Can you make your own luck?
    - o   Can you think of an opportunity that you have considered lucky, that may not have been considered lucky at a different time in your life?

Possible quotations to discuss with the class (you can find many more on the internet) are:

- 'It's not that I'm so smart, it's just that I stay with problems longer.' (Albert Einstein)
- 'I have no special talent. I am only passionately curious.' (Albert Einstein)

- 'I have always considered myself to be just average talent and that what I have is a ridiculously insane obsessiveness for practice and preparation.' (Will Smith)
- 'Chance favours the prepared mind.' (Louis Pasteur)
- 'Diligence is the mother of good luck.' (Benjamin Franklin)
- 'Opportunity is missed by most because it is dressed in overalls and looks like work.' (Thomas Edison).

You will find online a talent and luck PowerPoint presentation that you can use to guide/supplement this activity. It finishes with a video that outlines the main points and covers the '10,000-hour rule' from Matthew Syed's book *Bounce: The Myth of Talent and the Power of Practice.*

2. **Activity: Revisit challenge boards and demonstration of skills**

Refer back to challenge boards made in week 3 and ask each child to demonstrate the skill they have been practising. Emphasise the improvement they have made using growth mindset language. For example:

'You really tried hard.'

'You found a really good way to do that.'

'Keep trying and you will get there.'

'Your skipping is getting better and better.'

'Your catching has really improved; remember how many you could catch before?'

'There were hardly any mistakes this time.'

Get them to think about other things they might have been practising – e.g. How are they practising being a better friend? How are they practising being a Growing Learner?

3. **Activity: Inspirational people**

This activity aims to emphasise that even the people we most admire have had to work really hard. Give pupils a few moments to think about what makes people successful and who they most

(Continued)

(Continued)

admire. Then ask them for some examples of these role models and follow up with questions such as:

- Do you think [name of role model] had to work hard?
- Do you think everything was easy?
- Do you think they ever made mistakes?
- What do you think they did after making the mistake? – i.e. give up or pick themselves up and carry on?

Reflect on their answers. To conclude this activity, we suggest watching a video or two that show people's journeys to success. We have provided some suggestions on the video link list online. Encourage children to discuss the challenges that these people faced and how they overcame them. Emphasise the point that everyone needs to work hard; people aren't just born talented or lucky.

4. **Activity: Character development**

   For the final activity, ask children to create their own growth mindset individuals. Encourage them to be as imaginative as possible when coming up with their new characters. From all the themes you have covered in the last few sessions, ask them to give their traits and characteristics. Ask them to list the things their character enjoys and not focus solely on school, but also on hobbies and interests. This should act as a good way of recapping what they have learnt so far.

5. **Homework activity: People's Journeys to Success worksheet**

   To extend this session, ask children to do some research on one of their role models, either by finding out information in books or the internet, or by chatting to someone they admire – e.g. family, friends, teachers. We have provided a homework sheet with lots of questions to help guide their investigations.

PLENARY

Go over the main points of the session. The main areas to address are children's understanding of the words 'luck' and 'talent'. Remind them that although they are terms we hear used very often, they are not exclusively responsible for success; effort, persistence and learning from challenges and mistakes are much more important.

7.8 Week 8

KEY THEME

Consolidating key concepts.

LEARNING OUTCOMES

1. Recap and consolidate the key points from each of the weeks.

ACTIVITIES OVERVIEW

1. Homework recap.
2. Recap and mind-map: 'How to be a Growing Learner'.
3. Posters: 'How to be a Growing Learner'.
4. Glossary challenge.
5. Prepare 'expert-led' workshop for parents/other classes.

MATERIALS REQUIRED

- Large sheets of paper for mind-maps.
- Materials for making posters.
- Glossary challenge (available online).
- Workshop materials – e.g. posters, mind-maps and things created in previous weeks.

ACTIVITY DESCRIPTIONS

1. **Activity: Homework recap**

    To begin this session, ask pupils to report back to the rest of the class on the role model they chose to focus their homework on. Try to encourage them to really pay attention to the journey that the individual took in getting to where they are now.

    (Continued)

(Continued)

2. **Activity: Recap and mind-map: 'How to be a Growing Learner'**

Remind children of the themes from each week and make a list on the board of key messages emerging from each session. The most important points from the sessions are as follows:

- The difference between growth and fixed mindsets and associated approaches to learning.
- The brain is a muscle and can be strengthened/developed.
- The importance of resilience and not giving up when we face challenges.
- The importance of hard work, practice and effort.
- The importance of learning from mistakes.

After reminding children of the key themes from each week, make a big mind-map with the class about 'How to be a Growing Learner'. Write this in the middle of the 'spider' and ask children to volunteer ways to be a Growing Learner and add this to the diagram.

3. **Activity: Posters: 'How to be a Growing Learner'**

Based on the discussion, ask children to make their own posters on how to be a Growing Learner, potentially to display at the workshop (Activity 5). Explain that these are going to be put up to help teach other children how to be a Growing Learner. Tell them you want these to be full of information, but also to look nice. Encourage the pupils to use what they have learnt over the past seven weeks.

4. **Activity: Glossary challenge**

The glossary challenge is a sheet with key words and phrases from each of the different weeks, along with statements/definitions. These are in a jumbled order, so ask pupils to match the statements/definitions to the words by drawing lines from the word to its definition. This can be carried out individually or in small groups. Go through each answer with the class once everyone has finished.

5. **Activity: Prepare 'expert-led' workshop for parents/other classes**

Based on the activities in previous weeks, organise things for children to do in an 'expert-led' workshop. This workshop should be for children to show parents or other classes what they have learnt over the sessions. Either way, begin the workshop by telling the parents/

children a bit about what you have been doing and ask them to go and talk to the children about what they have learnt. You could choose children to show their challenge boards, stories or posters and anything else you have created along the way.

WHAT HAPPENS NEXT?

It is important that pupils are encouraged to continue using what they have learned over these sessions. The following section in your manual details some suggestions for what to do next and other activities that you can use to continue and reinforce the growth mindset approach.

7.9 Other materials and ideas for Key Stage 2

Where to go from here

Where possible, we recommend a 'whole-school approach'. Perhaps run a training day for the rest of the staff at your school based on your experiences from running the intervention. From this point, try to designate some time during regular staff meetings (perhaps once a month) to focus on how, as a whole school, you can change the school's culture to a growth mindset culture and, just as importantly, how you can *maintain* this change. This might also be the right time to share good classroom practice and have discussions about the school motto, reward systems, assembly content, corridor displays, etc. We also recommend using the intervention provided here throughout the school, so feel free to copy the materials you have been given and distribute them to each teacher within the school.

Work through the other ideas in this section to extend your eight weeks. Be open with the pupils about what you are doing with them; it has to be their choice to change their beliefs about intelligence and their approach to learning. The quicker they familiarise themselves with these concepts about beliefs and associated language, the better. Once all pupils have been introduced to the idea of mindsets, we recommend setting up a mindset peer-mentoring scheme – perhaps older pupils mentoring younger ones, or pupils you notice to hold a particularly strong growth mindset becoming 'mindsets champions' to mentor those who might be more fixed. Another option, where possible, is to bring parents on board. This could be implemented by running whole-school events around mindsets to show parents – e.g. plays and workshops, etc., or you could run a series of family learning sessions with pupils and their parents.

The key thing is to keep the message going; it can be useful to repeat these sessions each academic year (we have materials for all age groups) and to ensure that everyone in the school is using growth mindset language and praise. It is important, therefore, to run refresher staff training and consider using this during new staff induction.

The following pages outline some other activities that you might like to implement with your pupils, but by now we are sure that you have lots of your own ideas about what would work with your classes.

Other ideas

GROWTH TIME

At the end of a given piece of work (this can be in every lesson or just selected subjects), ask *all* children to spend 5–10 minutes improving their work. Refer to this as 'growth time' to help children realise that they can all improve their work. This should also help children view this time as rewarding, not as a punishment for those who are less able or less willing to engage with learning.

CLASS DISCUSSION ABOUT RESILIENCE (WITH DEMONSTRATION)

Talk to children about the concept of resilience, describing the difference between being a 'bouncy ball' or a 'sinking stone'. (You could demonstrate these metaphors using a bouncy ball and a stone in a jug of water.) Using these metaphors and/or demonstrations will help children to understand the difference between rebounding from set-backs, as opposed to giving up and not trying any more. Remind children about the importance of being a Growing Learner; even if we find things hard to start with, we can always improve. You might like to link these words to other related mindset terms, including perseverance and determination.

FRANKIE AND FRED (MINDSTERS) ACTIVITY

As we said at the beginning of this section, we have purposefully not included the Fred and Frankie Mindsters in any of our activities. You can include them in your growth mindset sessions however you like, but we thought it would be nice for classes to come up with their own characteristics for them – be it individually or in groups. We'd love to hear about anything you come up with.

LEARNING ABOUT IQ TESTS

You will find an article about IQ tests online. This article was written by our team for secondary pupils, and although it might be hard for younger pupils to grasp, you may still find it useful. The aim is to dispel the idea that intelligence is fixed and get pupils to realise that IQ tests are just one way of assessing specific aspects of intelligence and the results of these are not deterministic.

GROWING LEARNERS' PROBLEM-SOLVING ROUTINE

Learning to solve problems independently is a key stage in development. Introduce children to the Growing Learners problem-solving routine.

GROWING LEARNERS PROBLEM-SOLVING ROUTINE

A challenge is a chance to grow my brain!

1. What is the problem?
2. How can I solve the problem?
3. Solving the problem.
4. Did my solution work?

Explain that, as a class, this will be the new approach to solving all sorts of different problems and challenges, in lessons and in social situations – e.g. sharing, taking turns and interacting with others. To begin with, remind children that nothing is insurmountable and that challenges are not something to be frightened of; they are opportunities to grow our brains. You will find more information online, but the key stages are as follows:

1. Work out what the problem is.
2. Think about different ways to deal with the problem.

(Continued)

(Continued)

3. Try the solution.
4. Evaluate how well the solution works.

TEACHER–PUPIL REVERSAL

This activity encourages children to really understand fixed and growth mindsets in a learning setting and particularly from the teacher's perspective.

*   One teacher plays the role of a fixed mindset pupil and one teacher plays the role of a growth mindset pupil.
*   One or more pupils play the role of a teacher trying to teach a specific teaching point – schools have used a maths problem for this activity.
*   The fixed mindset teacher (in pupil role) responds by saying things like: 'I can't do it', 'It's too hard', 'Can I do an easier problem?', and so on. In contrast, the growth mindset teacher (in pupil role) responds by asking questions, working on different strategies, and making mistakes without being embarrassed, etc.
*   The rest of the class watches and discusses the activity and different responses.

CHALLENGE MOUNTAIN, FOCUSING ON STEPS TOWARDS SUCCESS

This activity works well with a wall display. A large picture of a mountain is displayed on a classroom wall, with labels going up the side of the mountain. At the summit of the mountain there is a challenge that a whole class would like to achieve. The labels going up the mountain represent the steps towards success. The goal can be anything such as learning how to swim (particularly if someone has a fear of swimming). Steps to success in this example might be things like getting into the pool, being splashed, swimming a few metres with a float, and so on. Alternatively, the challenge could be academic – e.g. learning times tables. Equally, pupils could have their own challenge mountains and set individual goals.

GRID DRAWING

The purpose of this activity is to provide a very visual demonstration of how using a different strategy can make a difficult task seem much easier.

- For this activity, you can either choose the pictures or photos that you would like pupils to draw copies of, or get them to select pictures themselves.
- Explain to pupils that you would like them to use a new strategy to copy these pictures by hand: the grid method.
- The grid method:

  o Take the picture you want to copy and draw a grid over it to break the picture into smaller squares.
  o On a fresh piece of paper, draw a grid with the *same number* of squares as there are in the grid on the picture that you want to copy (making these the same size will be easiest, but you can make this more difficult by telling pupils that you want them to do a bigger or smaller version of the original picture).
  o To make this easier, give both grids coordinates so that you don't end up copying the wrong square.
  o Then simply copy each square one by one.
  o This website gives a great description with pictures: www.wiki-how.com/Scale-Drawings-Using-the-Grid-Method

THINKING JOURNAL

This activity encourages self-reflection in a positive way and helps develop resilience.

- Each pupil has their own thinking journal in which they are encouraged to keep a record of their growth mindset journey.
- For example, they could use this to do the following:

(Continued)

(Continued)

- o Jot down when they have encountered something difficult, how this made them feel, and what strategies they are going to try to overcome the difficulty.
- o Note down when they are proud of something that they responded to in a growth mindset way.
- o Note down when they have helped other people to think in a growth mindset way.

There could also be a class thinking journal that everyone, including the teacher, contributes to.

GROWING LEARNERS STORY BOOKS

We have developed a range of books, some of which are available to buy from Amazon. These include:

- *George*
  - o Particularly useful for younger children.
  - o The story describes the life of a young puppy that feels very nervous about playing with other dogs. However, with some encouragement, he manages to overcome this fear.

- *Arthur the Wizard*
  - o Arthur is a young wizard desperate to learn how to do spells. The book follows Arthur's exciting journey to learn how to make spells, showing persistence in the face of challenges and mistakes, learning that the practice is the key to success.
  - o A good story with lovely illustrations for adults to read to younger children or for independent readers aged 6–10 years.

- *The Mystery of Mrs Raven*
  - o Jo has started at a new school, leaving her old school behind with all its familiarity and comfort.
  - o She is faced with the challenge of making new friends and meeting her mysterious new teacher, Mrs Raven.
  - o Follow Jo's journey of discovery as she starts finding out about her spooky new school.
  - o A good story for adults to read to younger children or for independent readers aged 8–11 years.

OTHER STORY BOOKS

There are a couple of other classic children's books that pick up on some important themes relating to growth mindsets. These include:

- *Little Red Hen*

  o   This provides a good opportunity to discuss the choices she made and the hard work she put in. Relate the characters in the story to the appropriate Mindster and ask children which 'voice' they might have been listening to.

- *Oh, the Places You'll Go!* (Dr Seuss)

  o   The story emphasises that we can all be what we want to be and reach our goals; we just need to work hard and believe in ourselves. It also reminds the reader that we might come across obstacles and life may not always be easy, but highlights the importance of being motivated and 'giving things a go'. This provides a good start for a discussion about resilience in that we might come across stumbling blocks, but we can overcome these if we are Growing Learners.

  o   Note there is some fixed mindset language in the book; depending on the age of the children, this could provide a source for further discussion. Refer to training day slides for more information on the implications of different types of language.

  NB: You could play the audio version of the book on YouTube – see link on the video link list online.

SCHOOL BEHAVIOUR AND REWARD POLICIES

After starting on their growth mindsets journey, many schools decide to change their behaviour and reward policies in line with the characteristics of a Growing Learners' approach. In particular, schools have focused rewards on effort, hard work and improvement, rather than 'absolute' ability. For example, a Learning Award certificate can be awarded to a child whenever they learn something new; this doesn't necessarily have to be academic, but anything that the child is proud of.

(Continued)

(Continued)

GROWING LEARNERS MENTORING PROGRAMME

A great way of continuing to develop what pupils have learnt in this programme is to get them to teach it to other pupils. Some schools that have adopted the growth mindset ethos have set up a peer-mentoring programme whereby older pupils work with younger pupils to support them with their work using growth mindset strategies, as well as teaching them about mindsets.

CHAPTER 8

ACTIVITIES FOR SECONDARY AND FURTHER EDUCATION

Notes using the lesson plans

The activities here have been divided into six themes. The themes are as follows.

1. Intelligence and IQ tests: introducing growth and fixed mindsets.
2. The brain: dealing with mistakes and challenges.
3. Mindset language: action plans.
4. Stereotypes: consequences.
5. The luck and talent myths: role models.
6. Consolidation of key themes.

Given the variability in age and ability of pupils across their secondary and college years, we have designed this programme to be flexible, enabling you to administer the activities that you feel are most appropriate for the cohort that you are using it with.

To that end, the activities and exercises are divided into six 'themes'. Each theme should be delivered chronologically (1 through to 6), but there is some degree of flexibility as to the activities that you choose to deliver within each theme. You will see that we have provided a suggested 'running order' for core activities within each theme, but this can be adapted to suit the needs of your class. Where possible, we have included alternative and additional activities, so if you feel that some of the core activities included are too advanced for the learning needs of your pupils, you can look to the additional and alternative activities included at the end of each theme and use these instead of, or in addition to, those suggested. The way in which you administer the themes is also flexible. For instance, you could break each theme up into shorter sessions to be implemented at regular intervals, perhaps in form time, across a few weeks. Alternatively, you could deliver longer sessions once a week, or designate a couple of days to an 'intensive' course whereby you go through the themes one after another. For older pupils, you could even allow them to choose the activities that most appeal to them. Whichever way you decide to do it, it is important to deliver the core activities (or the suggested alternatives if available) from each theme, and make sure that the themes are worked through in the order that they are presented within the manual.

Throughout the themes we have created worksheets to help pupils to keep a record of the key learning points from some of the more discussion-based or teacher-led activities. These may be too simplistic for older or more able pupils, so please use these where you feel appropriate. An alternative to these could be that pupils have workbooks dedicated to these sessions and make their own notes. How much of this is guided by you or pupil-led will depend on the ability of your pupils.

THEME 1: OVERVIEW

8.1 Intelligence and IQ tests: introduction to growth and fixed mindsets

LEARNING OUTCOMES

1. To think critically about intelligence and learn about IQ tests.
2. To identify barriers to learning and how to overcome these.
3. To understand the difference between growth and fixed mindsets, and to understand the impact that these different mindsets have.
4. To consider personal learning orientations and mindsets.

CORE ACTIVITIES

1. 'What is intelligence?' 'What makes you intelligent?': Mind-maps and group discussions.
2. Learning about IQ tests: magazine article, 'What does IQ really measure?' (available online).
3. Things you do and do not enjoy learning. Why? Mind-maps and class discussion.
4. Introducing theories of intelligence and mindsets: teacher-led presentation and class discussion (available online).
5. Recommended homework: reflective essay: 'Think about yourself. Do you have a growth or a fixed mindset? Is this different in different areas of your life? Why do you think that is?'

Alternative and additional activities are available online at https://study.sagepub.com/education/education-all-phases/ hoskins-growth-mindset-for-teachers

8.1 THEME 1: INTELLIGENCE AND IQ TESTS: INTRODUCTION TO GROWTH AND FIXED MINDSETS

Activity 1: 'What is intelligence?' 'What makes you intelligent?': Mind-maps and group discussions.

LEARNING OBJECTIVE

- To get pupils thinking about what intelligence actually is. This activity will also give you some insight into which mindset pupils hold more strongly.

MATERIALS REQUIRED

- Paper and pens.

ACTIVITY DESCRIPTION

- Begin this activity by getting pupils to brainstorm answers to each of these questions (individually or in small groups):

(Continued)

(Continued)

- o   What is intelligence?
- o   What makes you intelligent?

- • Working through each question individually, ask each individual or group to feed back two answers or examples to the class.
- • Encourage pupils to explain their answers and try to generate debate around answers that are particularly representative of a fixed or growth mindset.

The sorts of things that pupils might say in response to 'What is intelligence?' are:

- o   Something you are born with.
- o   How smart you are.
- o   There are different types of intelligence.

The sorts of things that pupils might say in response to 'What makes you intelligent?' are:

- o   Being a girl.
- o   Having clever parents.
- o   Lucky – just born that way.
- o   Being in a certain ability set.
- o   Being able to read.
- o   Being good at maths.
- o   Teachers.
- o   Listening in class.
- o   Working hard.

- • Once pupils have shared their thoughts about what intelligence is, discuss the *Oxford Dictionary* definition of 'intelligence', relating and comparing this to pupils' answers: 'Intelligence: The ability to *acquire* and apply knowledge and skills.'
- • You can conclude this activity by explaining to pupils that you are going to be learning a lot about the nature of intelligence over the next few weeks, and that this might change some of the answers and views that they have today.

It would be interesting to get pupils to keep their mind-maps from this activity as you could get pupils to redo this activity at the end of the intervention and compare their responses.

8.1 THEME 1: INTELLIGENCE AND IQ TESTS: INTRODUCTION TO GROWTH AND FIXED MINDSETS

Activity 2: Learning about IQ tests: magazine article, 'What does IQ really measure?'

LEARNING OBJECTIVE

- To dispel the idea that intelligence is fixed and get pupils to realise that IQ tests are just one way of assessing specific aspects of intelligence, and that the results of these tests are not deterministic.

MATERIALS REQUIRED

- IQ article (available online).
- IQ worksheet (available online).

ACTIVITY DESCRIPTION

- Begin this activity by writing 'IQ tests' on the board, and ask the class if they have heard of IQ tests.
- Following this, ask the class if anyone knows what IQ tests are, and write answers up on the board.
- The sorts of things that pupils might say in response to 'What are IQ tests?' are:

    o   Tests to measure how smart you are.
    o   Tests to measure your natural intelligence.
    o   A way of comparing how clever different people are.
    o   A way to test a person's potential.

- Give pupils the magazine article to read.
- After pupils have finished reading the article, give pupils the IQ activity sheet to fill in, or ask pupils to share their views about the article and encourage discussion in relation to their previous answers that are written on the board about IQ tests.

(Continued)

(Continued)

- Questions from the activity sheet:

  o What was the Binet-Simon scale intended to be used for?
  o What did Alfred Binet believe about intelligence?
  o What factors could affect a person's score on an IQ test?
  o Why do you think people continue to use IQ tests?
  o Now answer the question 'What are IQ tests?' again. Have your thoughts changed?

8.1 THEME 1: INTELLIGENCE AND IQ TESTS: INTRODUCTION TO GROWTH AND FIXED MINDSETS

Activity 3: Things you do and do not enjoy learning. Why? Mind-maps and class discussion.

LEARNING OBJECTIVE

- To get pupils to identify the real reasons why they might not enjoy all aspects of learning.

MATERIALS REQUIRED

- Paper and pens.

ACTIVITY DESCRIPTION

- Ask pupils to write down one thing that they really enjoy learning and one thing that they don't enjoy learning. These can be academic or non-academic.
- Then ask pupils to think, and make notes, about why they do or do not enjoy learning whatever they have selected.
- For the subjects that they have said they don't enjoy learning, ask pupils to think about what would make these more enjoyable.

  Examples of the 'whys' pupils might give for things they enjoy learning are:

  o It's fun.

- I'm good at it.
- My friends all do it.
- Because it's relevant to what I want to do when I am older.
- I find it easy.

Examples of the 'whys' pupils might give for things that they don't enjoy learning are:

- It's boring.
- I'm not very good at it.
- It's pointless.
- It's too hard.

- Try to get pupils to expand their 'whys':

  - Why is it fun/boring?

    - Is this related to how challenging/ rewarding they find it?
    - Is their conception of certain subjects or tasks a self-protection strategy? (e.g. they might say that maths is boring and that is why they don't pay attention in class or do their homework, but in truth they actually find it difficult but don't want to be seen trying if there is a risk of failing).

  - Why are you good at it/not good at it?

    - Get pupils to think about how much time they dedicate to learning (i.e. if you like something you tend to practise more).

  - Is it really pointless?

    - Try to get pupils to think about how it could be useful even if it might seem pointless now by asking what the outcome/ impact might be if they avoid something now.

  - Why do you find it easy/hard?

    - Get pupils to consider practice again. Even if they don't practise something that much but find it easy, is there something related that they practise a lot that might foster transferable skills?

- Conclude this session by making a class list of key characteristics of things that pupils enjoy learning and things that pupils don't enjoy learning.
- As a class, come up with an action plan for how they might embrace the challenge of tackling subjects that they don't enjoy learning. (See additional activities: Learn a new skill or Challenge Mountains.)

8.1 THEME 1: INTELLIGENCE AND IQ TESTS: INTRODUCTION TO GROWTH AND FIXED MINDSETS

Activity 4: Introducing theories of intelligence and mindsets: teacher-led presentation and class discussion

LEARNING OBJECTIVE

- To introduce pupils to the concepts of growth and fixed mindsets.

MATERIALS REQUIRED

- Presentation 'Theories of Intelligence' (available online).
- Theories of Intelligence worksheet (available online).

ACTIVITY DESCRIPTION

Tell the pupils that you are going to be learning about a relatively new theory of intelligence that will be the focus of the work you will be doing for the next few weeks. Also, tell pupils that after the presentation, you will be asking them how this relates to the other activities you have done so far.

- Go through the PowerPoint presentation titled 'Theories of Intelligence' (the additional worksheets have been designed to go alongside the presentation, so you could give these to pupils to fill in as you go along, or use these to guide discussion after the presentation).
- Possible questions to ask the pupils afterwards:
  - Now how would you answer the question 'What makes you clever?'
  - Think again about the subjects that you do and don't enjoy learning. Do you think that these attitudes might be due to your mindset?

8.1 THEME 1: INTELLIGENCE AND IQ TESTS: INTRODUCTION TO GROWTH AND FIXED MINDSETS

Activity 5 (Homework*): 'Think about yourself. Do you have a growth or a fixed mindset? Is this different in different areas of your life? Why do you think that is?'

*We suggest that this activity is set as homework, but you may run this as an in-class activity if you prefer.

LEARNING OBJECTIVE

- To get pupils to honestly consider their own approach to learning in relation to what they have learnt about mindsets.

MATERIALS REQUIRED

- Dependent on format chosen.

ACTIVITY DESCRIPTION

- Tell pupils that you would like them to write a short reflective essay based on what they have learnt about theories of intelligence and mindsets today, addressing the following questions:
  o Do you have a growth or a fixed mindset?
  o Is this different in different areas of your life? Why do you think that is?

- This doesn't have to be an essay if you would rather specify a different format. For example, you could get pupils to create presentations or posters.
- You can adapt this further if you wish to mould this to your subject. For example, you could get pupils to write a script for a play about a fixed or growth mindset character.
- Make sure that you discuss this homework before starting the next theme.

(Continued)

(Continued)

- The purpose of discussing the pupils' homework is primarily to recap what was covered in the first theme and identify any pupils who have not quite managed to grasp the concept of the two mindsets.
- The pupils' homework should provide a good insight into how your pupils view themselves and their own mindsets.
- Pupils could either discuss their homework with you individually, in small groups, or this could be done as a whole class.

THEME 2: OVERVIEW

8.2 The brain: dealing with mistakes and challenges

LEARNING OUTCOMES

1. To learn about the structure of the brain.
2. To learn about brain development in the context of learning.
3. To learn that mistakes and challenges are important parts of learning.
4. To understand that everyone faces challenges and makes mistakes, and that it is how we deal with them that determines success.

CORE ACTIVITIES

1. Brain presentation: teacher-led presentation and class discussion.
2. Taxi driver study video.
3. Our challenges and mistakes.
4. Feedback: Austin's butterfly and optional game.

Alternative and additional activities are available online at https://study.sagepub.com/education/education-all-phases/ hoskins-growth-mindset-for-teachers

8.2 THEME 2: THE BRAIN: DEALING WITH MISTAKES AND CHALLENGES

Activity 1: Brain presentation

LEARNING OBJECTIVE

- To provide scientific and concrete evidence that working hard and practising really can improve our skills and intelligence, by explaining the processes that take place in the brain when we are engaged in learning.

MATERIALS REQUIRED

- Presentation: The Brain (available online).
- The Brain worksheet (available online).

ACTIVITY DESCRIPTION

- Before you go through the brain presentation with the pupils, ask pupils if they still feel like there are certain things that they will just never be good at.
- Explain that it is natural to feel like that sometimes, and that we know that when you feel like that, you are more likely to just give up and not even bother trying.
- Introduce the brain presentation by saying that you are going to learn about the processes that take place in our brains while we are learning, and that this will hopefully help to make them feel more confident that they can improve at anything they want to as long as they hold a growth mindset throughout all aspects of their lives.
- Present the PowerPoint of the brain (available online) to the pupils.
- You can hand out the worksheets after the presentation, or you can hand these out before and allow pupils to fill this in as you go through the presentation.
- If you choose not to use the worksheets, then after the presentation, recap the main points and ask the class questions to check the pupils' understanding of the concepts (these may need to be explained further).

8.2 THEME 2: THE BRAIN: DEALING WITH MISTAKES AND CHALLENGES

Activity 2: Taxi driver study video

(Continued)

(Continued)

LEARNING OBJECTIVE

- To provide pupils with a memorable example of how practice and experience can actually change the structure of our brains, enabling us to be better at specific tasks or skills.

MATERIALS REQUIRED

- Taxi driver video (available online).
- Taxi Driver worksheet (available online).

ACTIVITY DESCRIPTION

- Watch the taxi driver video.
- Afterwards, recap and hand out the worksheets, or ask the class questions about the video.
- Examples of questions you could ask to promote discussion around what pupils have learnt so far are as follows.

  - How do you think what we have learnt about the brain relates to what we have learnt about growth and fixed mindsets?
  - Can you think of something that you can now do, but used to find really hard? Why do you think that is?
  - Is there anything that you still don't believe you would ever be able to do? Why?

The purpose of these discussions is to inspire the pupils to believe in themselves. Highlight that there is no reason why they cannot improve at anything; they just need to put their mind to it, work hard, and persevere.

8.2 THEME 2: THE BRAIN: DEALING WITH MISTAKES AND CHALLENGES

Activity 3: Our challenges and mistakes

LEARNING OBJECTIVE

- To highlight that making mistakes is just a natural part of the learning process. This activity is also designed to help pupils to understand that we are more likely to make mistakes when we are challenging ourselves, and it is challenging ourselves that leads to improvement.

MATERIALS REQUIRED

🖰 Michael Jordan video (see video link list).

ACTIVITY DESCRIPTION

- Show the Michael Jordan video (you may want to explain first that Michael Jordan is widely regarded as the greatest basketball player of all time).
- The purpose of this video is to generate discussion about mistakes.
- Possible questions you could ask following the video:
    o What do you think is the key message in this video?
    o How do you feel when you make a mistake?
    o Does making mistakes mean you are a failure?
    o Is it a good thing never to make mistakes?
    o When are you more likely to make mistakes?

- Points that you want to emphasise during discussion:
    o We can all feel embarrassed and deflated when we make mistakes but:
    o A fundamental part of having a growth mindset is not being afraid to make mistakes.
    o *Everyone* makes mistakes.
    o Mistakes do not mean that you are stupid or that you cannot do something.
    o Mistakes are opportunities to learn.
    o We often make mistakes when we are pushing our limits, and this is when our brain has to work the hardest.
    o If you don't make mistakes, then it's probably because you aren't challenging yourself enough.
    o Discuss some examples (babies learning to talk, learning a second language, learning to drive).

(Continued)

(Continued)

OUR OWN MISTAKES AND CHALLENGES

(You might want to begin the next part of this activity with one of your own examples to help pupils to feel comfortable.)

- Ask pupils to each write down a personal example of *two* occasions when they have made a mistake, encountered a kind of failure, or faced a difficult challenge.

    o One of these needs to be a time in which they dealt with this with a fixed mindset.
    o One needs to be a time in which they dealt with this with a growth mindset.
    o Ask pupils to be honest, and remind them that it will take time to not feel embarrassed about making mistakes, as it is normal to feel this way.

- Discuss pupils' examples as a class, asking questions such as:

    o What was the outcome?
    o How would approaching this with the opposite mindset have changed the outcome?
    o How did you feel at the time?
    o Did you learn anything from that experience?
    o Would you approach it differently now?

- Conclude by linking this discussion about mistakes to pupils' learning experiences:

    o For example, their mistakes can be useful for teachers as they highlight where the pupil might need more help.
    o On the flipside, if pupils aren't making mistakes, then it shows teachers that they might not be challenging pupils enough; if work is always perfect, then it could indicate that it is not stretching them appropriately.

8.2 THEME 2: THE BRAIN: DEALING WITH MISTAKES AND CHALLENGES

Activity 4: Feedback (and optional game)

LEARNING OBJECTIVE

- To emphasise that feedback, like mistakes, should be seen as a necessary and positive part of the learning process, and not something to feel deflated by.

MATERIALS REQUIRED

- Austin's butterfly video (see video link list).
- Paper and pencils (optional)
- Lego (optional)

ACTIVITY DESCRIPTION

- Show the video 'Austin's butterfly'.

  o Ask pupils why they think you have shown them this video. Were they impressed?
  o You want the key message here to be that learning is an iterative process and that mistakes and feedback are vital parts of this process.

- You could take this activity even further by asking pupils to attempt the 'Austin's butterfly' challenge (you could do this before or after showing the video).
- Put pupils into pairs, give each a picture and ask them to draw it. It is best to choose pictures that are often drawn as a simplified line drawing (e.g. a house, fish, butterfly or flower).
- After they have finished, ask them to provide each other with feedback on how they could make their drawing look more like the picture.
- Then ask them to have another go at drawing the picture on a new piece of paper, using the feedback they have just received to help them improve.
- Keep repeating this process of draft and feedback until pupils are happy with their own drawings and each other's.
- Keep each draft copy of the drawing so that pupils can see how they got to their end result and emphasise the 'journey' that got them there. The aim is to highlight that getting advice from others is

(Continued)

(Continued)

a good strategy to improve and that they shouldn't be disappointed when receiving feedback, or be afraid to ask for help.

LEGO GAME

- Pupils are put in groups of 4–5 and each group sits around a table.
- One person in the group is blindfolded.
- Each group is then given some Lego (or something else) put together in a certain way. The rest of the group have two minutes to examine the piece of Lego *in silence*. (The blindfolded person is allowed to touch the structure, too.)
- The Lego structure is then disassembled, and the group's task is to guide the blindfolded person to rebuild the structure (this should be timed).
- Only the blindfolded person can touch the pieces, but they cannot talk.
- The group cannot touch the Lego pieces, but they can help the blindfolded person by giving advice and instructions.
- Once it has been successfully reassembled, the group should record the time it took them.
- The group should discuss their strategies from their first go. The blindfolded person should give feedback as to what they found worked well, and advise the group as to how they could improve their instructions and advice – for example, one person talking at a time, with specific descriptions given about the direction of the pieces.
- Once the group agrees on their strategy, they do the task again to see if they can improve their time.

At the end of this task, discuss how the opportunity to give feedback to decide on a strategy can make a task easier.

THEME 3: OVERVIEW

8.3 Mindset language: action plans

LEARNING OUTCOMES

1. To learn about language associated with fixed and growth mindset.

2. To understand helpful and unhelpful language associated with learning.
3. To personally evaluate areas of learning that require more effort.

NB: Here is a quick recap about the impact of feedback and praise from the training day slides.

*   Avoid person-orientated praise.
*   Make praise and feedback process-orientated and/or task-orientated.
*   Why use process- and task-orientated feedback?

    o   Pupils at all levels can earn praise and encouragement.
    o   Creates stable self-esteem.
    o   Setbacks are interpreted as the result of a lack of effort, or inappropriate strategies, rather than 'not being clever'.
    o   This means that pupils can see a way to overcome challenges, rather than giving up.
    o   Helps to build resilience.

CORE ACTIVITIES

1. Class discussion of comments used to describe success and failure (to be revisited after Activity 3).
2. Statements and scenarios worksheets.
3. Carol Dweck's praise video (and optional additional worksheet).

    Revisit Activity 1

4. Action Plan Quiz.
5. Recommended homework: *Mindsets* magazine (read and discuss with family or friends, note down five key points from this to share with the rest of the class).

Alternative and additional activities are available online at https://study.sagepub.com/education/education-all-phases/ hoskins-growth-mindset-for-teachers

8.3 THEME 3: MINDSET LANGUAGE: ACTION PLANS

Activity 1: Class discussion of comments used to describe success and failure

(Continued)

(Continued)

LEARNING OBJECTIVE

- To enable pupils to identify the growth and fixed mindset messages that they hear.

MATERIALS REQUIRED

- Whiteboard.

ACTIVITY DESCRIPTION

- Ask pupils about the comments we hear when people talk about success and failure. For example, 'What do people say when you succeed on a task?'
- Make a column on the board (titled 'success') and write up pupils' answers (use bullet points).
- Then ask pupils 'What do people say when you fail a task?' Create a second column (titled 'failure') and write up pupils' answers.
- Try to get a good mixture of both fixed and growth mindset statements.
- *Leave these up on the board as they will be revisited after Activity 3.*

REVISITING ACTIVITY 1: CLASS DISCUSSION OF COMMENTS USED TO DESCRIBE SUCCESS AND FAILURE

- Revisit the original list of comments that you noted on the board.
- Work through each one and get the class to identify which are examples of growth mindset language and which are examples of fixed mindset language.
- You could also get the class to rephrase the fixed mindset comments into growth mindset language.

  Below are some examples of fixed mindset language.

  o   You got a great score on your maths test, Jimmy. You are such a smart boy!
  o   You are really clever.
  o   You are really good at maths.

- You're lucky, you have such a talent.
- You are so intelligent.
- That's great, aren't you a star?
- You are good at this.
- You are just not good at this.
- You don't have a natural talent for this.
- Never mind, you are good at others things.
- Let's try an easier one.
- No one in our family is academic, so don't worry about not doing well at school.
- No matter how hard you try you just won't be good at . . .

Below are some examples of growth mindset language.

- You got a great score on that exam, you must have revised lots.
- You have worked so hard on that – well done.
- You have really improved at maths.
- You have found a great strategy.
- You may not be very good at that now, but you will get there if you keep trying.
- Why don't you try it again?
- Why don't you try using a different strategy?
- It looks like you didn't put much effort into that piece of work.
- Don't give up – keep trying.

8.3 THEME 3: MINDSET LANGUAGE: ACTION PLANS

Activity 2: Statements and scenarios worksheets

LEARNING OBJECTIVE

- To get pupils to consider how the different growth and fixed mindset language that they hear might make them feel, and to think about ways of counteracting this by using their 'internal growth mindset voices'.

(Continued)

(Continued)

MATERIALS REQUIRED

⌐ Statements and scenarios worksheet (available online).

ACTIVITY DESCRIPTION

- Hand each pupil a copy of the worksheet to work through on their own.
- Once pupils have finished, go through these as a class (key points to cover are included in the teachers' copy of this worksheet).
- As you go through these examples, you want to emphasise the following points about fixed mindset comments:
  - ◦ Both positive and negative comments can be phrased in fixed mindset language.
  - ◦ These might make us feel better at the time, but there is a lot of evidence to suggest that these sorts of comments don't actually help us in the long term.
  - ◦ We will hear people (teachers, parents, friends, siblings) using fixed mindset language all the time, and the way to deal with this is not to challenge who we hear this language from, but to use our own 'internal growth mindset voices' to remind ourselves what is important (i.e. how much effort we have put in, how hard we have worked, what we have learnt, etc.).

8.3 THEME 3: MINDSET LANGUAGE: ACTION PLANS

Activity 3: Carol Dweck's praise video

LEARNING OBJECTIVE

- To demonstrate to pupils that experiments have actually shown that the different types of language we have been talking about influence pupils' motivation, enjoyment and achievement.

MATERIALS REQUIRED

- Carol Dweck's praise video (see video link list).
- Carol Dweck Video summary sheet (available online).

ACTIVITY DESCRIPTION

The purpose of this video is to demonstrate to pupils that experiments have actually shown that the different types of language we have been talking about influence pupils' motivation, enjoyment and achievement.

- Show the class the video and ask them what they think the key messages are.
- If the pupils struggle to get the key messages across, you may want to ask more specific questions, such as:

  o What was the impact of praising children for their intelligence?
  o Who did better – the children who were praised for effort or the children who were told they were really smart?
  o Why do you think the different types of praise had different effects?

- *Don't forget to now revisit Activity 1 (as detailed in Activity 1 description).*

OPTIONAL ADDITIONAL ACTIVITY

- The task that Carol Dweck talks about in the video was actually run as an experiment, so for older pupils, you may want them to read the Study Summary Sheet (available online), answer the questions and discuss this. For your own information, the full paper reference for the study that this video is referring to is included here:

Mueller, C.M. and Dweck, C.S. (1998) Praise for intelligence can undermine children's motivation and performance. *Journal of Personality and Social Psychology, 75*(1): 33.

8.3 THEME 3: MINDSET LANGUAGE: ACTION PLANS

Activity 4: Action plan quiz

LEARNING OBJECTIVE

- To get pupils to honestly evaluate their approach to learning and challenges, and to highlight where they might need to put in more effort. This quiz is also designed to encourage pupils to come up with a growth-mindset style action plan in order to take control of their own learning.

MATERIALS REQUIRED

⌲ Action Plan Quiz (available online).

ACTIVITY DESCRIPTION

It is important for pupils to realise also that having a growth mindset is only half the battle, as working hard is hard work.

- Give each child a copy of the quiz and ask them to fill it in individually.
- Pupils could copy the action plan section into their exercise books.
- It would be fantastic if you could discuss this with each pupil, but you could also ask pupils to share examples with the class of what they have written and ways in which they can help themselves to improve at 'x'.
- This is an activity that you may want pupils to complete again at a point later in time to see if they have achieved any of the goals they have set in the action plan.

8.3 THEME 3: MINDSET LANGUAGE: ACTION PLANS

Activity 5 (homework*): *Mindsets* magazine

* We have designed this activity to be set as homework, but you may adapt this to run as an in-class activity if you prefer.

LEARNING OBJECTIVE

- This magazine has been put together to provide a collection of articles that nicely cover some of the key messages about mindsets, as well as being a way of encouraging the pupils' parents to engage with some of the mindset messages.

MATERIALS REQUIRED

🖰 *Mindsets* magazine (available online).

ACTIVITY DESCRIPTION

- Give each student a copy of the *Mindsets* magazine.
- Some suggestions as to the homework you may set:
  - Summarise one of the articles for the rest of the class.
  - Read and discuss one of the articles with a family member or with friends, and feed their views back to the rest of the class.
  - Pick out five key points that they think support what they have learnt so far, or expand on what they have learnt so far.

DISCUSS HOMEWORK BEFORE STARTING THE NEXT THEME

- Find out which task pupils chose to do for their homework, and discuss the key points and article summaries as a class.
  - Ask pupils if they learnt anything new from this, or if they found anything that is a nice example of what they have learnt so far.
- Save discussing the views of family and friends for last, as this will lead nicely into the next task.
  - Ask pupils to be honest about what other people said about it.
- Were people receptive? Did people identify with the concepts and ideas? Did they come up against anyone who didn't identify with the concepts and ideas – i.e. someone with a very fixed mindset?

THEME 4: OVERVIEW

8.4 Stereotypes: consequences

LEARNING OUTCOMES

1. To learn about stereotypes (what they are and the fact that they are too general to be true).
2. To think about stereotypes in the context of learning (subject stereotypes, gender stereotypes, achievement stereotypes).
3. To appreciate that our decisions and responses to challenges have consequences and are our own responsibility.

NB: Growth mindset training has also been shown to reduce the effects of stereotype threat. You may want to read the following paper which discusses the effect of growth mindset training on closing the attainment gap between girls and boys in maths:

Good, C., Aronson, J. and Inzlicht, M. (2003) Improving adolescents' standardized test performance: an intervention to reduce the effects of stereotype threat. *Journal of Applied Developmental Psychology*, *24*(6): 645–s62.

CORE ACTIVITIES

1. What is a stereotype?
2. Linking stereotypes to learning, effort and mindsets.
3. Tree of consequences (recommended to be continued as homework).

8.4 THEME 4: STEREOTYPES: CONSEQUENCES

Activity 1: What is a stereotype?

LEARNING OBJECTIVE

- To get pupils to appreciate that they will encounter stereotypes all the time, but that they should remember that these are too general to be true. There are cases when the stereotypes are true, but they are not *always* true. It is also important to encourage pupils to realise that it is unfair to make such sweeping statements.

MATERIALS REQUIRED

🖰 Stereotype Sentence Sheets (available online).

ACTIVITY DESCRIPTION

- At the very beginning of the session, without explaining anything about stereotypes, provide each pupil with one of the A5 Stereotype Sentence Sheets (this can also be done in groups if you'd prefer).
- Ask the pupil to write a sentence about something they know about their character in the space provided and then put it to one side for now.
- Once pupils have finished writing their sentence, write the word 'stereotype' on the board and draw a box around it.
- Ask the pupils if they know what the word 'stereotype' means, or if they know what a stereotype is. Write any answers that are suitable on the board.
- If no pupils have responded, or once all willing pupils have given an answer, write the definition of stereotype up at the top of the board: 'Stereotype: an overly simple picture or opinion of a person, group or thing'.
- Ask the pupils to go back to the sentences they have written about men, women, old people and French people, and ask pupils to share these with the class.
- For each sentence, ask pupils whether they think these are facts or stereotypes? (This can be a difficult distinction for pupils to make, so try to ensure that the difference is highlighted when discussing pupils' sentences.)
- If all the comments are facts, then you may have to provide your own examples of on stereotypes that you have written on your own examples of the Stereotype Sentence Sheets.

(Continued)

(Continued)

- In cases where pupils have written down a stereotype, write these on the board and ask the class what they think about them.
- Examples:

  o   All old people are forgetful.
  o   Women are better cooks than men.
  o   Men are better drivers than women.
  o   All French people eat snails and frogs' legs.

- Annotate the stereotypes with pupils' comments – e.g. for the examples above, pupils might say that their dad always cooks dinner or their mum is a much better driver. If pupils don't offer responses freely, you may want to try asking specific questions for each one – e.g. 'Are all old people forgetful?'
- You want to encourage pupils to come up with examples of how they aren't true (obviously, they will also come up with supporting examples, too, which is fine, as you want to show that they can be true in some cases, but they aren't *always* true).
- Once you are confident that your class understands what a stereotype is, move on to the next activity, leaving the definition on the board.

You could keep the stereotype cartoons and display them in the classroom next to a 'Beware of stereotypes' sign, so the pupils can refer to them from time to time if needed.

8.4 THEME 4: STEREOTYPES: CONSEQUENCES

Activity 2: Linking stereotypes to learning, effort and mindsets

LEARNING OBJECTIVE

- To get pupils to understand the effects of stereotypes on our approaches to learning.

MATERIALS REQUIRED

- Stereotypes video (link available online).
- Stereotypes worksheet (available online).

ACTIVITY DESCRIPTION

STEREOTYPES SURROUNDING LEARNING

For this activity you can either just use the activity description given here, or you can also use the worksheet provided online as well.

- Leave the definition of the word 'stereotype' on the board.
- Ask pupils to think about stereotypes that surround education, learning, effort, or an extra-curricular activity that they take part in, and tell them to write it down on a piece of paper.
- After a few minutes, ask the pupils to put their hands up if they want to share their stereotype.
- Discuss each example with the class.
- First determine whether it is a stereotype, and then encourage the class to discuss what they think about that stereotype (i.e. cases where it is true and cases when it isn't).

Possible examples that you can use if the pupils struggle for ideas:

- o Boys are better at maths than girls.
- o Only girls work hard at school.
- o Science is a boys' subject.
- o Dancing is for girls.
- o Sports stars aren't very clever.

THE EFFECT OF STEREOTYPES AND APPROACHING STEREOTYPES WITH A GROWTH MINDSET

- Choose one of the pupils' examples from the previous activity and write it up on the board to work through.
- To demonstrate this activity we will use the example: Boys are better at maths than girls.
- Ask the class if they think stereotypes are examples of fixed or growth mindset language (the answer being that they are, of course, fixed).
- Now ask the class how stereotypes like this make them *feel*.
- For this example, you could ask questions like 'How might this make you feel towards maths if you were a girl?'

(Continued)

(Continued)

- You want to highlight that stereotypes send out fixed mindset messages. This example may make girls feel that there is no point in trying at maths.
- Finally, ask what the impact of this attitude would be (the answer being that it can perpetuate the stereotype).
- As you go through this for the different examples, aim to produce a flow chart that shows that this causes a cycle. For example:
- Ask the class what someone with a growth mindset would say about stereotypes.
- List pupils' comments on the board.
- You want to encourage comments like:

  o They aren't true.
  o Don't believe them, as you can do anything you want as long as you try hard.
  o Don't let them stop you from trying.
  o Anyone can get better at maths – they just have to try hard at it.

- You could now show the pupils the 'stereotype video' on the video link list, as this provides a nice summary of some of the ideas covered in the stereotypes sessions and mentions some scientific studies.

8.4 THEME 4: STEREOTYPES: CONSEQUENCES

Activity 3: Tree of Consequences

LEARNING OBJECTIVE

- To get pupils to think about the challenges and decisions that lie ahead of them, and to consider how a growth mindset may come into use.

MATERIALS REQUIRED

- Presentation 'Tree of Consequences' and handout (available online).

ACTIVITY DESCRIPTION

- For this activity, we want pupils to design a tree of consequences.
- Go through the PowerPoint example that we have provided to explain what we mean by a tree of consequences (still versions of full tree can also be found online).
- In order for pupils to construct their own tree of consequences, we advise that they either do a mind-map or a timeline first to get their ideas down (pupils may find that their Action Plan Quiz from week 2 comes in useful for this activity).

   o Ask pupils to start by thinking about something that they would like to do in the future – for example, their chosen career, somewhere they would like to travel, a language they would like to learn.

   o Pupils should then think about what smaller steps (challenges) they might need to work towards between now and then – for example, steps towards their chosen career, which could include improving in certain subjects, getting certain grades at GCSE and A Levels, work experience, university).

   o Pupils should also think about some possible mistakes, failures that they might face along the way and the possible ways of dealing with them – for example, they might only get a D grade in GCSE Maths, but they need a C to do the course they want to do at university. They would then have two options: to revise more and resit their exam (growth mindset), or give in and give up on their original career plans (fixed mindset).

   o Remind pupils that sometimes hard work doesn't always work, as we might hit stumbling blocks because we are using the wrong strategy and not because we aren't working hard. Ask each pupil to include at least one mistake, challenge or failure that could be the result of using the wrong strategy – for example, they might be struggling to memorise lists for an exam that would be easier to memorise using mnemonics.

- Once pupils have made a mind-map or a rough timeline, have a look over it and once you think there are enough steps, get pupils to make either a poster or a PowerPoint presentation of their tree of consequences. This could be a task that they finish for *homework*.

THEME 5: OVERVIEW

8.5 The talent and luck myths: role models

LEARNING OUTCOMES

1. To challenge pre-held beliefs about effort, talent and luck.
2. To identify the journeys of inspirational people.
3. To link these in with what we have learnt about mindsets, language, responses to challenges and failures, etc.

CORE ACTIVITIES

1. The luck and talent myths (and optional Violin Study Sheet).
2. Inspirational people's stories.
3. Why do some people feel embarrassed about doing well?
4. Research project on your own inspirational person (famous or not). Guided by worksheet (recommended to be continued as homework).

8.5 THEME 5: THE TALENT AND LUCK MYTHS: ROLE MODELS

Activity 1: The talent and luck myths

LEARNING OBJECTIVE

- To challenge pupils' pre-held beliefs about talent and luck, and to get them to redefine what talent and luck are from a growth mindset perspective.

MATERIALS REQUIRED

- Whiteboard.
- Talent and Luck worksheet (available online).
- Violin Study summary sheet (optional and available online).

ACTIVITY DESCRIPTION

For this activity, you can either just use the activity description given here to guide discussion or you can use the worksheets provided online as well.

- Write the words 'talent' and 'luck' on the board.
- Ask the class to define each of these words and once you have reached a consensus, write the agreed definition on the board.
- For your reference, here are the *Oxford Dictionary* definitions: talent: 'natural aptitude or skill'; luck: 'success or failure apparently brought by chance rather than through one's own actions'.
- Using the questions and quotes provided below, the point of this activity is to lead pupils towards seeing talent and luck in a growth mindset way:
  - Talent: from a growth mindset point of view, talent is considered to be 'the beginnings of an opportunity, and not a ticket to success'. We want pupils to realise that talent does not automatically lead to success, and that even people born with a natural affinity for something have to work hard.
  - Luck: from a growth mindset point of view, luck is considered to be 'preparation meeting opportunity'. We want pupils to understand that being prepared for opportunities is a way of increasing your own luck.
- Possible questions to ask and discussions to have about talent:
  - Is talent enough to ensure success?
    - How can you develop a talent?
    - If you don't have a natural talent for something, does that mean you won't be able to do it?
  - You could also ask the class if they have ever been told that they are talented at something, or if they have ever found that they picked up a skill much more quickly than other people. Ask them why they thought that was. Often, this happens when the new skill involves using skills that we have gained from other aspects of life.
    - People who have 'a natural talent' for certain sports tend to play a lot of other sports, meaning that the skills that

(Continued)

(Continued)

are required to be 'naturally good' at a new sport (such as fitness, stamina, hand–eye coordination) have been developed from practising other sports.

- People who are considered 'talented' are often just much more passionate about that particular activity, and this passion is what motivates them to keep practising and improving.
- A young child who enjoys playing football with their parents from an early age might be perceived as 'naturally talented' when they first start playing at school with other children who have never played, but this is actually just the result of previous experience.

- Possible questions to ask and discussion to have about luck:

  o Is luck the same for everyone?

    - Can you think of any examples where a situation might be lucky for someone but not for someone else? For example, a member of your football club is related to a famous football player who is coming to visit for the evening. Your friend has invited you and a couple of friends to go to the park for a practice session. However, you have left all your homework until the last minute, so you can't go. All your friends have done their homework, so they get to go.
    - Can you make your own luck?
    - Can you think of an opportunity that you have considered lucky, that may not have been considered lucky at a different time in your life?

- Possible quotations to discuss with the class (you can find many more on the internet!):

  o 'It's not that I'm so smart, it's just that I stay with problems longer.' (Albert Einstein)
  o 'I have no special talent, I am only passionately curious.' (Albert Einstein)
  o 'I've always considered myself to be just average talent and what I have is a ridiculously insane obsessiveness for practice and preparation.' (Will Smith)
  o 'Chance favours the prepared mind.' (Louis Pasteur)
  o 'Diligence is the mother of good luck.' (Benjamin Franklin)
  o 'Opportunity is missed by most because it is dressed in overalls and looks like work.' (Thomas Edison)

- Online, there is an optional worksheet that you can give to pupils called the Violin Study Summary which discusses the importance of practice. This worksheet provides a summary of the Violin Study by Ericsson et al. (1993) and some comprehension questions. This is pitched at quite a high level, so may only be suitable for older pupils.

8.5 THEME 5: THE TALENT AND LUCK MYTHS: ROLE MODELS

Activity 2: Inspirational people's stories

LEARNING OBJECTIVE

- To reinforce the lessons learnt about talent and luck by highlighting that even the people we admire and often idolise had to work hard and overcome challenges and mistakes to get to where they are.

MATERIALS REQUIRED

- Famous people worksheet (available online).

ACTIVITY DESCRIPTION

- Hand pupils the Famous People Worksheet (they could do this individually or in groups to help generate discussion).
- The first part of this worksheet involves linking well-known people to the achievements that they are most famous for (this is mainly to make sure that pupils are aware who all the people are before the next stage of the worksheet).
- The second part of the worksheet involves linking the same famous people to facts or comments that people said about them before they achieved success (some of these are very obvious, but some are not at all, which will hopefully generate some discussion).
- Once pupils have completed the worksheet, work through the answers, discussing the pupils' thoughts and reactions to these as you go through.

(Continued)

(Continued)

- Following on from this activity, and to make this as relevant to pupils as possible, ask the class to give examples of famous or successful people who they admire.
- Once the class gives you some examples, try to encourage them to explore why those people are successful by asking questions such as:
  - o Do you think [name of role model] had to work hard?
  - o Do you think everything was easy for them?
  - o Do you know/think they ever made mistakes?
  - o What do you think they did after making the mistake?

- List fixed and growth mindset qualities that pupils discuss on the board and explore these with the pupils.
- To conclude this activity, we suggest watching a video or two of inspirational videos which show people's journeys to success. There are plenty available online (we have provided some links on the video link list which is online).
- The pupils can then discuss the challenges that these people faced and how they overcame them.
- The take-home message from this discussion should be that people aren't just born talented or lucky (as demonstrated by the first worksheet), but that they succeeded because they were resilient to mistakes and challenges, worked hard and were often passionate about what they did.

8.5 THEME 5: THE TALENT AND LUCK MYTHS: ROLE MODELS

Activity 3: Why do some people feel embarrassed about doing well?

LEARNING OBJECTIVE

- To explore the reasons why some people can actually feel self-conscious and uncomfortable with achievements.

ACTIVITY DESCRIPTION

Up until now we have focused on the positives of working hard towards goals and achievements, but it is also important to consider that there are other factors that may stop people from trying as hard as they can. Therefore, the purpose of this discussion is for pupils to consider that some people can actually feel self-conscious and uncomfortable with achievements (especially academic achievements), as well as trying to encourage them to be sensitive to this.

NB: This discussion should be handled carefully, as it will involve discussions about teasing, bullying and anxiety. If you know that some of the pupils in your class might find this too personal, then you may wish to alter this discussion accordingly. This may be something that you could do with pupils one-to-one.

- You could introduce this discussion by saying something like, 'So far, we have talked a lot about the positives of working hard towards goals and achievements, but it is also worth thinking about some other factors that may stop people from working as hard or doing as well as they can.'
- You could just ask the class if anyone can think of anything, as they might come up with answers without prompting.
- If they don't come up with anything, you could prompt this discussion by asking questions such as:

  o 'Has anyone ever felt self-conscious or embarrassed when they have done well at something?' (You could ask why they have felt like this if you think they would be comfortable sharing it with the rest of the class.)
  o 'Has anyone ever not done as well as they can on purpose? Why?'
  o 'Have you ever lied about how much effort you put into a piece of work? Why?'

- Here are some reasons that we would recommend that you discuss with the class (pupils might come up with these themselves):

  o Sometimes people get teased and called names for doing well (this could be linked back to the stereotypes lesson – for example, 'people who are good at maths are nerds'.

    ▪ An important point you could raise here is that those who do tease others for doing well or down-grade others' achievements often do this as a means of self-protection.
    ▪ Another interesting point to consider here is that people who do well at certain things, such as sport, don't tend to be the victims of teasing as much as those who do well at other things.

(Continued)

(Continued)

- o   Sometimes people don't want others to know that they tried hard as they want others to think that they are naturally clever or talented (this links back to fixed mindsets).
- o   Sometimes people might be anxious about having to collect a prize in assembly, or having the attention put on them (this is sometimes typical of individuals who might have problems with anxiety disorders such as social phobia or generalised anxiety disorder).
- o   Sometimes people are worried that other people might think they are showing off.
- o   Is this a cultural issue?

- A nice way to end this discussion, and to link back explicitly to growth mindsets, is to ask those who have said that they do sometimes feel embarrassed about achievements and people knowing they have worked hard, whether they would feel this way if they knew that everyone had a growth mindset.

8.5 THEME 5: THE TALENT AND LUCK MYTHS: ROLE MODELS

Activity 4 (homework*): Role model research project

*We suggest that this activity is set as homework, but you may run this as an in-class activity if you prefer.

LEARNING OBJECTIVE

- To consolidate the key learning points from Theme 5 using role models that are more personally important to pupils.

MATERIALS REQUIRED

🖰 Inspirational people homework sheet (available online).

ACTIVITY DESCRIPTION

- The aim of this activity is to get pupils to do a mini research project on an inspirational person of their choice. This could be a famous person or a person they know.

- The homework sheet will help to guide the pupils in terms of the information that they should include.
- Pupils could simply complete the homework sheet, but we recommend that you get pupils to create a presentation (poster or PowerPoint) on their chosen person so that they can then give it to the rest of the class in the next session.

THEME 6: OVERVIEW

8.6 Consolidation of key themes

LEARNING OUTCOMES

1. Recap and consolidate the key points from each of the weeks.
2. Consider how we will use and implement what has been learnt in the future.

CORE ACTIVITIES

1. Role model presentations/discussion.
2. Recapping the key themes.
3. Jump Bump board game.
4. What we have learnt.

Alternative and additional activities are available online at https://study.sagepub.com/education/education-all-phases/hoskins-growth-mindset-for-teachers

8.6 THEME 6: CONSOLIDATION OF KEY THEMES

Activity 1: Role model presentations/discussion

LEARNING OBJECTIVE

- To highlight that the factors successful people share are hard work, perseverance, resilience and therefore a growth mindset. The other key point is that successful people also tend to have encountered lots of challenges along the way, and have also made mistakes that they have learnt from.

ACTIVITY DESCRIPTION

This activity will depend on which format you asked the pupils to complete their homework in. For example, you may wish for pupils to discuss their role model homework in small groups or get pupils to present their homework to the class.

8.6 THEME 6: CONSOLIDATION OF KEY THEMES

Activity 2: Recapping the key themes

LEARNING OBJECTIVE

• To recap and consolidate the key messages from each theme.

MATERIALS REQUIRED

• Whiteboard.

ACTIVITY DESCRIPTION

• Remind pupils of each of the themes that you have covered, and ask them to try to remember what they did and what they learnt about in each session.
• Make a list on the board of the key messages that were covered throughout the sessions.
• It would also be good to get pupils to go through their notes so that they can reflect on whether their opinions have changed or developed throughout the sessions – for example, this might be a good time to look at the first exercise in Theme 1, 'What is intelligence? What makes you intelligent?' to see if pupils would give different answers to this now.

8.6 THEME 6: CONSOLIDATION OF KEY THEMES

Activity 3: Jump Bump board game

LEARNING OBJECTIVE

- A fun way of consolidating some of the key messages throughout the intervention.

MATERIALS REQUIRED

- Computer and projector to display the game found online.
- A board (or paper) and pens for pupils to draw when required.
- Jump, Bump and Challenge Game instructions and answers (available online).
- Jump, Bump and challenge cards (available online).

ACTIVITY DESCRIPTION

- Copies of the instructions, answers and materials required for the game are all available online.
- The 'board' is designed so that this can be shown on a projector and controlled on the computer. The board includes movable counters, a timer and an electronic die. This was designed to fit a screen set to the resolution 1,600 by 900 pixels, so you may want to make sure that this displays properly before the lesson.
- You will need to print the Jump, Bump and challenge cards to play this game.

8.6 THEME: CONSOLIDATION OF KEY THEMES

Activity 4: What we have learnt

LEARNING OBJECTIVE

- To help pupils consolidate the key messages from the intervention by teaching others about it.

ACTIVITY DESCRIPTION

In order for pupils to consolidate what they have learnt from this programme, we recommend doing one of the following activities:

- Pupils could create presentations to teach other people about the benefits of growth mindsets (individually or in groups) and they could present these to other classes, to parents or in a school assembly.
- Based on the activities in the previous weeks, you could get pupils to arrange 'expert-led workshops' in which they show other pupils what they have learnt over the sessions.
- Pupils could write and perform a play that has alternate endings for characters (one ending being the result of dealing with a challenge or failure in a fixed mindset way, and one ending being the result of dealing with the same challenge).

8.7 Other materials and activities

Where to go from here

From this point, you could designate some time during regular staff meetings (perhaps once a month) to focus on how, as a whole school, you can change the school's culture to a growth mindset culture and, just as importantly, how you can maintain this change. This might include sharing good classroom practice and discussions about the school motto, reward systems, assembly content, corridor displays, etc. We also recommend using the intervention provided here throughout the school/college, so feel free to copy the materials you have been given and distribute them to each teacher within the school/college.

If you haven't already done so, work through the additional activities that are available online. Be open with the pupils about what you are doing with them; it has to be their choice to change their beliefs about intelligence and their approach to learning. The quicker they familiarise themselves with these concepts about beliefs and associated language, the better. Once all pupils have been introduced to the idea of mindsets, we recommend setting up a mindset peer-mentoring scheme – perhaps older pupils mentoring younger ones, or pupils you notice to hold a particularly strong growth mindset becoming 'mindsets champions' to mentor those who might be more fixed. Another option, where possible, is to bring parents on board. This could be implemented by running whole-school events around mindsets to show parents – e.g. plays and workshops, etc., or you could run a series of family learning sessions with pupils and their parents.

The key thing is to make sure that the sessions are repeated with new pupils each academic year (we have materials for all age groups) and to ensure that everyone in the school is using growth mindset language and praise. It is important, therefore, to run refresher staff training and consider during new staff induction. This could easily be managed in house, or again, get in touch if you would like our help with this.

The following pages outline some other activities that you might like to implement with your pupils, but by now we are sure that you have lots of your own ideas about what would work with your classes.

ACTIVITY 1: STUDENT SELF–APPRAISAL

You could consider getting pupils to reflect on their own work by completing a self-appraisal for each piece of work that they do. This could include the following questions:

- Was there anything you found hard? How did you overcome this?
- Is there anything you need more help with?
- What did you learn?

ACTIVITY 2: GROWING LEARNERS MENTORING PROGRAMME

A great way of continuing to develop what pupils have learnt in this programme is to get them to teach it to other pupils. Some schools that have adopted the growth mindset ethos have set up a peer-mentoring programme in which older pupils work with younger pupils to support them with their work using growth mindset strategies, as well as teaching them about mindsets.

ACTIVITY 3: THINKING JOURNAL

This activity encourages self-reflection in a positive way and helps develop resilience.

- Each pupil has their own Thinking Journal in which they are encouraged to keep a record of their growth mindset journey.

(Continued)

(Continued)

- For example, they could use this to:

  o Jot down when they have encountered something difficult, how this made them feel and what strategies they are using to try to overcome the difficulty.
  o Note down when they are proud of something that they responded to in a growth mindset way.
  o Note down when they have helped other people to think in a growth mindset way.

- There could also be a class Thinking Journal that everyone, including the teacher, contributes to.

ACTIVITY 4: GRID DRAWING

The purpose of this activity is to provide a very visual demonstration of how using a different strategy can make a difficult task seem much easier.

- For this activity, you can either choose the pictures or photos that you would like pupils to draw copies of, or get them to select pictures themselves.
- Explain to pupils that you would like them to use a new strategy to copy these pictures by hand: the Grid Method.
- The Grid Method:

  o Take the picture you want to copy and draw a grid over it to break the picture into smaller squares.
  o On a fresh piece of paper, draw a grid with the *same number* of squares as there are in the grid on the picture that you want to copy (making these the same size will be easiest, but you can make this more difficult by telling pupils that you want them to do a bigger or smaller version of the original picture).

- o To make this easier, give both grids coordinates so that you don't end up copying the wrong square.
- o Then simply copy each square one by one.

- This website gives a great description with pictures: www.wikihow.com/Scale-Drawings-Using-the-Grid-Method

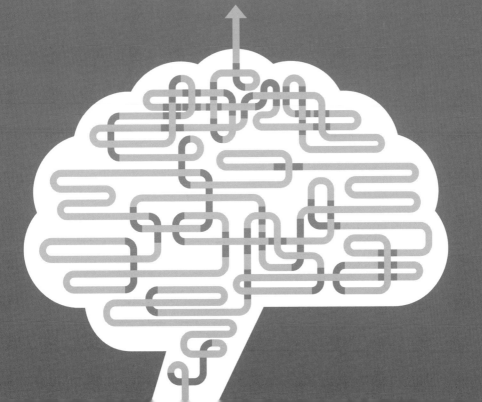

PART THREE

CHALLENGES QUESTIONS AND LOOKING AHEAD

CHAPTER 9
MYTHS, QUESTIONS AND CHALLENGES

SHERRIA HOSKINS AND JOANNA NYE

There are many consultants with varying degrees of expertise and experience of education and different levels of research literacy interpreting the work of researchers and adapting this to interventions for the classroom. There will therefore be a myriad of interventions available with just as much variety in quality, fidelity and effectiveness. Sadly, though, many misunderstand the original research and theory, oversimplify it and over-promise what a mindset intervention can achieve.

I (this refers to first author) would call on a quote from Adi Bloom from the *Times Educational Supplement* here who talks about educational attainment or, more precisely, lack of, as an entrenched issue – not something you can solve through a motivational poster or an Olympic athlete saying, 'Growth mindset! You can do it!' (*TES*, 2017). I could not agree more, but sadly it is some educational consultants and the media who have to some degree promoted this message. This in turn has led to a backlash of neighsayers who convey the opposite message – that mindset interventions are a fad, but with equal degrees of misunderstanding and oversimplification. I am often frustrated by the media presentations of my own work in this area. *The Guardian*, for example, described our intervention as being based on *the theory that anyone who tries can succeed*.

Mindset theory does not advocate that anyone who tries can succeed. It is a theory that explores how differences in our beliefs about intelligence can influence our motivation to learn – this includes trying hard, persevering in the face of failure, embracing challenge and exploring which strategies work for us. It is not rocket science to suggest that a learner who does more of this will have a better chance of succeeding. What we are trying to determine empirically is whether a mindset intervention (designed to test the theory) can support teachers to motivate children to approach learning this way. The message is not 'try harder and all will be solved'. It is not that simple. It is about exploring how teachers and a school culture can support the development of a belief system that motivates learners. It is also about having high expectations for all pupils regardless of the stereotypes that we might have about attainment related to the group they belong to – for example, stereotypes around socioeconomic status or gender.

Theory and research often don't offer simple answers, which can be frustrating for practitioners and educators. It is easy to misunderstand and over-simplify the original research and theory. This is confounded in the case of growth mindset work by the media attention, where it is presented as either a fad or a fix-all. It is neither. It is a rational theory with some promising research findings, but with much work still to be done with researchers and practitioners working together to find an effective way to translate this into classroom and parenting practice.

Since 2012, the Growing Learners team at the University of Portsmouth have worked with over 300 schools providing training and consultancy, and running several empirical research projects to test the effectiveness of an intervention, designed by the team. The intervention is based on theory and research, with the core being Carol Dweck's implicit theory of intelligence theory, or Growth Mindset.

During this work we have learnt a great deal about the complexities of moving theory and research into practice that we would like to share here. We hope that this chapter balances some of the myths, misunderstandings and oversimplifications that we have found.

'Just practise more'

One of the misinterpretations of the interventions is 'so you just need to practise more' or 'you just need to put in more effort'. Yes, practice and effort are necessary, but they are not sufficient. There are four elements that are often problematic in this message.

First, telling a child to practise more will be unlikely to have an impact. Changing mindsets interventions are not about telling children this – they are about increasing children's motivation to do this by developing a different belief system about the nature of intelligence.

"FIRST, TELLING A CHILD TO PRACTISE MORE WILL BE UNLIKELY TO HAVE AN IMPACT. CHANGING MINDSETS INTERVENTIONS ARE NOT ABOUT TELLING CHILDREN THIS, THEY ARE ABOUT INCREASING CHILDREN'S MOTIVATION TO DO THIS BY DEVELOPING A DIFFERENT BELIEF SYSTEM ABOUT THE NATURE OF INTELLIGENCE."

So the focus need also to be on unravelling myths about the nature of their abilities as something fixed that cannot develop. If children are supported to believe this, then they will develop a tendency to bounce back from failure and challenge with more effort and continued practice.

Second, a growth mindset can make the difference between someone who avoids challenge and failure and someone who embraces it for the sake of learning. Therefore, having a growth mindset will not influence your learning or learning outcomes if a learner is not being given the chance to challenge themselves. If classroom learning focuses on tasks that do not stretch pupils, then it is likely that the same level of learning will occur, as it did before a growth mindset was challenged, except for the pupils who were struggling in class. This is why we often see our mindset intervention influencing pupils who were already challenged, but not so often pupils that were doing fine already.

Further, another element is often missing. If you provide a challenge for children, they will make mistakes, and this needs to be allowed and supported. A learning environment that values mistakes as a learning opportunity needs to be built. Mistakes that are hidden are a missed learning opportunity for all. We use a mistakes board with the pupils that we work with, spending a few minutes each day noting the best mistakes and learning of the day.

Finally, persistence and effort after challenge and failure need to be meaningful, not just trying the same approach over and over again (unless that is resulting in development). Rather, a learner needs to be taught numerous strategies to explore if the first one fails and encouraged to explore these different strategies. Teachers do this all the time. The great thing about a growth mindset is that children become motivated to try them out, rather than avoiding a task that they have failed at the first time.

'You can't provide positive praise'

A clear message that comes from Carol Dweck's work is that you need to praise for effort and achievement, rather than providing *person-* or *attribute-* focused praise. However, this often gets interpreted as you can't praise at all, or you can only praise for effort, not for achievement. Both are myths.

The problem with giving person- or attribute-focused praise ('You are so good at maths – language just isn't one of your talents') is that it carries the implication that they will always succeed at maths but not at language. It is essentially saying, 'This is something that you are out of control of'. And what does that mean when they don't understand the next maths problem they encounter? Are they no longer that maths genius that they were supposed to be? No? Then self-esteem takes a hit, or they avoid the situation in future so they aren't revealed as an impostor.

In contrast, if we say, 'Great strategy, your sky looks really realistic in that drawing' or 'You got them all right because you persevered' or 'Some of these are wrong. I think that looking at the mistakes and having another go will help', then self-esteem is maintained in the face of challenge and failure, and your praise has provided the sense of control and the clues as to how to overcome that – effort, practice, exploring strategies.

'Mindset theory blames learners'

This couldn't be further from the truth. We are not looking to blame individuals or deny the fact that other system elements like school structures, educational policy or poverty, for example, influence attainment, rather mindset theory, and this intervention, can offer us insight into the psychological process via which these factors influence attainment: why it impacts some more than others.

For example, mindset could be one element influencing the relationship between attainment and socioeconomic status – e.g. via lower expectations for poorer pupils – and it is one that teachers can help to manage, even if we cannot change the whole education system. There will also be direct impacts like nutrition and access to resources, but this does not mean that there will not be equally powerful indirect impacts.

> "GROWTH MINDSET THEORY EXPLORES THE WAY IN WHICH THE LEARNER'S BELIEFS INFLUENCE THEIR MOTIVATION AND SO THEIR LEARNING BEHAVIOUR, ULTIMATELY INFLUENCING THEIR LEARNING OUTCOMES."

Growth mindset theory explores the way in which the learner's beliefs influence their motivation and so their learning behaviour, ultimately influencing their learning outcomes. Understanding the way the human mind works and influences behaviour does not mean that the solutions are situated in the individual, rather that we can now explore how the environment – for example, challenge in the classroom, room for mistakes, and teacher and parent language – can be changed to create a better learning environment for a child.

I also don't see examples of teachers using mindsets as a 'blaming' mechanism. It would be naive to suggest that others won't misuse this concept somewhere down the line, but that could happen without our research exploring if this theory works in practice.

"WHAT I EXPERIENCE IN MY WORK ARE MANY WONDER- FUL TEACHERS TRYING TO SUPPORT PUPILS TO COPE WITH A VERY DIFFICULT EDUCATION SYSTEM AND STILL THRIVE."

What I experience in my work are many wonderful teachers trying to support pupils to cope with a very difficult education system and still thrive. They are seeking tools to help them in this goal. We want to be able to offer another tool, but only when that tool has been thoroughly researched, only when we know if it works.

'Mindsets will affect all pupils in the same way'

From our research and interventions, we have found that high-attaining pupils and students with a fixed mindset may have a higher chance of developing anxiety issues. Further, developing a growth mindset may have more of an impact on the academic outcomes for particular children – those already struggling or with a poor learner identity, such as those receiving free school meals or with low socioeconomic status – than those who are attaining low marks at the time of the intervention and have experienced much challenge or failure up to that point. Why is this? The answer lies in what we briefly mentioned above regarding challenge being necessary for a growth mindset to positively impact on learning. If everything that you have done so far as a learner had a successful outcome, then you have no need for growth mindset; it is a message that will be, well, just irrelevant to you. Carol Dweck described a pupil who said, 'You mean, I don't have to be stupid?' on hearing the growth mindset message. Imagine what a child who has always attained might make of the same message – perhaps, 'You mean, I'm not always going to be clever?' Mindset work needs to take these differences into account. We recommend working with pupils openly on growth mindset interventions, giving space to explore each individual's perspective on it, not simply imposing one-size-fits-all interventions that are 'done to' pupils.

'It is too late by the time they get to me'

Quite often teachers who we work with are concerned that it is too late to help the age group that they work with, fearing that the damage has been done already. In psychology, there are many developmental theories that refer to critical stages of development – e.g. for language, where, if there is an impact at one stage, this delay will be difficult to unravel later. We have so far not experienced this with mindsets. We've worked with children from the age of three, right up to university students and adults, and we've seen that anyone can develop a growth mindset.

> "WE'VE WORKED WITH CHILDREN FROM THE AGE OF THREE, RIGHT UP TO UNIVERSITY STUDENTS AND ADULTS, AND WE'VE SEEN THAT ANYONE CAN DEVELOP A GROWTH MINDSET."

It seems that the trick is to be open with children. If you are going to change the way you praise your child or the type of behaviours that you encourage, let them know why you are doing it. Tell them all about growth mindsets. Remember that a change in the way you talk about performances and effort for a child who has never heard this before can be demoralising. They may wonder, 'Why did they say I tried hard? It must mean I didn't do well.' This is why it is so important, particularly with older children, that we introduce the concept of mindsets and explain to them, 'So we, as teachers, are going to focus on effort and strategy and your growth, not on how well you did compared to others'. The older children become, the more they need this context to understand the change, but the better they are able to understand that they are part of an intervention that the whole class or school is doing together.

False growth mindsets

One other issue that we have seen is the tendency to give pupils messages much like that which Adi Bloom talks of above – motivational mindset messages. This is sometimes followed by an evaluation of the impact of these messages measured via self-report items that repeat the said motivation words and ask pupils to indicate the degree to which they agree or disagree with these positive mindset statements. This will be heavily impacted by what we call social desirability – i.e. the pupils know what the assessor wants them to say. In addition, it measures a learning of the culturally accepted way of thinking, not a genuine change in cognition – i.e. belief in the nature of intelligence. We refer to this as a false growth mindset. For this reason, it is critical that we don't tell children what to say, then measure what they say – this is not going to make any difference to children's learning and attainment. For this reason, we advise that rather than measure mindsets, educators assess their intervention by measuring learning orientations – whether pupils display mastery or helplessness when they face challenge and failure. We have produced and tested an assessment of orientation that we share in the 'how to do it' manual in this book.

"IN OUR EXPERIENCE, FOR MINDSET INTERVENTIONS TO BE SUCCESSFUL, THEY REQUIRE A GOOD UNDERSTANDING OF THE THEORY AND RESEARCH ALONGSIDE USE BY AN EXPERT EDUCATOR WHO WILL APPLY IT WITH CARE AND UNDERSTANDING OF THE EDUCATIONAL CONTEXT IN WHICH THEY WORK AND THE PUPILS THEY WORK WITH. THIS CAN WORK BEST WHEN EDUCATORS AND RESEARCHERS WORK TOGETHER, AND IS EVEN BETTER WHEN PARENTS AND CARERS ARE INVOLVED TOO."

In our experience, for mindset interventions to be successful, they require a good understanding of the theory and research alongside use by an expert educator who will apply it with care and understanding of the educational context in which they work and the pupils they work with. This can work best when educators and researchers work together and is even better when parents and carers are involved too.

CHAPTER 10

LOOKING AHEAD: WHAT'S NEXT?

SHERRIA HOSKINS

Looking ahead, I would appeal to researchers and practitioners alike to keep exploring and questioning mindset both in the 'lab' theoretically and in the classroom. What we cannot do is apply this theory unquestioningly or develop interventions without understanding their nuanced impacts. In the classroom we need to evaluate and refine as we go, and in the lab we need to continue to explore some key unanswered questions. There is so much that we still need to learn theoretically about mindsets and we need much more experience, reflection and refinement of interventions in the classroom.

"THERE IS SO MUCH THAT WE STILL NEED TO LEARN THEORETICALLY ABOUT MINDSETS AND WE NEED MUCH MORE EXPERIENCE, REFLECTION AND REFINEMENT OF INTERVENTIONS IN THE CLASSROOM."

The questions that I would suggest we still need to answer about mindsets, beyond the overarching question of whether it works in the classroom, are as follows.

The research/theoretical questions

- Are mindsets subject-specific or generalised, or both?
- Are there critical age ranges for the development of different mindsets after which it is much harder to change these?
- How do we effectively measure mindsets and the behaviours that we expect to result from different mindsets without measuring false growth mindsets or children's desire to please us?

The applied questions

- What are the critical elements of mindset interventions that schools could focus on? Is it the learning from failure, the development of different learning strategies, rather than one so that children can try alternatives in the face of challenge, the focus on effort for praise and reward, the belief system about the nature of intelligence, or something that we haven't even tried yet?
- How do we support teachers to evaluate the programmes they use and develop when they have so little time?

This is by no means an exhaustive list. They are just a few that I reflect on.

I would appeal to practitioners and researchers to keep talking to each other and working together to ensure that we share our learning with each other. We need to be respectful of the different skills and knowledge that we bring to education. We also need to understand that our respective fields bring a myriad of different terminologies that we might misunderstand.

In my field, there is a whole literacy around theory and research, and most formidably impenetrable is the language of research methods and statistics. Researchers need to endeavour to make this clearer in their communications, but practitioners need also to understand (not helped by media interpretations of statistics) that there are no simple answers. For example, any researcher will know the frustration of not achieving the magic 5% confidence level, also known as reaching statistical significance, since many who are not familiar with research methods and statistics might assume that without statistical significance there is no impact.

In our pupil workshops, reported in 2013 (https://educationendowment-foundation.org.uk/projects-and-evaluation/projects/changing-mindsets/), after our intervention, there was an increase in the intervention group of two months' additional attainment, compared to the control group. This is a meaningful difference and was systematic in that it was found for most intervention pupils in both numeracy and literacy attainment. However, the change was not statistically significant.

Statistical significance tells us how confident we can be that a change in any outcome variable (in this case, academic attainment in literacy and maths) is due to the intervention, rather than due to chance or some other factor that we did not measure. For numeracy attainment, there was a 76% probability that the increased attainment was due to the intervention. For literacy attainment, there was a 93% chance that the increased attainment was due to the intervention. However, something is only considered statistically significant when there is at least 95% confidence in the change being due to the intervention (represented statistically as a P (probability) value of less than 0.05). So, for this randomised control trial, we can only say that for literacy we were approaching a significant effect.

In this and other research, there can be many reasons that the results may not be statistically significant.

- There is no impact of the intervention and there never will be for the following reasons.

  ○ The theory/research on which the intervention is based might be wrong/erroneous.
  ○ The theory/research might not be applicable to the classroom because of other influencing factors that are controlled for in the lab.

- The theory/research could work, but the intervention needs to be refined.

  ○ The intervention developed, based on the theory/research, might not have been true enough to the theory (low fidelity).
  ○ The intervention did not operate for long enough to have an impact.

- The intervention is good, but there are methodological issues that resulted in statistical significance not being reached.

  ○ The post-intervention data was collected too soon or too long after the intervention (a fading of results over time or not long enough for change in behaviour to influence a change in attainment).
  ○ The statistical power of the study may have been weak – meaning that we could not find a significant difference even if one existed in reality simply because of the maths. We know from the final analysis of our own work that because of the drop-out of some schools from the study, we didn't have enough participants to reach statistical power.

o   The control group (those who did not receive the intervention so they could be compared to those who did) became contaminated. This means that they became aware of the intervention materials or even received elements of the intervention or a similar intervention. This was our experience of a large-scale randomised control trial in which some of the schools selected at random to be in the waiting control group were so disappointed that they were not to receive the mindset intervention for eight months that they began to deliver mindset curriculum themselves.

By way of a final word, only when interventions are co-created by academics and practitioners with an open mind and a refusal to 'sell' or expect a fad or a fix-all can we even hope that theory will translate to the classroom to make any real difference to learning and achievement.

"ONLY WHEN INTERVENTIONS ARE CO-CREATED BY ACADEMICS AND PRACTITIONERS WITH AN OPEN MIND AND A REFUSAL TO 'SELL' OR EXPECT A FAD OR A FIX-ALL CAN WE EVEN HOPE THAT THEORY WILL TRANSLATE TO THE CLASSROOM TO MAKE ANY REAL DIFFERENCE TO LEARNING AND ACHIEVEMENT."

We hope that this book goes some way to achieve that open-minded and honest dialogue.

REFERENCES

Aguilar, L., Walton, G. and Wieman, C. (2014) Psychological insights for improved physics teaching. *Physics Today*, 67(5): 43–9.

Ames, C. (1992) Goals, structures and motivation. *Journal of Educational Psychology*, 84(3): 261–71.

Anderson, S.C. and Nielsen, H.S. (2016) Reading intervention with growth mindset approach. *Proceedings of the National Academy of Sciences*, 113(43): 12111–13. DOI: 10.1073/pnas.1607946113

Archer, J. (1994) Achievement goals as a measure of motivation in university students. *Contemporary Educational Psychology*, 19: 430–446.

Aronson, J., Fried, C.B. and Good, C. (2002) Reducing the effects of stereotype threat on African American college students by shaping theories of intelligence. *Journal of Experimental Social Psychology*, 38 (2): 113–25. DOI: 10.1006/jesp.2001.1491

Ashmore, T. (2009) *What impoverishes young people's aspirations?* High Wycombe: National Educational Trust.

Baird, G.L., Scott, W.D., Dearing, E. and Hamill, S.K. (2009) Cognitive self-regulation in youth with and without learning disabilities: academic self-efficacy, theories of intelligence, learning vs. performance goal preferences, and effort attributions. *Journal of Social and Clinical Psychology*, 28(7): 881–908.

Bandura, A. (1977) Self efficacy: Towards a unifying theory of behavioural change. *Psychological Review*, 84(2): 191–215.

Bandura, A. (1997) The nature and structure of self-efficacy. *Self-efficacy: The Exercise of Control* (pp. 1–35). New York: W.H. Freeman.

Belenky, D.M. and Nokes-Malach, T.J. (2012) Motivation and transfer: The role of mastery-approach goals in preparation for future learning. *Journal of the Learning Sciences*, 21(3): 399–432. DOI: 10.1080/10508406.2011.651232

Bempechat, J., London, P. and Dweck, C.S. (1991) Children's conceptions of ability in major domains: An interview and experimental study. *Child Study Journal.*

Benenson, J.F. and Dweck, C.S. (1986) The development of trait explanations and self-evaluations in the academic and social domains. *Child Development*, 1179–87.

Biddle, S.J., Wang, C.J., Chatzisarantis, N.L. and Spray, C.M. (2003) Motivation for physical activity in young people: Entity and incremental beliefs about athletic ability. *Journal of Sports Sciences*, 21(12): 973–89. DOI: 10.1080/02640410 310001641377

Blackwell, L. S., Trzesniewski, K. H. and Dweck, C. S. (2007) Implicit theories of intelligence predict achievement across an adolescent transition: A longitudinal study and an intervention. *Child Development*, 78(1), 246–3. DOI:10.1111/j.1467-8624.2007.00995

Boaler, J. (2009) *The Elephant in the Classroom*. London: Souvenir Press.

Boaler, J. (2015a) *What's Math Got To Do With It? How Teachers and Parents Can Transform Mathematics Learning and Inspire Success* (rev. edn). New York: Penguin.

Boaler, J. (2015b) *Mathematical Mindsets: Unleashing Students' Potential Through Creative Math, Inspiring Messages and Innovative Teaching*. Chichester: John Wiley & Sons.

Boaler, J. and Selling, S.K. (2017) Psychological imprisonment or intellectual freedom? A longitudinal study of contrasting school mathematics approaches and their impact on adults' lives. *Journal for Research in Mathematics Education*, 48(1): 78–105.

Boaler, J., Dieckmann, J.-A., Pérez-Núñez, G., Sun, K-L. and Williams, C. (2018) Changing students' minds and achievement in mathematics: The impact of a free online student course. *Frontiers in Education*, 3. DOI=10.3389/feduc. 2018.00026

Boyd, P. and Ash, A. (2018) Mastery mathematics: Changing teacher beliefs around in-class grouping and mindset. *Teaching and Teacher Education*, 75, 214–23. Available online at: https://doi.org/10.1016/j.tate.2018.06.016

Boylan, M., Maxwell, B., Wolstenholme, C., Jay, T. and Demack, S. (2018) The mathematics teacher exchange and 'mastery' in England: The evidence for the efficacy of component practices. *Education Sciences*, 8(4): 202. DOI: 10.3390/educsci8040202. Available online at: www.mdpi.com/2227–7102/8/4/202

Brady, A. and Alleyne, R. (2018) Resilience and growth mindset in sport and physical activity. In Brady, A. and Grenville-Cleave, B. (2018) *Positive Psychology in Sport and Physical Activity: An Introduction*. London: Routledge.

Brandt, D. (1984) Is that all there is? Overcoming disappointment in an age of diminished expectations. New York: Poseidon Press.

Broome, P. (2001) The gender-related influence of implicit theories of one's intelligence with regard to academic performance in introductory physics classes. In A. Ziegler (ed.) *Antecedents of motivation and behaviour: The role of implicit theories* (pp. 100–28). Lengerich: Pabst.

Buchmann, C. and Dalton, B. (2002) Interpersonal Influences and Educational Aspirations in 12 Countries: The Importance of Institutional Context. *Sociology of Education,* 75(2): 99–122. DOI:10.2307/3090287

Burnette, J. L., O'Boyle, E. H., VanEpps, E. M., Pollack, J. M. and Finkel, E. J. (2013) Mind-sets matter: A meta-analytic review of implicit theories and self-regulation. *Psychological Bulletin,* 139: 655–701.

Butler, R. (1998) Age trends in the use of social and temporal comparison for self-evaluation: Examination of a novel developmental hypothesis. *Child Development,* 69(4): 1054–73. DOI: 10.1111/j.1467-8624.1998.tb06160.x

Cain, K.M. and Dweck, C.S. (1995) The relation between motivational patterns and achievement cognitions through the elementary school years. *Merrill-Palmer Quarterly,* 41(1): 25–52.

Ceballo, R., McLoyd, V.C. and Toyokawa, T. (2004) The influence of neighborhood quality on adolescents' educational values and school effort. *Journal of Adolescent Research,* 19(6): 716–39.

Chapman, R.S. and Hesketh, L.J. (2000) Behavioral phenotype of individuals with Down syndrome. *Specific Behavioral/Cognitive Phenotypes of Genetic Disorders,* Special Issue, 6(2): 84–95.

Chen, J.A. and Pajares, F. (2010) Implicit theories of ability of Grade 6 science students: Relation to epistemological beliefs and academic motivation and achievement in science. *Contemporary Educational Psychology,* 35(1): 75–87. Available online at: https://doi.org/10.1016/j.cedpsych.2009.10.003

Chen, P., Chavez, O., Ong, D.C. and Gunderson, B. (2017) Strategic resource use for learning: A self-administered intervention that guides self-reflection on effective resource use enhances academic performance. *Psychological Science,* 28(6): 774–85.

Cheng, S. and Starks, B. (2002) Racial differences in the effects of significant others on students' educational expectations. *Sociology of Education,* 75(4): 306–27.

Choi, I. and Nisbett, R.E. (1998) Situational salience and cultural differences in the correspondence bias and actor-observer bias. *Personality and Social Psychology Bulletin,* 24(9): 949–60.

Cimpian, A., Arce, H.M.C., Markman, E.M. and Dweck, C.S. (2007) Subtle linguistic cues affect children's motivation. *Psychological Science,* 18(4): 314–16. DOI: 10.1111/j.1467-9280.2007.01896

Cimpian, A., Hammond, M.D., Mazza, G. and Corry, G. (2017) Young children's self-concepts include representations of abstract traits and the global self. *Child Development,* 88(6): 1786–98.

Claro, S., Paunesku, D. and Dweck, C.S. (2016) Growth mindset tempers the effects of poverty on academic achievement. *Proceedings of the National Academy of Sciences,* 113(31): 8664–8. DOI: 10.1073/pnas.1608207113

Coan, J.A. and Allen, J.J.B. (2004) Frontal EEG asymmetry as a moderator and mediator of emotion. *Biological Psychology,* 67(1–2): 7–50.

Cogdill, S.H. (2015) Applying research in motivation and learning to music education: What the experts say. Update. *Applications of Research in Music Education,* 33(2): 49–57. Available online at: https://doi.org/10.1177/8755123314547909

Cohen, G.L., Garcia, J., Apfel, N. and Master, A. (2006) Reducing the racial achievement gap: A social-psychological intervention. *Science,* 313 (5791): 1307–10.

Coleman, J.A., Galaczi, A. and Astruc, L. (2007) Motivation of UK school pupils towards foreign languages: A large-scale survey at Key Stage 3. *Language Learning Journal,* 35(2): 245–81. DOI: 10.1080/09571730701599252

Costa, A. and Faria, L. (2018) Implicit theories of intelligence and academic achievement: A meta-analytic review. *Frontiers in Psychology*, 9: 829. DOI: 10.3389/fpsyg.2018.00829

Crust L. and Clough P.J. (2011) Developing Mental Toughness: From Research to Practice. *Journal of Sport Psychology in Action*, 2:1, 21-32. DOI: 10.1080/21520704.2011.563436

Cury, F., Da Fonseca, D., Zahn, I. and Elliot, A. (2008) Implicit theories and IQ test performance: A sequential mediational analysis. *Journal of Experimental Social Psychology*, 44(3): 783–91.

Cutts, Q., Cutts, E., Draper, S., O'Donnell, P. and Saffrey, P. (2010). Manipulating mindset to positively influence introductory programming performance. In Proceedings of the 41st ACM Technical Symposium on Computer Science Education (pp. 431–5). ACM.

Dai, T. and Cromley, J.G. (2014) Changes in implicit theories of ability in biology and dropout from STEM majors: A latent growth curve approach. *Contemporary Educational Psychology*, 39(3): 233–47. Available online at: https://doi.org/10.1016/j.cedpsych.2014.06.003

Daly, I., Bourgaize, J. and Vernitski, A. (2019) Mathematical mindsets increase student motivation: Evidence from the EEG. *Trends in Neuroscience and Education*, 15: 18–28. Available online at: https://doi.org/10.1016/j.tine.2019.02.005

Davis, V.W. (2016) Error reflection: Embracing growth mindset in the general music classroom. *General Music Today*, 30(2): 11–17. Available online at: https://doi.org/10.1177/1048371316667160

Davis-Kean, P.E. (2005) The influence of parent education and family income on child achievement: The indirect role of parental expectations and the home environment. *Journal of Family Psychology*, 19(2): 294–304.

Degol, J.L., Wang, MT. and Zhang, Y. (2018) Youth Adolescence 47: 976. DOI: 10.1007/s10964-017-0739-8

Deighton, J. et al. (2017) Longitudinal pathways between mental health difficulties and academic performance during middle childhood and early adolescence. *British Journal of Developmental Psychology*, 36(1): 110–26.

Department for Children, Schools and Families (DCSF) (2009) In T. Ashmore, *What Impoverishes Young People's Aspirations?* High Wycombe: National Educational Trust.

Department for Education (2014) Performance descriptors for use in key stage 1 and 2 statutory teacher assessment for 2015/2016. London: Department for Education.

Department for Education (2015) Available online at: www.gov.uk/government/uploads/system/uploads/attachment_data/file/399005/SFR06_2015_Text.pdf

Department for Education and Employment (1998) *Statistics of Education: Schools in England 1997.* London: HSMO.

Department for Education and Skills (2007) Gender and education: The evidence on pupils in England. Available online at: http://webarchive.nationalarchives.gov.uk/20090108131525

Diener, C.I. and Dweck, C.S. (1978) Analysis of learned helplessness – continuous changes in performance and strategy, and achievement cognitions following failure. *Journal of Personality and Social Psychology*, 36(5): 451–62.

Donohoe, C., Topping, K. and Hannah, E. (2012) The impact of an online intervention (brainology) on the mindset and resiliency of secondary school pupils: A preliminary mixed methods study. *Educational Psychology*, 32(5): 641–55.

Doron, J., Stephan, Y., Boiché, J. and Le Scanff, C. (2009) Coping with examinations: Exploring relationships between students' coping strategies, implicit theories of ability, and perceived control. *British Journal of Educational Psychology*, 79, 515–28.

Du Sautoy, M. (2016) Reckon you were born without a brain for maths? Highly unlikely. *The Guardian*, 26 March. Available online at: www.theguardian.com/education/2016/mar/26/reckon-you-were-born-without-a-brain-for-maths-highly-unlikely (accessed 14.02.18).

Dweck, C.S. (1996) Implicit theories as organizers of goals and behaviour. In P.M. Golwitzer and J.A. Baugh (eds) *The Psychology of Action: Linking Cognitions and Motivation to Behaviour* (pp. 69–81). New York: Guildford Press.

Dweck, C.S. (1999) *Self-theories: Their Role in Motivation, Personality, and Development*. Philadelphia, PA: Psychology Press.

Dweck, C.S. (2002) The development of ability conceptions. In A. Wigfield and J.S. Eccles (eds) *Development of Achievement Motivation* (pp. 57–88). San Diego, CA: Academic Press.

Dweck, C.S. (2006) *Mindset: How You Can Fulfil Your Potential*. New York: Random House.

Dweck, C.S. (2007) *Mindset: The New Psychology of Success*. New York: Random House.

Dweck, C.S. and Leggett, E.L. (1988) A social-cognitive approach to motivation and personality. *Psychological Review*, 95, 256–73. DOI: 10.1037/0033-295X.95.2.256

Eccles, J.S. Schools, academic motivation and stage-environment fit. In R.M. Lerner and L. Steinberg (eds.) *Handbook of Adolescent Psychology* (2nd edn, pp. 125–53). Hoboken: Wiley.

Eccles, J.S. and Jussim, L. (1992) Teacher expectations II: Construction and reflection of student achievement. *Journal of Personality and Social Psychology*, 63(6): 947–61.

Eccles, J., Adler, T.F., Futterman, R., Goff, S.B., Kaczala, C.M., Meece, J.L. and Midgley, C. (1983) Expectancies, values, and academic behaviours. In J.T. Spence (ed.) *Achievement and Achievement Motivation* (pp. 75–146). San Francisco, CA: W.H. Freeman.

ECU Gender and education: The evidence on pupils in England (2017). Available online at: http://webarchive.nationalarchives.gov.uk/20090108131525 ECU

Egan, S.J., Wade, T.D. and Shafran, R. (2011) Perfectionism as a transdiagnostic process: A clinical review. *Clinical Psychology Review*, 31, 203–12.

Elliott, A.J. and Harackiewicz, J.M. (1996) Approach and avoidance achievement goals and intrinsic motivation: A mediational analysis. *Journal of Personality and Social Psychology*, 70, 461–75.

Enea-Drapeau C., Carlier M. and Huguet P. (2017) Implicit theories concerning the intelligence of individuals with Down syndrome. *PLoS ONE*, 12(11): e0188513. Available online at: https://doi.org/10.1371/journal.pone.0188513

Equality in Higher Education: Statistical Report 2017. Available online at: www.ecu.ac.uk/publications/equality-in-higher-education-statistical-report-2017/

Ericsson, K.A., Krampe, R.T. and Tesch-Römer, C. (1993) The role of deliberate practice in the acquisition of expert performance. *Psychological Review*, 100(3): 363–406.

Eysenck, H.J. (1965) *Fact and Fiction in Psychology*. Middlesex: Penguin.

Fergusson, D.M. and Horwood, L.J. (1997) Gender differences in educational achievement in a New Zealand birth cohort. *New Zealand Journal of Educational Studies*, 32(1): 83–96.

Fink, A., Cahill, M.J., McDaniel, M.A., Hoffmann, A. and Frey, R.F. (2018) Improving general chemistry performance through a growth mindset intervention: Selective effects on underrepresented minorities. *Chemistry Education Research and Practice*, 19: 783–806. DOI: 10.1039/C7RP00244K

Flanigan, A.E., Peteranetz, M.S., Shell, D.F. and Soh, L.-K. (2017) Implicit intelligence beliefs of computer science students: Exploring change across the semester. *Contemporary Educational Psychology*, 48: 179–96. Available online at: https://doi.org/10.1016/j.cedpsych.2016.10.003

Flett, G.L. and Hewitt, P.L. (2014) A proposed framework for preventing perfection-ism and promoting resilience and mental health among vulnerable children and adolescents. *Psychology in Schools*, 51(9): 899–912. Special Issue: Perfectionism in the School Context, November.

Francis, B. (2000) Gender and achievement. *Boys, Girls and Achievement: Addressing the Classroom Issues* (pp. 1–5). Abingdon: RoutledgeFalmer.

Frey, K. and Ruble, D.N. (1985) What children say when teacher is not around: Conflicting goals in social comparison and performance assessment in the class-room. *Journal of Personality and Social Psychology*, 48(3): 550–62.

Frith J., Sykes R. (2015) *The Growth Mindset Coaching Kit*. Independent Publishing Network: London.

Genicot, G. and Ray, D. (2017) Aspirations and inequality. *Econometrica*, 85(2): 489–519.

Gershenson, S. and Papageorge, N. (2018) The power of teacher expectations: How racial bias hinders student attainment. *Education Next*, 18(1): 64. *Academic OneFile* (accessed 11.06.19)

Good, C., Aronson, J. and Inzlicht, M. (2003) Improving adolescents' standardized test performance: An intervention to reduce the effects of stereotype threat. *Journal of Applied Developmental Psychology*, 24(6): 645–62.

Goodman, A. and Gregg, P. (2010) Poorer children's educational attainment: How important are attitudes and behaviour? York: Joseph Rowntree Foundation.

Goyette, K. (2008) College for some to college for all: Social background, occupa-tional expectations and educational expectations over time. *Social Science Research*, 37(2): 461–84. DOI:10.1016/j.ssresearch.2008.02.002

Grenfell, M. and Harris, V. (2013) Making a difference in language learning: The role of sociocultural factors and of learner strategy instruction. *Curriculum Journal*, 24(1): 121–52.

Grolnick, W., Frodi, A. and Bridges, L. (1984) Maternal control style and the mastery motivation of one-year-olds. *Infant Mental Health Journal*, 5(2): 72–82.

Grolnick, W. S. and Slowiaczek, M. L. (1994) Parents' Involvement in Children's Schooling: A Multidimensional Conceptualization and Motivational Model. *Child Development*, 65: 237-252. DOI:10.1111/j.1467-8624.1994.tb00747.x

Guardian article: www.theguardian.com/education/2016/may/10/growth-mindset-research-uk-schools-sats

Gunderson, E.A., Gripshover, S.J., Romero, C., Dweck, C.S., Goldin-Meadow, S. and Levine, S.C. (2013) Parent praise to 1- to 3-year-olds predicts children's motivational frameworks 5 years later. *Child Development*, 84(5): 1526–41. DOI: 10.1111/cdev.12064

Gurria, A. (2016) PISA 2015 results in focus. *PISA in Focus*, 67: 1.

Gutman, L.M. and Schoon, I. (2013) The impact of non-cognitive skills on outcomes for young people: Literature review. Institute of Education: Education Endowment Foundation. Available online at: https://educationendowmentfoundation.org.uk/public/files/Publications/EEF_Lit_Review_Non-CognitiveSkills.pdf. Department for Education and Skills (2007).

Haimovitz, K. and Dweck, C.S. (2016) What predicts children's fixed and growth intelligence mindsets? Not their parents' views of intelligence but their parents' views of failure. *Psychological Science*, 27, 859–69. DOI: 10.1177/0956797616639727

Hallam, S. (1997) What do we know about practising? Towards a model synthesising the research literature. In H. Jørgensen and A.C. Lehmann (eds) *Does Practice Make Perfect? Current Theory and Research on Instrumental Music Practice*, pp. 179–231. Oslo: Norwegian State Academy of Music.

Hamlin, J.K., Wynn, K. and Bloom, P. (2007) Social evaluation by preverbal infants. *Nature*, 450(7169): 557.

Harris, A. (2004) The "Can-Do" Girl versus the "At-Risk" Girl. *Future Girl: Young Women in the Twenty-First Century* (pp. 13–35). London: Routledge.

Haycock, L.A., McCarthy, P. and Skay, C.L. (2011) Procrastination in college students: The role of self-efficacy and anxiety (electronic version). *Journal of Counselling and Development*, 76: 316–27.

Henderson, V. and Dweck, C. (1990) Motivation and achievement. In S.S. Feldman and G.R. Elliot (eds) *At the Threshold: The Developing Adolescent* (pp. 308–29). Cambridge: Havard University Press.

Heyman, G.D. and Compton, B.J. (2006) Context sensitivity in children's reasoning about ability across the elementary school years. *Developmental Science*, 9(6): 616–27.

Heyman, G.D., Dweck, C.S. and Cain, K.M. (1992) Young children's vulnerability to self-blame and helplessness: Relationship to beliefs about goodness. *Child Development*, 63(2): 401–15.

Heyman, G.D., Gee, C.L. and Giles, J.W. (2003) Preschool children's reasoning about ability. *Child Development*, 74(2): 516–34.

Hicks, C.M., Liu, D. and Heyman, G.D. (2015) Young children's beliefs about self-disclosure of performance failure and success. *British Journal of Developmental Psychology*, 33(1): 123–35.

Hill, N. E. and Taylor, L. C. (2004) Parent-school involvement and children's academic achievement: Pragmatics and issues. *Curr. Direct. Psychol. Sci.* 13: 161–164.

Hofer, B.K. and Pintrich, P.R. (1997) The development of epistemological theories: Beliefs about knowledge and knowing and their relation to learning. *Review of Educational Research*, 67: 88–140.

Hong, Y.Y., Chiu, C.Y., Dweck, C.S., Lin, D.M.S. and Wan, W. (1999) Implicit theories, attributions, and coping: A meaning system approach. *Journal of Personality and Social Psychology*, 77(3): 588–99.

Horwitz, E.K. (1999) Cultural and situational influences on foreign language learners' beliefs about language learning: A review of BALLI studies. *System*, 27(4): 557–76. DOI: 10.1016/S0346-251X(99)00050-0

Horwitz, E. (2001) Language anxiety and achievement. *Annual Review of Applied Linguistics*, 21, 112–26. DOI: 10.1017/S0267190501000071

House of Commons Education Committee (2010–11) *Behaviour and Discipline in Schools*. Vol. 11. Available online at: www.publications.parliament.uk/pa/cm201011/cmselect/cmeduc/516/516ii.pdf (accessed 25.11.12).

Hulleman, C.S., Durik, A.M., Schweigert, S.B., Harackiewicz, J.M. (2008) *Journal of Educational Psychology*, 100(2): 398–416.

Jackson, C. (2006) 'I don't want them to think I'm thick': Academic motives for 'laddishness'. *Lads and Laddettes in School* (pp. 24–36). Maidenhead: Open University Press.

Ji, L.J., Peng, K. and Nisbett, R.E. (2000) Culture, control, and perception of relationships in the environment. *Journal of Personality and Social Psychology*, 78(5): 943.

Jones, B.D., Wilkins, J.L.M., Long, M.H. and Wang, F. (2012) Testing a motivational model of achievement: How students' mathematical beliefs and interests are related to their achievement. *European Journal of Psychology of Education*, 27(1): 1–20.

Jourden, F.J., Bandura, A. and Banfield, J.T. (1991) The impact of conceptions of ability on self-regulatory factors and motor skill acquisition. *Journal of Sport and Exercise Psychology*, 13(3): 213–26.

Jowett, N. and Spray, C.M. (2013) British Olympic hopefuls: The antecedents and consequences of implicit ability beliefs in elite track and field athletes. *Psychology of Sport and Exercise*, 14(2): 145–53.

Jussim, L. and Harber, K. D. (2005) Teacher expectations and self-fulfilling prophecies: Knowns and unknowns, revolved and unresolved controversies. *Personality and Social Psychology Review*, 9(2): 131–55.

Kalaja, P., Barcelos, A.M.F., Aro, M. and Ruohotie-Lyhty, I.R. (2015) *Beliefs, Agency and Identity in Foreign Language Learning and Teaching*. Basingstoke: Palgrave Macmillan.

Kasimatis, M., Miller, M. and Marcussen, L. (1996) The effects of implicit theories on exercise motivation. *Journal of Research in Personality*, 30(4): 510–16. Available online at: https://doi.org/10.1006/jrpe.1996.0037

Kelley, S.A., Brownell, C.A. and Campbell, S.B. (2000) Mastery motivation and self-evaluative affect in toddlers: Longitudinal relations with maternal behaviour. *Child Development*, 71(4): 1061–71.

King, R.B. (2012) How you think about your intelligence influences how adjusted you are: Implicit theories and adjustment outcomes. *Personality and Individual Differences*, 53(5): 705–9.

Kintrea, K. (2009) Aspirations, attainment and social mobility in disadvantages areas. *European network for housing research*.

Law, Y.-K. (2009) The role of attribution beliefs, motivation and strategy use in Chinese fifth-graders' reading comprehension. *Educational Research*, 51(1): 77–95. DOI: 10.1080/00131880802704764

Laws, D. (2013) Closing the achievement gap. Published speech. Available online at: www.gov.uk/government/speeches/closing-the-achievement-gap

Layard, R. (2011) Time for action. *New Scientist*, 210(2808).

Lederman, N.G. (1999) Teachers' understanding of the nature of science and classroom practice. Factors that facilitate or impede the relationship. *Journal of Research in Science Teaching*, 36: 916–29.

Leerkes, E.M., Blankson, A.N., O'Brien, M., Calkins, S.D. and Marcovitch, S. (2011) The relation of maternal emotional and cognitive support during problem solving to pre-academic skills in preschoolers. *Infant and Child Development*, 20(6): 353–70.

Lepper, M.R. and Greene, D. (1975) Turning play into work: Effects of adult surveillance and extrinsic rewards on children's intrinsic motivation. *Journal of Personality and Social Psychology*, 31(3): 479–86.

Li, Z. (2016) The magnitude of teacher expectation effects: Differences in students, teachers and contexts. *International Journal of Learning, Teaching and Educational Research*, 15(2): 76–93.

Licht, B.G. and Dweck, C.S. (1984) Sex differences in achievement orientations: Consequences for academic choices and attainments. In M. Marland (ed.) *Sex Differentiation and Schooling*. London: Heinemann.

Lou, N.M. and Noels, K.A. (2016) Changing language mindsets: Implications for goal orientations and responses to failure in and outside the second language classroom. *Contemporary Educational Psychology*, 46: 22–3.

Lou, N.M. and Noels, K.A. (2017) Measuring language mindsets and modeling their relations with goal orientations and emotional and behavioral responses in failure situations. *The Modern Language Journal*, 101: 214–43. doi:10.1111/modl.12380

Luo, W., Lee, K., Ng, P.T. and Ong, J.X.W. (2014) Incremental beliefs of ability, achievement emotions and learning of Singapore students. *Educational Psychology*, 34(5): 619–34. DOI: 10.1080/01443410.2014.909008

Magid, R. W. and Schulz, L. E. (2015) Quit while you're ahead: Preschoolers' persistence and willingness to accept challenges are affected by social comparisons. *CogSci*. Available online at: https://cbmm.mit.edu/sites/default/files/publica tions/15_Cogsci_Magid%26Schulz.pdf

Malka, A. and Covington, M.V. (2005) Perceiving school performance as instrumental to future goal attainment: Effects on graded performance. *Contemporary Educational Psychology*, 30(1): 60–80.

Malouff, J., Schutte, N., Bauer, M., Mantelli, D., Pierce, B., Cordova, G. and Reed, E. (1990) Development and evaluation of a measure of the tendency to be goal oriented. *Personality and Individual Differences*, 11: 1191–200.

Martin, A.J., Papworth, B., Ginns, P., Malmberg, L.-E., Colllie, R.J. and Calvo, R.A. (2015) Real-time motivation and engagement during a month at school: Every moment of every day for every student matters. *Learning and Individual Differences*, 38: 26–35. Available online at: https://doi.org/10.1016/j.lindif. 2015.01.014.

Matthes, B. and Stoeger, H. (2018) Influence of parents' implicit theories about ability on parents' learning-related behaviors, children's implicit theories, and children's academic achievement. *Contemporary Educational Psychology*, 54: 271–280. Available online at: http://dx.doi.org/10.1016/j.cedpsych.2018.07.001

Meece, J.L. and Holt, K. (1993) A pattern analysis of students' achievement goals. *Journal of Educational Psychology*, 85, 582–90.

Mercer, S. and Ryan, S. (2009) A mindset for EFL: Learners' beliefs about the role of natural talent. *ELT Journal*, 64(4): 436–44. Available online at: https://doi. org/10.1093/elt/ccp083

Middleton, M. J. and Midgley, C. (1997) Avoiding the demonstration of lack of ability: An underexplored aspect of goal theory. *Journal of Educational Psychology*, 89(4): 710–718. Available online at: http://dx.doi.org/10.1037/0022-0663.89.4.710

Miedel, W.T. and Reynolds, A.J. (2000) Parent involvement in early intervention for disadvantaged children: Does it matter? *Journal of School Psychology*, 37(4): 379–402. DOI: 10.1016/S0022-4405(99)00023-0

Miu, A.S. and Yeager, D.S. (2015) Preventing symptoms of depression by teaching adolescents that people can change: Effects of a brief incremental theory of personality intervention at 9-month follow-up. *Clinical Psychological Science*, 3(5): 726–43.

Mofield, E.L. and Parker Peters, M. (2018) Mindset misconception? Comparing mindsets, perfectionism, and attitudes of achievement in gifted, advanced, and typical students. *Gifted Child Quarterly*, 62: 327–49.

Molway, L. and Mutton, T. (2019) Changing mindsets in the modern foreign languages classroom: An intervention combining intelligence theories and reading strategies. *The Language Learning Journal*. DOI: 10.1080/0957 1736.2018.1554693

Mueller, C.M. and Dweck, C.S. (1998) Praise for intelligence can undermine children's motivation and performance. *Journal of Personality and Social Psychology*, 75(1): 33–52. DOI: 10.1037/0022-3514.75.1.33

Mullensieffen, D., Harrison, P., Caprini, F. and Francourt, A. (2018) Investigating the importance of self-theories of intelligence and musicality for students' academic and musical achievement. *Frontiers in Psychology*, 6: 1702. DOI=10.3389/ fpsyg.2015.01702

Mystkowska, A. (2014) The role of mindsets in foreign language learning: A person-in-context perspective. In W. Szubko-Sitarek, L. Salski and P. Stalmaszczyk (eds) *Language Learning, Discourse and Communication* (pp. 133–47). New York: Springer.

Nicholls, J. G. (1978) The development of the concepts of effort and ability, perception of academic attainment, and the understanding that difficult tasks require more ability. *Child Development*, 49(3): 800–814.

Nicholls, J. G. (1979) Development of perception of own attainment and causal attributions for success and failure in reading. *Journal of Educational Psychology*, 71(1): 94–99.

Nisbett, R. E. and Miyamoto, Y. (2005) The influence of culture: holistic versus analytic perception. *Trends in cognitive sciences*, 9(10): 467–473.

Nisbett, R. E., Peng, K., Choi, I. and Norenzayan, A. (2001) Culture and systems of thought: holistic versus analytic cognition. *Psychological review*, 108(2): 291.

Nussbaum, A. D. and Dweck, C. S. (2008) Defensiveness Versus Remediation: Self-Theories and Modes of Self-Esteem Maintenance. *Personality and Social Psychology Bulletin*, 34(5): 599–612. DOI: 10.1177/0146167207312960

Noyes, A. (2009) Participation in mathematics: What is the problem? *Improving Schools*, 12(3): 277–88. Available online at: https://doi.org/10.1177/1365480 209342682

Ofsted (2010/2011) The Annual Report of Her Majesty's Chief Inspector of Education, Children's Services and Skills. Available online at: https://assets.publishing. service.gov.uk/government/uploads/system/uploads/attachment_data/file/ 379294/Ofsted_20Annual_20Report_2010-11_20-_20full.pdf

OECD (2016) 'PISA 2015 Results in Focus', PISA in Focus, No. 67, OECD Publishing, Paris. Available online at: https://doi.org/10.1787/aa9237e6-en

Olson, K. and Dweck, C.S. (2009) Social cognitive development: A new look. *Child Development Perspectives*, 3(1): 60–5.

Ommundsen, Y. (2001) Self-handicapping strategies in physical education classes: The influence of implicit theories of the nature of ability and achievement goal orientations. *Psychology of Sport and Exercise*, 2(3): 139–56. DOI: 10.1016/s1469-0292(00)00019-4

Ommundsen, Y. (2003) Implicit theories of ability and self-regulation strategies in physical education classes. *Educational Psychology*, 23(2): 141–57. DOI:10.1080/01443410303224

Ommundsen Y., Roberts G.C., Lemyre P. and Miller B.W. (2005) Peer relationships in adolescent competitive soccer: Associations to perceived motivational climate, achievement goals and perfectionism. *Journal of Sports Sciences*, 23:9: 977–989. DOI: 10.1080/02640410500127975

Parsons, J., Adler, T., Futterman, R., Goff, S., Kaczala, C, Meece, J. and Midgley, C. (1983) Expectancies, values and academic behaviors. In J.T. Spence (ed.) *Perspectives on Achievement and Achievement Motivation* (pp. 75–146). San Francisco, CA: Freeman.

Patston, T. and Waters, L. (2015) Positive instruction in music studios: Introducing a new model for teaching studio music in schools based upon positive psychology. *Psychology of Well-Being*, 5(10). DOI: 10.1186/s13612-015-0036-9

Paunesku, D., Walton, G.M., Romero, C., Smith, E.N., Yeager, D.S. and Dweck, C.S. (2015) Mind-set interventions are a scalable treatment for academic underachievement. *Psychological Science*, 26(6): 784–93.

Peacock, M. (2001) Pre-service ESL teachers' beliefs about second language learning: A longitudinal study. *System*, 29(2): 177–95. DOI: 10.1016/S0346-251X(01)00010-0

Plaks, J.E. and Stecher, K. (2007) Unexpected improvement, decline, and stasis: A prediction confidence perspective on achievement success and failure. *Journal of Personality and Social Psychology*, 93(4): 667–84.

Pomerantz, E. M. and Kempner, S. G. (2013) Mothers' daily person and process praise: Implications for children's theory of intelligence and motivation. *Developmental Psychology*, 49(11): 2040–46.

Rattan, A., Good, C. and Dweck, C.S. (2012) 'It's ok—Not everyone can be good at math': Instructors with an entity theory comfort (and demotivate) students. *Journal of Experimental Social Psychology*, 48(3): 731–37.

Rawsthorne, L.J. and Elliot, A.J. (1999) Achievement goals and intrinsic motivation: A meta-analytic review. *Personality and Social Psychology Review*, 3(4): 326–44.

Rhem, J. (1999) Pygmalion in the classroom. *The National Teaching and Learning Forum*, 8(2): 1–4.

Rholes, W.S., Blackwell, J., Jordan, C. and Walters, C. (1980) A developmental study of learned helplessness. *Developmental Psychology*, 16(6): 616–24.

Robins, R.W. and Pals, J.L. (2002) Implicit self-theories in the academic domain: Implications for goal orientation, attributions, affect, and self-esteem change. *Self and Identity*, 1(4): 313–36.

Rosenthal, R. and Jacobson, L. (1968) Pygmalion in the classroom. *The Urban Review*, 3(1): 16–20.

Rosenthal, R. and Jacobson, L. (1992) *Pygmalion in the Classroom: Teacher Expectation and Pupils' Intellectual Development*. New York: Irvington Publishers.

Ruble, D.N., Parsons, J.E. and Ross, J. (1976) Self-evaluative responses of children in an achievement setting. *Child Development*, 990–97.

Ruiselová, Z. and Prokopcáková, A. (2005) Coping style and anxiety in relation to the implicit theory of intelligence. *Studia Psychologica*, 47(4): 301–7.

Salomon, G. (1984). Television is "easy" and print is "tough": The differential investment of mental effort in learning as a function of perceptions and attributions. *Journal of Educational Psychology*, 76: 647–58.

Schleider, J. L., Abel, M. R. and Weisz, J. R. (2015) Implicit theories and youth mental health problems: A random-effects meta-analysis. *Clinical Psychology Review*, 35: 1–9. DOI:10.1016/j.cpr.2014.11.001

Schleider, J. and Weisz, J. (2018) A single-session growth mindset intervention for adolescent anxiety and depression: 9-month outcomes of a randomized trial. *Journal of Child Psychology and Psychiatry*, 59, 160–70.

Schmidt, L.A. and Trainor, L.J. (2001) Frontal brain electrical activity (EEG) distinguishes valence and intensity of musical emotions. *Cognition and Emotion*, 15(4): 487–500.

Schunk, D.H. (1996) *Learning Theories: An Educational Perspective* (2nd edn). Englewood Cliffs, NJ: Merrill.

Seegers, G. and Boekaerts, M. (1996) Gender-related differences in self-referenced cognitions in relation to mathematics. *Journal for Research in Mathematics Education*, 215–40.

Seligman, M.E., Reivich, K., Jaycox, L., Gillham, J. and Kidman, A.D. (1995) *The Optimistic Child*. New York: Houghton Mifflin.

Shim, S. S., Cho, Y. and Wang, C. (2013) Classroom goal structures, social achievement goals, and adjustment in middle school. *Learning and Instruction*, 23: 69–77.

Sinclair, S., McKendrick, J. H. and Scott, G. (2010) Failing young people? Education and aspirations in a deprived community. *Education, Citizenship and Social Justice*, 5(1): 5–20. Available online at: https://doi.org/10.1177/1746197909353564

Skelton, C. (2001) Theorizing masculinities. *Schooling the Boys: Masculinities and Primary Education* (pp. 39–61). Buckingham: Open University Press.

Slater, M.J., Spray, C.M. and Smith, B.M. (2012) 'You're only as good as your weakest link': Implicit theories of golf ability. *Psychology of Sport and Exercise*, 13(3): 280–90. DOI: /10.1016/j.psychsport.2011.11.010.

Sloboda, J.A. (1996) The acquisition of musical performance expertise: Deconstructing the "talent" account of individual differences in musical expressivity. In K.A. Ericsson (ed.) *The Road to Excellence: The Acquisition of Expert Performance in the Arts and Sciences*. Mahwah, NJ: Erlbaum.

Smiley, P.A. and Dweck, C.S. (1994) Individual differences in achievement goals among young children. *Child Development*, 65(6): 1723–43.

Smiley, P.A., Coulson, S.L., Greene, J.K. and Bono, K.L. (2010) Performance concern, contingent self-worth, and responses to repeated achievement failure in second graders. *Social Development*, 19(4): 779–98.

Smiley, P.A., Tan, S.J., Goldstein, A. and Sweda, J. (2016) Mother emotion, child temperament, and young children's helpless responses to failure. *Social Development*, 25(2): 285–303.

Smith, B.P. (2005) Goal orientation, implicit theory of ability, and collegiate instrumental music practice. *Psychology of Music*, 33(1): 36–57. Available online at: https://doi.org/10.1177/0305735605048013

Snow, M.A., Padilla, A.M. and Campbell, R.N. (1988) Patterns of second language retention of graduates of a Spanish immersion program. *Applied Linguistics*, 9(2): 182–97. Available online at: https://doi.org/10.1093/applin/9.2.182

Spray, C.M., Wang, C.K.J., Biddlea, S.J.H., Chatzisarantisc, N.L.D. and Warburton, V.E. (2010) An experimental test of self-theories of ability in youth sport. *Psychology of Sport and Exercise*, 7: 255–67.

Stevenson, H.W., Lee, S.Y., Chen, C., Stigler, J.W., Hsu, C.C., Kitamura, S. and Hatano, G. (1990) Contexts of achievement: A study of American, Chinese, and Japanese children. *Monographs of the Society for Research in Child Development*, 55(1/2): i–119.

Stipek, D.J. and Daniels, D.H. (1988) Declining perceptions of competence: A consequence of changes in the child or in the educational environment? *Journal of Educational Psychology*, 80(3): 352.

Stipek, D.J. and Daniels, D.H. (1990) Children's use of dispositional attributions in predicting the performance and behavior of classmates. *Journal of Applied Developmental Psychology*, 11(1): 13–28.

Stipek, D.J. and Gralinski, J.H. (1991) Gender differences in children's achievement-related beliefs and emotional responses to success and failure in mathematics. *Journal of Educational Psychology*, 83(3): 361.

Stipek, D. and Gralinski, J.H. (1996) Children's beliefs about intelligence and school performance. *Journal of Educational Psychology*, 88(3): 397–407.

Stipek, D. J. and MacIver, D. (1989) Developmental change in children's assessment of intellectual competence. *Child Development*, 60: 521–38.

Stipek, D., Recchia, S. and McClintic, S. (1992) Self-evaluation in young children *Monographs of the Society for Research in Child Development*, 57(1): 100.

Stodolsky, S., Salk, S. and Glaessner, B. (1991) Student views about learning math and social studies. *American Educational Research Journal*, 28: 89–116.

Stoet, G. and Geary, D.C. (2018) The gender-equality paradox in science, technology, engineering, and mathematics education. *Psychological Science*, 29(4): 581–93. Available online at: https://doi.org/10.1177/0956797617741719

Strand, S. (2015) Ethnicity, deprivation and educational achievement gaps at age 16 in England: Trends over time. Department for Education (Research Report 439B). Available online at: www.academia.edu/15177342/

Tarbestsky, A.L., Collie, R.J. and Martin, A.J. (2016) The role of implicit theories of intelligence and ability in predicting achievement for Indigenous (Aboriginal) Australian students. *Contemporary Educational Psychology*, 47: 61–71. Available online at: https://doi.org/10.1016/j.cedpsych.2016.01.002

TES article: www.tes.com/news/school-news/breaking-news/new-study-puts-growth-mindset-theory-test

Thorley, C. and Cook, W.A.J. (2017) *Flexibility For Who? Millennials and Mental Health in the Modern Labour Market*. Unspecified. Institute for Public Policy Research.

Todor, I. (2014) Investigating "the old stereotype" about boys/girls and mathematics: Gender differences in implicit theory of intelligence and mathematics self-efficacy beliefs. *Procedia – Social and Behavioral Sciences*, 159: 319–23.

Tull, M.T., Gratz, K,L., Salters, K. and Roemer, L. (2004) The role of experiential avoidance in posttraumatic stress symptoms and symptoms of depression, anxiety, and somatization. *The Journal of Nervous and Mental Disease*: 192(11): 754–61.

Turner-Bisset, R. (2007) Performativity by stealth: A critique of recent initiatives on creativity. Education 3–13, 35(2): 193-203. DOI: 10.1080/03004270701318007

Turok, I., Kintrea, K., St Clair, R. and Benjamin, A. (2009) Shaping educational attitudes and aspirations: The influence of parents, place and poverty: *Interim Report*. School of Social and Political Sciences, Glasgow University.

Van-Yperen, N.W. and Duda, J.L. (1999) Goal orientations, beliefs about success, and performance improvement among young elite Dutch soccer players. *Scandinavian Journal of Medicine and Science in Sports*, 9(6): 358–64. Available online at: https://doi.org/10.1111/j.1600-0838.1999.tb00257.x

Vella, S.A., Cliff, D.P., Okely, A.D., Weintraub, D.L. and Robinson, T.N. (2014) Instructional strategies to promote incremental beliefs in youth sport. *Quest*, 66(4): 357–70. DOI: 10.1080/00336297.2014.950757

Von Suchodoletz, A., Trommsdorff, G. and Heikamp, T. (2011) Linking maternal warmth and responsiveness to children's self-regulation. *Social Development*, 20(3): 486–503.

Walton, G.M. and Cohen, G.L. (2007) A question of belonging: Race, social fit, and achievement. *Journal of Personality and Social Psychology*, 92, 82–96.

Wang, C.K.J. and Biddle, S.J.H. (2001) Young people's motivational profiles in physical activity: A cluster analysis. *Journal of Sport and Exercise Psychology*, 23(1): 1–22. Available online at: https://doi.org/10.1123/jsep.23.1.1

Warren, F., Mason-Apps, E., Hoskins, S., Devonshire, V. and Chanvin, M. (2019) The relationship between implicit theories of intelligence, attainment and socio-demographic factors in a UK sample of primary school children. *British Educational Research Journal*. DOI:10.1002/berj.3523

Warrington, M., Younger, M. and Mclellan, R. (2003) Under-achieving boys in English primary schools. *Curriculum Journal*, 14(2): 139–56.

Wenden, A. (1998) Metacognitive knowledge and language learning. *Applied Linguistics*, 19(4): 515–37. DOI: 10.1093/applin/19.4.515

Wigfield, A., Byrnes, J.P. and Eccles, J.S. (2006) Development during early and middle adolescence. *Handbook of Educational Psychology*, 2: 87–113.

Wong-On-Wing, B. and Lui, G. (2007) Culture, implicit theories, and the attribution of morality. *Behavioral Research in Accounting*, 19(1): 231–46.

Yeager, D.S., Walton, G.M., Brady, S.T., Akcinar, E.N., Paunesku, D., Keane, L., Kamentz, D., Ritter, G., Duckworth, A.L., Urstein, R., Gomez, E.M., Markus, H.R., Cohen, G.L. and Dweck, C.S. (2016) Teaching a lay theory before college narrows achievement gaps at scale. *Proceedings of the National Academy of Sciences of the United States of America*, 113(24): E3341–E3348.

Younger, M., Warrington, M., Gray, J., Ruddack, G., Mclellan, R., Bearne, E., Kershner, R. and Bricheno, P. (2005) *Raising Boys' Achievement in Secondary Schools*. Available online at: www.education.gov.uk/publications/eOrdering-Download/RR636.pdf (accessed 25.11.12).

Zentall, S. R. and Morris, B. J. (2010) Good job, you're so smart: The effects of inconsistency of praise type on young children's motivation. *Journal of Experimental Child Psychology*, 107(2): 155–163. DOI:10.1016/j.jecp.2010.04.015

Zhao, W. and Dweck, C. S. (1994) Implicit theories and vulnerability to depression-like responses. Unpublished manuscript: Columbia University.

Ziegert, D.I., Kistner, J.A., Castro, R. and Robertson, B. (2001) Longitudinal study of young children's responses to challenging achievement situations. *Child Development*, 72(2): 609–24.

INDEX